more. Information may be located quickly by using the index on the back cover flap (which also serves as a handy bookmark).

The contributors

London-based Insight Guides editor **Lesley Gordon** produced this edition of *Insight Guide: Bermuda*. The original edition was produced by **Martha Ellen Zenfell**, editor-in-chief of Insight's North American titles.

Two Bermuda-based writers were enlisted to provide new chapters: **Roger Crombie**, a chartered accountant-turned financial writer contributed the finance feature, *Sun and Savings*; **Alexandra O'Reilly**, a newspaper and magazine journalist, wrote *Modern Bermuda*.

No Insight Guide update can be attempted without on-the-spot, insider assistance, and for this book, our man in Bermuda was **Charles H. Webbe**, former public relations manager for the island's Department of Tourism and a reporter in both Bermuda and Britain. He wrote the original articles on food and music and patiently rooted out the answers to our editorial team's unending stream of queries.

Contributors to the original guide included English historian and writer **Rowlinson Carter**. **Marian Robb** wrote about art and culture on the island; **Don Grearson** explored life at the docks. **Nancy Acton** contributed a series of personality profiles; **Chris Gibbons** tackled sport; **Rebecca Zuill** wrote the piece on flora and fauna.

Two other notable members of the writing team included the late **David Allen**, former Minister of Tourism, and **David F. Raine** (architecture and sailing), his history of St George's is on sale locally.

Invaluable help with the original picture research was given by **John Adams**, at the time custodian of the island's visual and printed heritage at the Bermuda Archives. Contemporary images were provided by **Carl** and **Ann Purcell**, with additional images supplied by snappers **Bob Krist** and **Dave G. Houser**

For the first edition **Derek Brightwell** of Bermuda Tourism and **Pippa Grive** were enthusiastic in their assistance, while **Charlie Hampton** and **Kristel Valaydon** provided help with the current edition. **Sue Johnston** rewrote *Festival Fever*. Bermuda resident and journalist, **Liz Jones**, provided text about local character, Johnny Barnes and also keeps this book up to date.

Map Legend

▬ ▪ ▪	International Boundary
▬ ▬ ▬	Parish Boundary
▬ ▪ ▬	National Park/Reserve
▬ ▬ ▬	Ferry Route
✈ ✦	Airport: International/Regional
🚌	Bus Station
❶	Tourist Information
✉	Post Office
✝ ✝	Church/Ruins
✝	Monastery
☪	Mosque
✡	Synagogue
🏰	Castle/Ruins
⌂	Mansion/Stately home
∴	Archaeological Site
∩	Cave
𝟏	Statue/Monument
★	Place of Interest

The main places of interest in the Places section are coordinated by number with a full-colour map (e.g. ❶), and a symbol at the top of every right-hand page tells you where to find the map.

INSIGHT GUIDE
BERMUDA

CONTENTS

Maps

Bermuda **168**

Hamilton **172**

Hamilton Environs **198**

The West End **224**

Royal Naval Dockyard **229**

Harrington Sound **242**

The East End **256**

Inside front cover:
Western Bermuda
Inside back cover:
Eastern Bermuda

Introduction

Life on the Rock **15**

History

Decisive Dates **28**

Beginnings: Isle of Devils **31**

Governors and Witchcraft **41**

Wars and Early Tourists.......... **57**

From Slavery to Harmony **69**

Features

Modern Bermuda **77**

Island Architecture **85**

Festival Fever **91**

Sailing the Seas **97**

Bermuda Sports **105**

The Visual Arts................... **113**

Calypso Culture **118**

Treasure Island **123**

Food for Thought **129**

Life on the Docks **135**

Wild Birds and
Genteel Flowers **141**

The Bermuda Triangle **148**

A Winter's Tale **155**

An aerial view
over Warwick.

Travel Tips

Getting Acquainted . . **282**

Planning the Trip **283**

Practical Tips **286**

Getting Around **288**

Where to Stay **289**

Where to Eat **294**

Sites **296**

Festivals **298**

Sport and Leisure . . . **299**

Nightlife **300**

Shopping **301**

Further Reading **302**

◆ **Full Travel Tips index
is on page 281**

Places

Introduction **167**

Hamilton **171**

Hamilton Environs **195**

The Railway Trial **213**

The West End **223**

Harrington Sound **241**

The East End **255**

The Small Islands **275**

Information panels

Spies at the Princess Hotel **63**

Dancin' in the Street **156**

Bermuda Shorts **182**

Sun and Savings **188**

Hurricanes **200**

The Salvaging of the
Sea Venture **230**

Notes for Nervous Drivers **249**

Johnny Barnes **266**

LIFE ON THE ROCK

Culturally suspended between Britain and the United States,
Bermuda sets itself apart and revels in its difference

Bermuda has popped up in the oddest ways, originally as the result of a seismic shift in the Atlantic Ocean, and more recently as a synonym for a popular style of short trousers. Scholars might more readily associate the name with Shakespeare's *The Tempest* or perhaps with the lyrical flow of Andrew Marvell who, not alone among poets, wrote lovingly of Bermuda without even setting foot there.

One writer who did get there was Tom Moore, the 19th-century Irish poet. The object of his desire was, scandalously, the teenage bride of one of the colony's worthiest citizens. The latter understandably felt that Bermuda could manage without any more itinerant poets for the time being.

Naturalists might think of Bermuda in terms of the cahow, a bird as much the symbol of a unique environment as the dodo was of Mauritius. Gourmets once sang the praises of the Bermuda onion, arrowroot and even the potato. The arrowroot is now extinct on the island as the cahow almost was. Sailors will talk of Bermuda rigging, the thrilling Bermuda dinghy or of the mysteries of the Bermuda Triangle. It was in the last context that a pastor from California, having studied the Bible, proclaimed that Bermuda, in his opinion, was a signpost to one of two entrances to Hell.

No income tax

For tourists who do not wish to ponder such matters, Bermuda is an enduringly fashionable resort of magnificent ocean-going yachts, a sunny, temperate climate, brilliant beaches, championship golf courses and friendly people who routinely exchange cordial greetings with total strangers. To this list the permanent colony of expatriates would undoubtedly wish to add, in a whisper: "And so little tax."

PRECEDING PAGES: Bermuda's ceremonies often take place out of season; schoolgirls; black and white harmony; designer beach.
LEFT AND RIGHT: life on the Rock.

The Atlantic Ocean all around "The Rock", as Bermudians call their island, is abysmally deep. The islands were produced by a volcano which sent a needle of rock soaring 3 miles (5 km) up from the seabed. Other, more distant volcanic activity produced what are, by comparison, gentle underwater humps. The broad crown of this rocky pinnacle did not quite reach the surface, but jagged extremities did. Thus exposed in water that was reliably not colder than 65°F (18°C) because of the Gulf Stream, the tips attracted tiny coral creatures whose shells were compressed with sand over the next 70 million years to form a 250-ft (76-metre) cap of limestone – in other words, Bermuda.

In due course these lumps were vegetated by flotsam, a random process relying on incalculable odds. Migratory birds, alighting on this lonely spot 600 miles (966 km) east of Cape Hatteras, North Carolina, introduced other forms of life. By some means, Bermuda acquired a truly native creature, a lizard known as the skink. The more celebrated frog that contrives to make a whistling sound by rubbing its legs together is a 19th-century trespasser from the West Indies, as is the bass section of the nocturnal chorus, a giant toad brought in to combat cockroaches.

The first humans ashore were 16th-century European sailors, usually the victims of shipwrecks on the huge encirclement of reefs, a reminder of the volcanic crown which remains, for the most part, about 50 ft (15 metres) beneath the surface to provide some of the world's best scuba-diving. The vivid clarity of the water and its even temperature invited (and

were the first human inhabitants of consequence. By then the ecology had developed a long way from flotsam and bird droppings. The islands – seven large ones interspersed with scores of smaller ones – were thickly covered in cedar and palmetto trees; the waters teemed with turtles, oysters and hitherto unknown types of fish, many so trusting or stupid that the settlers could scoop them out by hand.

In spite of their fearful reputation, the birds proved to be as innocently trusting as the native fish. The Rev. Hughes, Bermuda's first clergyman, wrote with amazement of birds strolling nonchalantly among a row of boiling pots as if

still invites) underwater exploration as naturally as snow put Norwegians on skis.

A Bermudian anticipated modern scuba-diving by descending with his head inside an upturned barrel. It was a crude contraption but it enabled him to remain submerged for 40 minutes and his services were in great demand by treasure hunters locally and in the Bahamas. The reefs around Bermuda are a museum of marine mishaps, compulsive viewing for experienced divers with tanks, snorkellers or simply spectators dry and comfortable in the many observation boats that run excursions.

English settlers shipwrecked on their way to the new colony of Jamestown, Virginia, in 1609

volunteering to jump in with friends and relatives who already occupied them.

Closer acquaintance with conditions in Bermuda revised the Spanish view that it was the forbidding "Isle of Devils". The cedar was excellent building material, in particular for boats, because it was so fine-grained. Palmetto leaves provided plenty of thatch and furthermore this useful tree grew heads that could be cooked like a cabbage and delicious red berries, with juice that was both potable and potent. The diet of seabirds and fish was augmented by wild hogs, which had multiplied prolifically from breeding pairs left behind by Spanish sailors.

The ecology of a remote archipelago in the mid-Atlantic was so delicately balanced that even the introduction of a few hogs threw it out. The hogs brought the cahow perilously close to extinction by digging up its burrowed eggs. Man's attempt to settle the islands had opened up a Pandora's box. An accidental invasion of ship-borne rats stripped the islands bare like a plague of locusts. Most of the vegetation was burnt in a desperate attempt to halt the rats.

The cedars recovered but were reduced over the years in the interest of profitable boat-building. The last straw for the cedar trees was a scale insect epidemic in the 1940s.

fundamentalists would doubt or question that it is in almost every respect very much better.

Economic evolution

Natural Bermuda was fascinating but could not sustain an economy. The early settlers were great dreamers. While governors cajoled them into building forts and undertaking other public works, they pinned their hopes on uncovering buried treasure or on the easy pickings of casual piracy. The discovery on a beach of a large lump of ambergris, part of a whale's stomach used in the making of scent, caused frantic excitement because it was worth at least its weight

Men could not turn back the clock, but they did the next best thing by introducing a rich variety of flora that would never have reached Bermuda by natural means. The result is marvellously lush, turning the whole colony into what could easily pass as a botanical garden. The amount of land set aside for conservation is especially commendable in view of the pressure on space. The fact that 95 percent of the plants were foreign, even if they now grow wild, means that Bermuda is not what it was in the early days of settlement, but only botanical

LEFT AND ABOVE: history is re-enacted in the town of St George.

in bullion. No more appeared because, rather like oysters and pearls, only sick whales produced ambergris, and whales around Bermuda were then bursting with rude and robust health.

Tobacco cultivation started promisingly but petered out. The settlers turned unromantically to growing potatoes, but that didn't work either. Problems on the American mainland – the Revolutionary and Civil Wars, prohibition – dangled tantalising black market profits, but they did not represent the basis of long-term growth. Any prediction that Bermuda would one day be in the top division of international wealth-per-capita would have been blamed on the mind-numbing effect of palmetto juice.

Sounder economic prospects evolved around New Englanders who wanted to warm themselves during the winter but could not afford the time, long before air travel, to sail as far south as the Caribbean. They took their cue from Princess Louise, daughter of Queen Victoria and wife of the Marquess of Lorne, Governor General of Canada. Her winter holiday in Bermuda in 1883 attracted considerable publicity, enough to get entrepreneurs busy on a hotel that was completed a few years later and duly named after her, the Princess.

One of the curious Americans who came to see what people were talking about was Mark

nating yet wearisome turmoil of New York, the Western metropolis, and in 48 hours find yourself in a pure and balmy atmosphere, a silent restful land, where modern progress has yet to remove the rust of antiquity and obliterate ideas of old-fashioned simplicity." He recommended the colony "especially to the person who is tired and nervous, run down in body and mind. Its tranquillity is soothing, and furthermore it is remarkably free from repellent blemishes".

Such enthusiastic endorsements were difficult to reconcile with *A Plaine Description of the Barmudas*, published in 1612: "nothing but gusts, storms and foul weather".

Twain, who evidently had a rough passage. "Bermuda is paradise", he remarked, "but you have to go through Hell to get to it". The reference to paradise helped to redress the colony's balance in literary circles after some of Anthony Trollope's unflattering comments: "There can be no place in the world as to which there can be less said than there is about this island…"

Travel writers were soon passing judgement on this new destination. William Brownell Hayward was satisfied; his verdict is as appropriate now as it was when he handed it down a century ago. "You leave ice, snow, dirt, noise, bustle, the glitter of wealth, the sordidness of poverty, all the elements that combine to make the fasci-

Tourism – then and now

The tourist industry, then as now, was geared to the well-heeled visitor. The yachts that call throughout the summer, the standard of the hotels and golf courses with seemingly not a blade of grass out of place banish any doubt on that score. With the need to import practically everything, prices were never going to be low.

A 19th-century English visitor complained about shortages, but seemed to have the situation under control: "Preserved meats from Fortnum & Mason, however, are very useful as a reserve on days when it is impossible to procure fresh meat of a tolerable kind." He was not keen on local cuisine, declaring that: "the females make wretched bad cooks". However, he was particularly impressed by a novelty, ice from America. He thought the importers, Gosling & Co. (still in business on Hamilton's Front Street), deserved the thanks of the whole community. "Applied to the forehead, it will sometimes stave off and at all times mitigate fevers; and sore eyes, occasioned by the glare of the sea, or the white buildings, are greatly relieved by the application of ice two or three times a day."

The islands were soon able to make their own ice, and visitors did not long have to concern themselves with emergency reserves from

is merely a compilation of facsimile menus without editorial comment; there are humbler establishments that can't or won't advertise but shouldn't be ruled out on those grounds. Chowder is uniformly good, especially with a few drops of sherry pepper sauce, a local speciality. Bars carry every imaginable form of drink. Palmetto juice is unfortunately no longer obtainable – barmen put their creative talents into rum concoctions.

Supermarkets brimming with delicacies of every description are the badges of a society with surplus money to spend. The articles on sale reveal the extent to which Bermuda

Fortnum & Mason. Few modern travellers would regret the passing of boiled palmetto heads as a staple, even if they were said to be better than the cabbages they resembled, although it is a pity that more recent local specialities like codfish with bananas, shark hash and conch stew are not as widely available as they were.

Hotels and restaurants lean toward "international" cuisine and maintain high standards at corresponding prices. *Dining Out in Bermuda*

LEFT: Mark Twain on holiday in Bermuda.
ABOVE: unidentified man with dog, *circa* 1895.
ABOVE RIGHT: "Mark Swan" *circa* 1890.

depends on the United States for its supplies. The logistics of life are concealed, however, behind a facade echoing traditional England, including the ritual of afternoon tea, dressing for dinner (which, for men, leaves open the option of Bermuda shorts) and similar police uniforms, complete with hard hats.

Mid-Atlantic mentality

Historically, Bermudians have seen themselves as being apart from the Caribbean, culturally suspended between Britain and the US, a curious blend of influences from the 19th and 20th centuries. However, the 21st century has brought a change of outlook.

In 2002 CARICOM (Caribbean Community) accepted Bermuda as an associate member. Supporters of the move argue that many Bermudians have Caribbean ancestry and that today the island has more cultural ties with the Caribbean than it does with Britain.

Certainly, the island retains a formality more British than British. Men who would presume to ride a moped shirtless, or enter a store or restaurant in a state of undress are frowned upon. The thought of topless sunbathing makes Bermudians shudder. Alcohol must not be consumed in a public place and there are strict rules against littering. Afternoon tea remains a ritual

As a self-governing British colony, the official position is that Bermuda could become fully independent for the asking. The issue has been raised from time to time but there is evidently no pressing desire to change the *status quo*.

Not Miami

Appearances matter greatly, to the extent that Colonel Sanders, of Kentucky and fried chicken fame, was *persona non grata*, along with other well-known franchises, in case their presence and especially their ubiquitous signboards made Bermuda look too much like Miami. The colonel, his goatee and chickens

in some of Bermuda's hotels. And a "good morning", "afternoon" or "evening" is mandatory before any kind of transaction. On the other hand, to Europeans, the island is more like America. Bermudians, after all, tend to soften their consonants and they often have a more than healthy respect for the US dollar.

The islands demography is changing, however, since foreign workers needed for international business, hotels and restaurants now come from all over the world. Once the island pottered along like a well-managed estate, now it buzzes to a global tune. But conservatism is still key, especially where religion is concerned. Places of worship on the island are always packed.

were eventually conceded a discreet roost away from Hamilton's genteel harbour. There was a McDonald's, in the grounds of the US Naval Air Station on St David's Island. However, when the base closed in 1995, the burger-and-fries haven't shut down at the same time.

Stout resistance to one American innovation, the automobile, crumbled during World War II when the war effort was acknowledged as more important than Bermuda's long-standing antipathy. The ban on cars had been made official before World War I, when one which had slipped through the net, a machine known as "The Scarlet Runner", frightened a horse into bolting and nearly caused a man's death. The ban stood throughout the first war, the military having to move their equipment around in horse-drawn carts, as they were still doing in the early days of the second.

A few years earlier the governor, Sir Reginald Hildyard, had resigned in a rage when the Legislature refused to let him have an official car. Bermudians were content with their horse-drawn buses, boats, bicycles and, from 1931, a narrow-gauge railroad that ran from Somerset to St George's and is now a picturesque trail for hikers.

While the guiding principle in the design of Bermuda's roads had traditionally been to make them no wider than was necessary to roll a

on drivers convicted of scorching about at all of 30 mph. Taxis are plentiful and the service provided by the pastel pink buses is exemplary.

Cars are limited to one per residential unit. With the decision that parts of the same house were allowed to qualify as residential units if they had self-contained cooking facilities or met other structural requirements, the islands rocked on their volcanic perch to the rhythm of hasty D.I.Y. home improvements. Other rules were piled on: a moving car had to contain the registered owner or a member of the owner's family; anyone selling a car could not buy another for at least one year. Some of the rules were relaxed in

barrel, the military vehicles that crammed the islands during World War II needed rather more space. The improved roads weakened the case for re-imposing the ban after the war, but there was nevertheless a fierce argument before the Legislature relented in 1946.

The joys of private motoring paled as a quart of cars tried to wriggle into a pint pot. There are no self-drive hire cars; the most an independent traveller can aspire to is a moped. The maximum speed limit is an undebatable 20 mph (35 kph), with courts imposing six-month bans

LEFT: a "birdcage" for all seasons.
ABOVE: an enthusiastic spectator.

the late 1990s, such as friends may now drive each other's cars with the owner's permission.

Interchangeable currency

Nevertheless, Bermuda knows what to do to earn the compliment that visitors bestow when at last they come across a worthy recipient: the place "works". The telephone system certainly deserves the accolade – not surprisingly, since it is an essential part of Bermuda's expanding role as an off-shore tax haven for international companies. For the same reason, bank tellers do not stare at foreign notes as if they had dropped from Mars. American and Bermudian dollars are on par and fully interchangeable, and Bermudians consider their dollar every bit as good as the mainland version.

By contrast, the supply of hot water – that other yardstick of the less intrepid tourist – is more problematical. The water does run and it is hot, but some taps open counter-clockwise, others not, which would not be too bad if pairs of taps were consistent. As it is, trying to adjust the temperature of a shower with taps that rotate in opposite directions could be an unwelcome early morning challenge for visitors staying in an otherwise admirable private guest house. Nevertheless, the milk on the breakfast table will always be fresh.

elsewhere, like Lightbourne. People whose names get into the newspapers – in the social columns or through answering charges in the magistrate's court – appear to be drawn from the same small pool of families. The same names also loom large in the colony's colourful history, applied impartially to heroes and villains.

"The great difficulty in the colony", an army officer once sniffed, "is where to draw the social line. Except professional persons, all the best families, with scarcely an exception, are employed in retail trade, of a kind that, in the mother country, is considered somewhat incompatible with the social position of a gentleman.

Taxis have meters; not only do drivers scrupulously switch them on and off, they are knowledgeable and engaging guides. One does not haggle over prices in the shops along Hamilton's beautifully preserved waterfront; they sell cashmere and fine china, and good quality souvenirs.

Bermuda's name game

The names on some of the waterfront shops (such as Frith) and on bottles of sherry pepper sauce (Outerbridge) are among those that dominate the telephone directory. Columns are devoted not so much to "Smith" and "Jones" (though Smith is a local name) but to names that would be unusual

Even the lawyers and the clergy have, for the most part, relatives who keep, or are subordinates in retail stores."

In the next breath, however, he removed the sting. "Yet to confound these gentlemen with petty English traders, on account of similarity of occupation, would be both illiberal and unjust." He followed that up with an observation that anticipates the spirit that people employed in the tourist industry bring to their jobs in the present age. "The setting up of a new store was considered not merely as a profitable speculation, but also as a most praiseworthy and patriotic act."

A roll call of Bermudian names no longer carries any reliable indication, if one were sought, of race, colour or class. The impression of a population divided among only a few, huge extended families is the result of slaves adopting the names of their masters when they were freed. None had surnames before then, and many had arrived in Bermuda from the Caribbean with Spanish first names that were quickly Anglicised.

The numbers of whites and blacks in Bermuda were quite evenly balanced from *circa* 1623, 11 years after the arrival of the first settlers. The blacks made up 60 percent of the total population, the balance including Portuguese immigrants and the descendants of

the United States during the turbulent 1960s. The system that was enforced in Bermuda until then was in all but name that of apartheid: separate schools, separate seating or total segregation in public places such as hotels, restaurants, churches and cinemas, and a grave stigma was attached to the idea of mixed marriages.

The battle had almost been won when Governor Sir Richard Sharples and an aide were assassinated in 1973 as they strolled in the grounds of Government House. The conviction and execution of two black men, one a convicted armed robber who had murdered

Native Americans whose high-boned features are apparent in some persons of mixed blood. Slavery, as practised in Bermuda, was probably as relaxed as slavery could be, but that did not make it a sinecure and there were several attempted uprisings, the strangest being at the instigation of Irish slaves (Cromwell's victims and, by all accounts, thoroughly unsatisfactory servants) who wanted to stamp out Protestantism on the island.

The pressure for integrated racial equality was fuelled by the civil rights movement in

before, lit a fuse which threatened to tear Bermuda apart. Two guests and an employee died after an arson attack on the Southampton Princess Hotel. The rioting ended before the arrival of British troops, but this did not prevent a flood of cancelled hotel reservations.

The scars of racial confrontation have healed to the extent that they are now less visible. The process may have been accelerated by the realisation that everyone was in the same proverbial boat and that the economic consequences of public disorder would sink it. As far as visitors are concerned, there is no such thing as a no-go area, but caution is advised, especially if walking alone at night.

LEFT: heavenly images.
ABOVE: Vince Cann, taxi guide extraordinaire.

While Bermuda is relatively safe, the scourge of drugs and all that they imply has had an impact. And petty theft, such as handbag snatching, is an irritant. Try to keep hotel doors and windows locked too.

No ghettos

Bermuda is affluent in a way that small oil-producing states are not. Wealth is distributed far more evenly among the population, so there are no slums or ghettos and little of the so-called ghetto mentality. It vies with Luxembourg for the highest per capita Gross Domestic Product. There is virtually full employment and

even menial jobs may pay $30-plus an hour with no deductions for income tax unless a small "hospital tax" is so regarded.

Revenue for the usually balanced national budget is raised through indirect taxation. Percentages added to hotel bills and a departure tax (included in the cost of airline and cruise tickets) are aimed at visitors, but everyone pays the duty levied on imported goods – a category that embraces most items. Expectations are high, and it is not unusual for ambitious people to hold down two or even three jobs.

Although the size of the population remains relatively stable, the affluent younger generation aspire to home ownership, and meeting

these expectations adds to the pressure on limited space. The price of an ordinary family house rose to $300,000 by the early 1990s. Now it is about $1.4 million for a three bedroom house and $900,000 for a condominium, in spite of measures to shield prices from the influence of eager foreign buyers. Today they may not buy property with an annual rental value of less than $153,000 for a house and $32,000 for a condominium and, once bought, there are restrictions on what they can do with it. A foreigner may not bequeath a property to another foreigner; nor, for that matter, may a Bermudian to a non-Bermudian.

The country has unfortunately attracted the drugs trade, not only because there are people who can afford to buy drugs but also because of Bermuda's position as a logical transhipment point for traffic originating in the Caribbean and Central America. The tragic concomitant of drug abuse has been dirty needles and a near epidemic of Aids. When Bermuda buried its 100th Aids victim in 1989, some of the glitter had gone from its achievement of being ninth in the table of Gross Domestic Product.

This single blemish on Bermuda's otherwise elegant gentility will not intrude on visitors, nor does it deter some from extending their stay – for a year or two! The rules, alas, are tight. A foreigner can only take a job that has been advertised three times locally without producing a suitable candidate. In practice, the only jobs available are either specialised or involve working at unsocial hours. Work permits are valid for up to three years, after which the job must be re-advertised. Visitors are not allowed to land in Bermuda without a return ticket. Regulations state that no foreigner may have a work permit for longer than six years unless that individual is considered essential. The permit may then be extended for a maximum of three further years.

As the following history shows, the early days of Bermuda were notable for intermittent spells of mutinous laziness and drunken anarchy – a clumsy way of saying, in many cases, that a freak of nature had produced a place that was too good to be squandered on work. The modern visitor to Bermuda may be inclined to concede the point. ❑

LEFT: outside the Anglican Trinity church in Hamilton.
RIGHT: one man and his dog.

Decisive Dates

Circa **70,000 BC** The Bermudian islands begin to emerge from a chain of volcanoes.

AD 1503 The islands are visited by Spanish explorer, Juan de Bermudez.

1543 An inscription carved at Spanish Rock confirms the existence of an early shipwreck survivor.

1593 The vessel carrying Henry May is shipwrecked; he provides the earliest description of the islands for the English government.

1609 Shipwreck of Sir George Somers and passengers aboard *Sea Venture*, whilst bound for

Virginia, marks the beginning of a permanent settlement on the islands.

1610 Sir George Somers dies on Bermuda, his body is shipped back to England. King James I grants a charter to the Virginia Company to colonise the islands.

EARLY COLONISTS

1612 Arrival of first colonists from England aboard *The Plough*. Under the first governor, former ship's carpenter Richard Moore, they settle mainly on St George Island.

1615 The Virginia Company sells the island to its shareholders, who form the Somers Island Company to undertake the colony's development.

1616 First Assizes; the first Native American and black settlers arrive, many brought as slaves.

1617 Richard Norwood completes the first island survey, dividing the island areas into tribes, later called parishes.

1620 The State House and the first jail are built.

1651 Witchcraft trial of Jeane Gardiner who was executed in St George.

1684 Somers Island Company dissolved and the legal status of colony reassessed. Bermuda becomes a crown colony.

1712 St Peter's Church is partially destroyed by a storm, but rebuilt within a year.

1722 Government House is built on a hillside overlooking St George.

1731 A serious outbreak of Yellow Fever.

1775 Bermudian involvement in "The Gunpowder Scandal", which gives support to American colonists during the War of Independence.

1784 Joseph Stockdale establishes the first newspaper press and prints the first issue of the *Bermuda Gazette*.

1790 Legislation is passed to build a town to be called Hamilton.

1809 Construction work commences on Royal Naval Dockyard.

1815 The capital moves from St George to Hamilton.

1824 Convict labour arrives from Britain to help with the construction of Royal Naval Dockyard.

1834 Emancipation of slaves.

1846 Gibb's Hill lighthouse is built, designed by William Facy.

1861 The American Civil War sees Bermuda commercially active on both sides.

1871 The Causeway opens, forging a road link between East End and Hamilton.

1879 St David's lighthouse is built.

1887 The first telephone link between St George and Hamilton is established.

1899 The Causeway is destroyed by a tidal wave that hits the south coast.

1901 South African Boer prisoners of war arrive in Bermuda. The first automobile arrives.

1902 The first Somerset-St George cricket "Cup Match" is held.

1906 The first Newport-Bermuda yacht race.

1915 Initial contingent of Bermuda Volunteer Rifle Corps heads off to World War I (1914–18).

1920 The 300th anniversary of Parliament.

1931 The Bermuda Railway commences island-wide service from St George to Somerset.

1940 A British World War II censorship station is established at the Hamilton Princess Hotel.

AMERICAN INFLUENCE

1941 The US Government starts to build military bases and an airport, including a Naval Air Station on St David's Island.

1944 Wealthy, property-owning women are granted the right to vote.

1946 Introduction of automobiles. Political activist, Dr E.F. Gordon, travels to London to petition for racial and economic parity.

1951 The "extinct" cahow bird is rediscovered in Bermuda. The Royal Naval Dockyard closes.

1953 The Bermuda "Big Three" Conference is attended by Winston Churchill (Britain), Dwight Eisenhower (USA) and Joseph Lanial (France).

1958 The wreck of the *Sea Venture* is discovered.

1959 A boycott of Bermuda's segregated theatres leads to the desegregation of most public places.

THE BIRTH OF THE CIVIL RIGHTS MOVEMENT

More than a century after Emancipation in 1834, Bermuda was still strictly segregated. Bermuda's white minority had the pick of jobs, sole access to the significant capital, the best education and the best seats at cinemas. However, the British colonial wind of change and the American civil rights movement were gathering strength, and black Bermudians dared to dream of equality. At first led by labour leader Dr E.F. Gordon, the thrust toward racial and economic parity started in earnest after World War II. Then in the mid-1950s a young black dentist, Dr Stanley Ratteray, returned to the island after studying in Canada, where no segregation existed. Ratteray formed the non-political Progressive Group. They called on black Bermudians to protest cinema segregation. The group converged outside the theatre, refusing to go in and pressuring others not to enter either. It may seem innocuous – a boycott of the cinema – but it worked. And local union man Calvin Smith said: "Within 15 days, the theatre owners capitulated by removing seating restrictions based on race. Removal of colour bars in hotels and restaurants followed shortly thereafter."

The movement to improve quality of life for black Bermudians was not over and Bermuda experienced several periods of social unrest. Over the next decade the black population achieved the vote, the reduction of racial barriers in employment and the desegregation of schools.

PRECEDING PAGES: *Flatts Inlet* by Thomas Driver.
LEFT: Winston Churchill and Dwight D. Eisenhower meet for the Bermuda Conference in 1953.
RIGHT: Bermuda is a British Dependent Territory.

NO TO INDEPENDENCE

1961 Anti-discrimination legislation is passed.

1965 Universal adult suffrage introduced.

1968 A Constitutional Conference establishes Bermuda's self-governing colony status.

1971 Sir Edward Richards becomes Bermuda's first black premier.

1973 Bermuda's Governor, Sir Richard Sharples and his aide-de-camp, Hugh Sayers, are assassinated.

1983 Bermuda becomes a British Dependent Territory, later called a British Overseas Territory.

1995 A referendum is held as to whether Bermuda should secede from the British Commonwealth. It fails. The US Naval Air Station is closed.

1997 Pamela Gordon becomes first female premier.

1998 Jennifer Smith becomes the first female to be elected as premier.

2002 Bermuda applies to join CARICOM.

2003 The Progressive Labour Party (PLP) wins the first general election held under the new constitution. The premier, Jennifer Smith, resigns three days later and is replaced by Alex Scott. In September Hurricane Fabian, a category 3 storm, strikes Bermuda causing considerable damage.

2005 Trimingham Brothers department store, together with its acquired store, H.A.&E. Smith, closes after 163 years in business.

2007 The PLP wins the general election under the leadership of Dr Ewart Brown. ❑

TEMPEST.

BEGINNINGS: ISLE OF DEVILS

A shipwreck brought the first English visitors to Bermuda – a place first thought to be inhabited by evil creatures, but later described as a land of plenty

Alfred Hitchcock could have taken the idea for his film *The Birds* from the terrifying reception given to Bermuda's first visitors, shipwreck victims clawing their way to shore. Bombardment by diabolical birds apart, the islands were notorious. "The islands of the Barmudas", a 1612 document noted, "as every man knoweth that hath heard or read of them, were never inhabited by a Christian or heathen people but were ever esteemed and reputed a most prodigious and enchanted place, affording nothing but gusts, storms and foul weather, which made every navigator and mariner to avoid them as Schylla and Charybdis or as they would shun the Devil himself." Sir Walter Raleigh was more matter of fact: "a hellish sea for thunder, lightning, and storms".

The earliest Spanish sailors to the New World were well aware of the islands because their return voyage took them up the coast of Florida until they picked up the westerly trade winds. The crescent-shaped archipelago was the point at which they changed course for the Azores and home. They had no desire to go ashore nor to linger in the area because it was an obvious stalking ground for pirates hoping to intercept Spanish *cargazoone* of sugar and tobacco, the latter a novelty that had quickly become a craze throughout Europe. King James I of England deplored the habit: "the barbarous and beastly manners of the wild, godless and slavish Indians... so vile and stinking a custom".

Horror story

One of the first Englishmen to sail past Bermuda added to the bad publicity. He saw a monster rising from the depths. "From the middle upwards", he noted, "he was proportioned like a man, of the complexion of a mulatto or tawny Indian".

The islands were first visited, as far as anyone knows, by Juan de Bermudez in 1503. The hostile birds that taunted him were described in some detail by a subsequent visitor, Captain

LEFT AND RIGHT: illustrations from *The Tempest.*

Diego Ramirez, another Spaniard whose ship ran aground opposite what is known as Spanish Point. From his description the birds were obviously the celebrated cahow, about the size of a pigeon but with a three-foot wingspan. They were black and white, he said, web-footed and had very strong longish beaks with white saw-

like edges which curved at the tip. "When we landed", the Captain wrote, "they came to us, perched on our heads, uttering a multitudinous chorus of cries... such an outcry and varying clamour that one cannot help being afraid".

Ramirez tried to comfort his alarmed crew. "The sign of the Cross at them!" he shouted. "We are Christians." A negro who had gone ashore with a lantern let out a howl. "The devil is carrying off the negro", gasped Ramirez. "All ashore!"

"It was these nightbirds!" he wrote. "So many came to the light and dashed against the negro that he could not defend himself with his club, neither could the men who went to his help either. Finally we solved the mystery and they brought more than 500 birds to the ship. We cooked them with hot water and they were so fat and good that every night the men went hunting and we dried and salted more than 1,000 for the voyage besides what the men ate... They are so plentiful that 4,000 could be killed at the same spot in a single night."

Catching fish presented no problem either. Ramirez wrote: "great numbers of fish; groupers, parrot fish and especially red snappers which are so stupid that we caught them in our hands with pointed sticks and bent nails". There was evidence of earlier shipwrecks in an old mast and pieces of shaped wood, but no

sign of life. Ramirez's account lay forgotten in the archives of Seville for 350 years, but news of the birds had spread. Bermuda was fixed in mariners' minds as the Isle of Devils.

By 1511 the islands were included in Spanish charts. Bermudez returned in 1514 or 1515 with Gonzales Ferdinando d'Oviedo, who had been privy to discussions between Queen Isabella of Spain and Columbus about the latter's ambitions. Bermudez and d'Oviedo intended to drop off on Bermuda a stock of hogs which would provide a source of fresh meat for passing ships. However, the weather prevented their landing.

A few years afterward, a Portuguese vessel on the way home from San Domingo wedged itself between two rocks on a reef. The crew were able to salvage all but the hull and, over the next four months, built a new ship out of local cedar to return to San Domingo. One of the stranded sailors passed time carving into a rock the initials "R" and "P"– probably "Rex Portugaline" – and the date, 1543. The so-called Spanish Rock (the carving was until recently attributed wrongly to a Spaniard, and controversy still reigns on this topic) is in the Spittal Pond nature reserve and bears a bronze casting of the original inscription.

Exactly 50 years later it fell upon Henry May to become the first recorded Englishman to set foot on Bermuda. He was being given a passage home in a French ship commanded by a Monsieur de la Barbotière. The crew were well aware of Bermuda's notorious reefs and, under the impression that they had safely passed them, "threw aside all care, and gave themselves up to carousing. Amid this jollity, about midnight, the ship struck with such violence as to make it evident that she must speedily sink".

It took all the next day to reach land, by which time they were "tormented" by a thirst that was relieved by the discovery of a rock filled with rainwater. The land, May noticed, was an unbroken forest of cedar.

"Now it pleased God before our ship did split that we saved our carpenters' tools, else I think we would be there till this day," he wrote. "And having recovered the aforesaid tools, we went roundly about the cutting down of trees and in the end built a small bark of some 18 tons for the most part with tronnels and very few nails... Instead of pitch we made lime and mixed it with the oil of tortoises." They had 13 live tortoises as food for the voyage and, eventually, "it pleased God to set us clear of the island, to the no little joy of us all..."

Involuntary settlers

While Spain prevaricated for a century over whether Bermuda was worth settling, the English had their sights set on North America. The first settlement in Virginia had failed, so in 1609 a more determined effort was initiated. A new Virginia Company, given a charter by King James, campaigned to raise funds and enlist volunteers for the expedition. In spite of the earlier failure, Virginia was promoted as "earth's only paradise". The response was enthusiastic and, even before the charter was sealed, its list of "Adventurers" (today's "financial investors") included 21 peers, 96 knights, 53 captains, 28 esquires and an assortment of 400 other citizens. Shakespeare had friends and patrons among them and took, like most of England, a keen interest in the enterprise.

A flotilla of eight ships assembled in Plymouth to convey the new settlers, about 600 in all. The admiral was Sir George Somers, a shareholder in the company who had sailed with Drake and Raleigh and done a little piracy on the side before entering Parliament as the member for Lyme Regis in Dorset. He was then 60 years old. The master of the flagship, *Sea*

role. The most distinguished passenger was Sir Thomas Gates. Like Somers, he had sailed with Drake and was on his way, accompanied by his secretary, William Strachey, to become Governor of Virginia.

On 23 June, after what had until then been a smooth voyage, "a dreadful storm and hideous began to blow from out the northeast, which swelling and roaring as it were by fits, some hours with more violence than others, at length did beat all light from the heaven, which so like a hell of darkness turned black upon us, and overmastered the senses so that the terrible cries and murmurs of the winds shook even those of

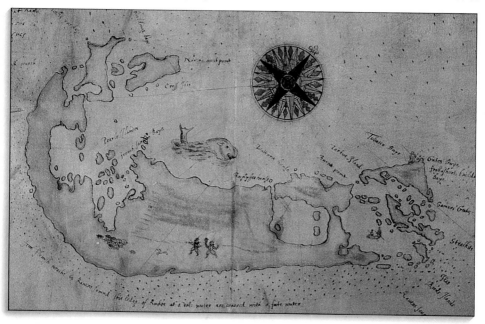

Venture, was Captain Christopher Newport, a veteran of three previous crossings to Virginia. He knew the storms of the Atlantic well and had confidence in his ship, a fully rigged and fairly heavily armed galleon.

Sea Venture carried 150 passengers. Among artisans and farmers heading for a new life was an ostentatious fellow who wore a cape, feathered hat and sword and travelled with a servant. Henry Paine described himself as a "gentleman", although he was heading for a small place in Bermuda's history in a less flattering

our company who were best prepared to face them". This graphic account of the storm, by Strachey, almost certainly provided Shakespeare with material for *The Tempest*.

"Fury added to fury", Strachey continued, "one storm urging a second more outrageous than the former… It could not be said to rain, the waters like whole rivers did flood in the air". The *Sea Venture* sprang leaks, which the crew attempted to stop with pieces of beef. All hands took a turn at the pumps, not least the admiral and governor-designate and "gentlemen who had never had an hour's work in their lives".

Sea Venture had a cargo of 12,000 lbs (5,400 kg) of biscuits, the prospect of finding

LEFT: statue of Sir George Somers.
ABOVE: map of Bermuda, 1609–15.

fresh food in Virginia being poor. Mixed with the deluge of rain and sea water, the biscuits practically turned into cement and clogged the pumps. The crew thought they were doomed and began "taking their last leave… until their more joyful and happy meeting in a more blessed world". The passengers, too, were "commending our sinful souls to God" when on the fourth day of the storm Sir George Somers, "peering through the curtain of fine rain, described land".

Sea Venture was still a mile (1.6 km) from land when it struck a reef. The women and children were put into the longboat with Sir

them, did willingly share with the hogs for them". The head of the tree "is very good meate, either raw or sodden, it yieldeth a head which weigheth about 20 lb, and is farre better meate than any cabbage". Another interesting discovery, albeit one with mixed blessings, was that the juice of the berries made a potent drink.

A mysterious sniffing noise heard during the night proved to be an inquisitive wild hog, indirect evidence that someone had succeeded in introducing these animals where Ramirez had failed. The only indigenous mammal on the islands was a lizard called the skink, a snake-like creature now found only on the islets in

ORDER ACANTHOPTERYGII.

FAMILY SERRANIDÆ.

30

SERRANUS GUTTATUS
EPENEPHELUS GUTTATUS
Hind ⅖
July 1876.

Thomas standing at the prow. On reaching shallow water he leapt out and proclaimed: "Gates, his bay!" Luckily, *Sea Venture* was wedged between two rocks and over the next few days the crew were able to salvage the cargo, including hogs and the ship's dog, and strip the vessel of useful timbers. This left only the ribcage of the ship, which rolled over and sank.

Misgivings about being stuck on the frightful Isle of Devils were pleasantly revised. The palmetto tree not only provided leaves which could be used as shelter but the berries, said Silvester Jourdain, were "very pleasant and wholesome" and "upon which the hogs do most feed; but our men finding the sweetness of

Castle Harbour. Apparently oblivious to danger, the hog allowed its back to be stroked, and did not object when a rope was wound around its hind legs. It was the first of many such gullible meals.

The 60-year-old admiral, former pirate and sitting MP, had a small fishing boat built while the longboat was being fitted with a deck for the voyage to Virginia. Sir George's first day out in the new boat produced no fewer than 500 fish. "Fish is there so abundant", Jourdain wrote later, "that if a man steppe into the water, they will come round about him, so that men were (reluctant) to go out for feare of byting". The fish were "very fat and sweete". Mullet and pilchard were caught by the thousand, and, attracted by lights, enough crayfish could be taken in a night to feed the entire population.

Whales were frequent visitors, and the stranded settlers once watched a sword fish and thresher shark chasing a whale. "The sword fish with his sharp and needle fin pricking him into the belly when he would sink and fall into the sea, and when he started upwards from his wounds, the thresher with his large fins like flails beating his above water." The indefatigable admiral visited one of the smaller islands and returned with 32 more hogs as well as confirmation that there seemed to be no snakes,

hook. He embellished his map with a drawing of the dog chasing hogs with a human entourage dressed in baggy Elizabethan costume and feathered hats. It was partly in recognition of his detailed map-making that the company decided to call the islands after him, killing two birds with one stone by throwing in a sainthood to appease England's patron.

One of Sir George's trusted men was put in command of the converted longboat for the voyage to Virginia. Picking a route through the reefs was always going to be dangerous, so it was agreed that a watch would be kept on St David's Island by day and beacons left burn-

ORDER TELEOCEPHALI.
FAMILY SCARIDÆ.

9

PSEUDOSCARUS CÆRULEUS
(D. rare) ¼

Scale full size

rats or mosquitoes anywhere, although there were many flies and large cockroaches. To conserve supplies, hogs were slaughtered only when the weather prevented fishing. The ship's dog, fully recovered from its ordeal, proved a cunning hunter of wild hogs, fastening its teeth into their hind legs.

Reasonably satisfied about the food supply, Sir George went off for days on end in his little boat to map the islands. He discovered an archipelago of seven main islands and many smaller ones aligned roughly in the shape of a fish

LEFT AND ABOVE: from *Fishes of Bermuda*, painted by Lady Lefroy between 1871 and 1877.

ing at night for their return on completion of the mission or, in an emergency, before. Gates's assiduous secretary took his turn at a point since known as Strachey's Watch. In the event, the precautions came to nothing: the longboat was neither seen nor heard of again.

Unwilling to stake all on the longboat reaching Virginia, Gates and Somers got to work separately on two new ships – a hint of the division that existed between the passenger-colonists and the professional seamen in the party. The construction of Gates's boat, *Deliverance*, took place close to where he had proclaimed his bay and had a monopoly, bar one small item, on the materials salvaged from the *Sea Venture*. The work was under the supervision of the ship's carpenter, Richard Frobisher. The name of the building site, originally Frobisher's Building's Bay, is more generally referred to now around St George's merely as Building's Bay.

In the circumstances, the design and construction of *Deliverance* was an extraordinary achievement. The full-size replica on Ordnance Island in St George's is awesome. Although more modest in size (30 as opposed to 80 tons), Somers' ship, *Patience*, was perhaps an even greater feat. The only part of the stricken *Sea Venture* that went into it was a single iron bolt. The rest was built of local cedar and held

The rebels told Gates that they wanted to build a third ship on one of the other islands to take them back to England. Gates disingenuously seemed to agree to their demands. *Ex officio*, however, he had the right to nominate the island concerned, and the one he had in mind was a rocky outcrop. Of course, he added, the men would have to fend for themselves. The rebellion melted; work on the *Deliverance* resumed. The governor was dismayed that the ship's carpenter was among the rebels. He was reduced in the governor's estimation to nothing more than "one who made much profession of Scripture, a mutinous and dissembling imposter".

together by carved, wooden dowels. The seams of the 30-ton craft were caulked with a mixture of wax, crushed coral rock and turtle oil. No trace of the ship remains.

The pace of the work on the ships in stifling heat caused considerable grumbling, especially among those who began to feel that they were probably better off where they were, rather than pushing on to the hardships of food shortages, a disagreeable climate and the troubles connected with restless Native Americans in Virginia. The sailors' aspirations leant towards the luxurious life available in England on the proceeds of Spanish treasure, which they were confident of finding if only they had time to look for it.

Bloody murder

Over at his building site on "The Main" (island), Sir George had to deal with a murder. The murderer, Edward Waters, was bound to the body of his victim to await hanging in the morning. His shipmates freed him during the night and he fled into the woods. He was later pardoned and allowed to return to work.

While this was going on, the first baby was born in Bermuda. The father was John Rolfe, who later made history in Virginia by taking as a second wife the Native American princess Pocahontas. The baby did not survive.

The incipient mood of mutiny was revived by the doings of the questionable "gentleman",

Henry Paine. He stole weapons and distributed them to conspirators. Paine then became involved in an argument with a captain of the guard, striking him in a flood of expletives which "would offend the modest ear too much to express it in his own phrase". The plot spilled out and the governor decided matters had gone too far: Paine would hang immediately. "…And the ladder being ready, after he had made many confessions, he earnestly desired, being a Gentleman, that he might be shot to death, and towards evening he had his desire; the sun and his life setting together." Henry Paine thus earned the questionable distinction of being the

The two fugitives watched from their hiding place as the two ships picked a way through the reefs and, bound for Virginia, drew out of sight.

Jamestown, when *Deliverance* and *Patience* arrived there in 1610, was miserable. Some of the settlers whose ships had ridden out the hurricane which wrecked *Sea Venture* fared less well against the Native Americans and had already been murdered. The survivors were on the verge of evacuating, when relief arrived in the person of Lord de la Ware. It remained to persuade the truculent Native Americans to trade some of their corn, and Sir George Somers, spotting his opportunity, said that he knew of some

first of many people to be executed in Bermuda.

Two of the conspirators, Christopher Carter, a veteran of the earlier, half-hearted mutiny, and Waters, the reprieved murderer, went into hiding and turned a deaf ear to entreaties to give themselves up. They had still not reappeared when *Deliverance* and *Patience* were ready to leave for Virginia, although it seems that Somers may have been nurturing the hope of an early return to Bermuda and had secretly appointed them "caretakers" in the meantime.

LEFT: the replica of *Deliverance*.
ABOVE: Somers and the *Sea Venture*.
RIGHT: Somers' grave in 1905.

hogs that might appeal to them. The hogs in question were, of course, situated in Bermuda, and Sir George proposed collecting them in *Patience*.

It will never be known exactly what Somers' intentions were – did he really care, for example, whether the Indians ever saw the hogs? – but Carter and Waters were apparently expecting him. They were no longer in hiding and rowed out to meet *Patience*. The strain of the voyage was too much for the old admiral, however, and he returned only to die. His body was embalmed and put aboard *Patience* for onward passage to Lyme Regis, his parliamentary seat, but his heart was removed and placed in what is now the Somers Garden in St George's. A

plaque with some dreadful doggerel by a later governor, Nathaniel Butler, marks the spot.

The hog mission forgotten, *Patience* now sailed for England, leaving Carter and Waters to resume their vigil. They had additional company in the person of one Edward Chard and the *Sea Venture*'s dog, a situation which was to become the basis of Washington Irving's historical tale *Three Kings of Bermuda*.

Three kings

What Matthew Somers, who returned to England with his father's body, had to report about Bermuda persuaded the Virginia Company to establish an offshoot, the Somers Island Company. The King granted a charter which empowered the company to colonise and govern the island in accordance with English law.

Back in Bermuda, the "three kings" were industrious, clearing Smith's Island to plant a variety of crops, including tobacco, and salting vast quantities of pork for the winter. They were one day scouring the beach in Somerset for pearls when they came across a more valuable prize. Ambergris, the smelly contents of a sick whale's stomach, was a key ingredient in the production of scent and worth £3 an ounce in London. One of the pieces they found weighed 80 lbs (36 kg), enough to set them up for life.

The ambergris, like any treasure or pearls that might be found, legally belonged to the company. The men decided that the company did not need to know about their discovery. Chard claimed the bulk for himself because he had actually spotted it. Carter and Waters disputed this, the beginning of a "most hot and violent contention" that lasted two years. It obsessed them even when fishing and on one occasion led to "a fierce combat" with oars. After toppling overboard, they continued the struggle in the water. The dog was roused into joining another of their fist-fights and in the excitement bit Waters, his nominal master. Carter emerged as the peace-maker and hid all weapons.

Instead, they resolved to build a boat which would take them to Newfoundland with their precious cargo. From there, they would not have to wait long for a passage to England. Just then, however, a ship threaded cautiously through the reefs. The first intentional settlers had arrived. ❑

LEFT: *St George's* by Thomas Driver.

GOVERNORS AND WITCHCRAFT

A succession of colourful governors shaped early Bermuda and its settlers,
who made the transition from pirates to farmers to accomplished shipbuilders

Bermuda's first official governor, Master Richard Moore, a former ship's carpenter, was full of good intentions. He was impressed by what the "three kings" had achieved when they weren't fighting over the secret ambergris, although he immediately moved the main settlement from Smith's Island to St George's. One of Moore's first tasks was to build a small, thatched church on the site of the present St Peter's, which, even in its later guise, still qualifies as "the oldest Anglican church in continuous use in the western hemisphere".

Silk route

Moore's second priority was the construction of forts to ward off the Spanish. He asked the "three kings" about commercial prospects such as pearls, tobacco, whales, silk, yellow wood – and ambergris. They told him what they knew. On the specific point of ambergris, however, no – none at all.

In fact, they were already conspiring with the captain of the newly arrived ship to sneak off with "their" ambergris. The captain indiscreetly mentioned its existence to one of his passengers, Edwin Kendall, who was intrigued. The story leaked, and Carter tried to save his skin by confessing all to Moore. Chard and Kendall were promptly locked up, and, without much fuss, Chard was sentenced to death. A gallows was erected on the island where the replica of *Deliverance* now stands, but virtually as the rope went round his neck Chard's sentence was commuted to three years' imprisonment.

The first of Moore's forts – he planned to fortify all the obvious seaward approaches, especially what is known as Castle Island – was named after Gates. In Spain, the Duke of Medina Sidonia, a name forever linked to the Armada, was proposing to attack the 200 settlers "and send them off to England".

The urgency in preparing defences diverted the energy that would otherwise have gone into

essential food production. The hogs had depleted the burrowed eggs of the cahows on the populated islands, and the men had depleted the hogs. Moore needed more help from the company, and so he decided that the best way to drum it up was to use the fabulous potential of ambergris as bait. Instalments of it were duly

despatched to England at enticing intervals.

In the meantime, there were complaints about the work load because of the rush to build forts. Two men were so persistent in their moaning that Moore had them charged, mentioning in passing that the penalty on conviction would be death. "One fell dead of palsy on the spot and the other was so frightened by the event that he reformed."

An invasion of a different type nearly finished off the young colony completely. Daniel Elfrith, an English pirate, was warmly received when he turned up with a Spanish prize loaded with grain. As the grain tumbled out, so too, however, did rats – ravenous creatures that

LEFT: Carter House.
RIGHT: picturesque cannon at Gates' Fort.

devoured anything and everything as in an Old Testament plague. When they had eaten through one island, they swam to the next. Dogs killed them by the thousand, cats went wild and grew fat on them, but nothing could stop the rats. They were found in the stomachs of fish that had swallowed them whole as they swam in shoals across channels.

Settlers continued to arrive but couldn't be fed. For Bermuda this was "starving time". Moore dispersed the population to islands where there were fewer rats. The Rev. Lewis Hughes, a Welsh Puritan, was sent to Cooper's Island, which still had a good stock of cahows.

nurses had no great liking for their responsibilities; so, rather than bother with fishing for food, they merely slaughtered the company's few remaining cattle. When asked what had happened to the cattle, they said the beasts had gone swimming to escape the heat – and drowned. Men loath to work disappeared into the woods and lived off crabs and snails. One of them surfaced long afterward "with never a rag on his back but yet with a good store of fat on his belly".

The Puritan Hughes was appalled at the amount of excessive drinking. The heaviest drinkers were to be found in Somerset and

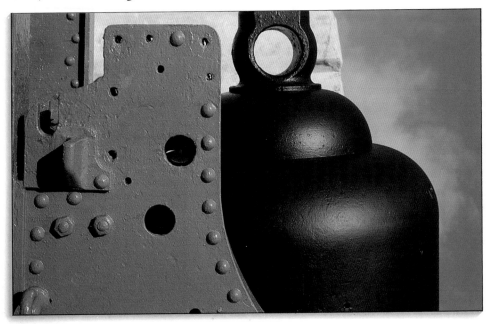

He hated his companions – "ungodly, slothful and heartless men" who were "so greedy that they would not wait until their meat was cooked but more like dogs than Christians did devour it blood raw". He described the scene on the island: "Every cabin had pots and kettles full of birds boiling, and others roasting on spits while the living wild birds walked among the people in the cabins, making their strange noises as though begging to be taken." The diet of undercooked cahow proved to be too rich for the settlers' weak stomachs and many died.

An isolation camp was established at Port Royal for sick colonists who were supposed to be cared for by healthy ones. The reluctant

St George's, and if ever the two should meet anything could and probably would happen. On just such an occasion, one of the revellers dropped dead. The inquest found him guilty of causing his own death. Hughes wrote approvingly of what happened next. The body was placed on the road with a stake through it; the survivors were made to wear placards on their backs which read: "These are the companions of him which killed himself with drinking." One was taken to the whipping post; another, a soldier, was saddled across a cannon. The ensuing explosion "did shake him terribly".

Hughes was equally pleased about the punishment meted out to whores. "For their comfort and to cool them a little they are now and then towed at a boat's tail up and down the harbour." The self-righteous but nevertheless plucky Puritan was later revealed as someone who enjoyed, or anyway indulged in, a fairly adventurous sex-life himself.

Eventually, on 14 March 1614, the long-anticipated Spanish "invasion" took place. Two merchantmen on their way home from San Domingo had been ordered to find out what was happening in the colony. They saw smoke rising from two forts, one made of timber, the other of masonry, about 330 ft (100 metres) apart. The colonists mistook the ships for

sky-high. The men "tramped back and forth and all over it" but no explosion occurred and it was perhaps as well that only one of the cannons worked. Moore took over its operation personally. His initial shot sailed over the main mast of the first ship. His second hit the rigging and the Spaniards turned tail. They could not have known that only a single cannon ball was left in the arsenal.

The jubilant governor expected the company's congratulations for his repulsion of the Spaniards. Instead, the next communication was yet another pestering request for more ambergris, with the implication that Moore

English vessels bringing supplies. They went out in two launches to meet them and were "a musket shot off" when they realised their potentially fatal mistake.

The alarm sent Governor Moore hurrying to the fort on Castle Island. The fruit of two years' labour was about to be tested. In the excitement, the defenders very nearly perpetrated what would have been a spectacular own goal. One of them knocked over a keg, spilling enough gunpowder to blow the whole place

might be keeping some back for himself. Moore felt he had to clear his name and set off for London. He managed to vindicate his actions but decided against returning to Bermuda. He joined up with Raleigh and was later killed in action.

Drunken anarchy

The arrangements Moore made for the running of Bermuda in his absence were described as "the very worst that he ever committed during the whole of his abode, for not any one of these thus put in authority were fit for the place or capable of the employment". The plan was that the colony should be run

LEFT: military hardware.
ABOVE: settlers enjoyed a potent drink made from the berries of the palmetto tree.

by a council of six, each member taking turns at being governor for a term of one month.

Lots drawn, the first of them was Charles Caldicott, and at once there was an indication of what the future held. All work ceased. No further progress was made on Moore's cherished fortifications, nor on the farms. The only interruption of a leisurely existence of swimming, pleasure boating, eating palmetto berries and drinking the juice was the need to make stills that would provide a wider choice of liquor, and to repair an old Spanish ship for the purposes of piracy. Caldicott and two of his governor colleagues assembled a crew of 36

eager, would-be pirates. Those who stayed behind were promised a share of the spoils. "Afterwards roving at sea", noted the surveyor Richard Norwood, who had declined to join them, "they were driven to great extremity and at last, as I have heard, taken by the Spaniards who hanged up divers of them, and what became of the rest I know not".

With Caldicott at sea in 1615, the next governor in line was a Captain Mansfield who "had only so much more wit than his fellows as to help him to be so much the more vicious". He declared a policy of "general leave to play so that now the bravest fellow was he who could drink deepest, bowl best with soccer shot

in the Governor's garden and win the most loblolly", the last being a popular gruel.

Mansfield reluctantly made way for Christopher Carter, one of the former "three kings". He had been rewarded for spilling the beans about the ambergris with the title to Cooper's Island. He was convinced the island held Spanish treasure and was too busy trying to dig it up to have any time for affairs of state. With no one to egg them on, the settlers slipped happily into bone idleness.

The tempo of "perpetual night" did not change under Carter's successor, Captain Kendall, the following month. "Not a hoe, axe, pickaxe or shovel was so much as once heard in the streets; not an oar seen or heard unless when their stout stomachs compelled them to it." Evidently resigned to not finding the elusive treasure, even Carter was content to "sit still, eat and especially drink at his ease and to the full".

With three of the governors-designate still occupied at sea, whereabouts unknown, the prospect of another month of Mansfield in command distressed those in the colony who were not part of his coterie. He affected best behaviour while there was a supply ship in port, which would soon be returning to England with the latest news. As soon as it left, however, he reverted to type, confiscating for his own use all the drink the ship had delivered, a year's supply for the whole colony. The amazing drinking bout that followed had the colonists turning to The Rev. Hughes for guidance.

On getting wind of the stirrings, Mansfield and his "Bacchanalian crew" occupied Warwick fort above the town, stocked up with ammunition, raised a flag and dared anyone to challenge them. Hughes went to remonstrate with him. Mansfield dared not harm Hughes, but he arrested one of his supporters and tortured him so badly that he had to be sent to Carter on Cooper's Island to recuperate in private.

Ostensibly to give the colony a treat, but in reality because he had finished the company drink, Mansfield declared public celebrations. Led by heralds and flying the governor's flag, he traversed his domain, leaving one settlement for the next as soon as he had drunk what the inhabitants had to offer.

Having consumed every drop they could uncover throughout Bermuda, Mansfield and his entourage returned to St George's to ponder their next move. News of a Flemish ship in distress, and the possibility that it was carrying gold – not to mention the odd bottle or two – sent governor and friends rushing to the shore. The wreck yielded only a disappointing £20. Mansfield said he would look after it personally.

He had cleverly concealed his excesses from the officers and crew of the returning supply ship, but that did not explain to the company's satisfaction why a ship meant to return brimful with local produce, especially tobacco, was empty. Colonies like Bermuda were founded for no other reason than profit, so something had to be done. The man chosen to restore order and profits was Daniel Tucker, planter.

"weighted with irons, and kept upon the ground night and day in grievous pain".

To prevent any further such misunderstandings from occurring again, the governor posted a proclamation that "whosoever shall use any art or means to the disgrace of any member of this plantation, or give any backbiting, slanderous disgraceful words... shall on the first offence ask public forgiveness upon their knees in church. And for continuance... to be whipped and ask the like public forgiveness with addition of such further punishment as shall be inflicted upon them".

Tucker's subjects soon learnt to recognise

Stern discipline

Dan Tucker's experience as a planter in Virginia had impressed on him "the improvement... wrought by stern discipline". He demonstrated his convictions at once. A drunk heckled him while he was introducing himself to the population; the man was removed from the room and was subsequently hanged. Henceforth, Tucker announced, a drummer would wake everyone up at dawn for serious work. Another protester naively raised his voice and was immediately sent to prison,

warning signs. "When in a morneinge his hatt stoode on one side or such a coloured sute of cloathes was worne, there was noe comeinge nere him all that whole daye." Hoping that safety lay in numbers, most of the work force threatened a go-slow strike. Tucker rose early the following morning to "cudgell with his owne hands not fewer than fortie of his poore workmen" before breakfast.

His methods were at least a tonic for the economy. He cleared the ground for planting and had timber squared for building purposes. Plantains, sugar cane, figs, pines, cassava and pawpaws were imported from the Bahamas, and replacement hogs from Virginia. Tucker did not want to

LEFT: Bermuda is ringed with ancient forts.
ABOVE: the Old Rectory dates from 1705.

be too dependent on tobacco, but it was not long before he was able to send 30,000 lb (13,600 kg) back to the company, the first significant return on its investment in Bermuda.

Whaling was less successful. The sperm whales that swam past Bermuda in early spring were too fast and powerful for conventional whaling methods. The whalers were able to strike with harpoons but after "many trialls, hazards, adventures and many rayleinges against poor Mistris Fortune, not so much as one piece of whale" was landed. When wounded, the whales were "exceedingly fierce".

Tucker tackled the rat problem with the same

ties for not reporting such talk, so witnesses put him under arrest with the intention of delivering him to Tucker.

Pollard was on his way to Tucker in a small boat when the governor passed in another boat going the other way. Tucker was "so deep in thought that they had difficulty in stopping him", but Pollard's captors were able to draw alongside and present him with their prisoner. "Fretting at being thus waylaid", Tucker told them to lock him up in St George's until he returned. "I have more serious thinges to thincke of at this time," he remarked. He then spotted Rich, who was an ordinary passenger in

iron discipline he used on his men. As neither dogs, cats, traps nor poison had worked against the rats, he decided to burn the islands – not once but twice. Acre upon acre of valuable cedar went up in smoke to the distress of the owners, some of whom had powerful friends and relatives in the company. Among them were Robert Rich, who was related to the Earl of Warwick, and William Pollard, a gentleman of the household of the Earl of Pembroke.

Rich and Pollard had both made known their opposition to Tucker, the latter going so far as to say that rather than supply any more workers for Tucker's public works "he himselfe would lie in yrons for them". There were grave penal-

the same boat. "Lock him up while you're about it," he ordered.

Tucker was two weeks returning. Pollard and Rich prudently acknowledged their offence as "heynous" and "submitted wholly to the Governours mercye". He "thereupon that he might shewe... that he always proceeded with mercye rather than justic, not only remitted their transgressions, but instantly restored them to their formers places of command".

What had been occupying Tucker's mind when the boats crossed was a devious scheme that was to contribute to his ultimate downfall. A survey had just shown that the islands were larger than had been supposed when the land was distributed among the "tribes" named after the principal Adventurers of the Somers Island Company, men like Sir Edwyn Sandys and William Cavendish, Earl of Devonshire. (These "tribes" were the forerunners to today's parishes.) In addition to these private holdings, each divided into 50 "shares", there was "public land" amounting to about one-seventh of the colony which was supposed to produce sufficient revenue to pay the salaries of the governor, sheriff, clergy and others. Ordinary settlers were expected to work this public land and in certain circumstances they could even end up owning parcels of it.

hectares) to Bermuda than had previously been realised. Tucker was determined to have the lot. An "overplus" of 200 acres was vague, however, so Tucker ordered Norwood to rig the survey so that the unsuspected acres were specifically in the very valley which Norwood had recommended as being of "fatte and lustye soyle".

Tucker decided to erect a house. The site of the house, between Southampton and Sandys, meant that timber felled at St David's had to be "squared and framed… by the choysest workmen" at St George's before being "conveyed in flotes as near to the overplus as he could, and from thence to be haled, by the strength of

The survey was undertaken by Richard Norwood, who was sent to Bermuda to look for pearls. After failing to find any, he hollowed a canoe out of a tree trunk and proceeded to paddle around the islands doing a survey that stands the test of time remarkably well. Before he set off, Tucker asked him to keep an eye open for some good, unoccupied land to which he could then lay claim. He was entitled to three shares – that is, 75 acres (30 hectares).

Norwood did better than that. He discovered that there were actually 200 more acres (80

LEFT: Bermudian cedar tree before and after.
ABOVE: close-up of St Peter's Church cedar door.

men, to the place wher he appointed". No remuneration was offered for any of this work although some of the labourers "were well payd with sound cudgellinge by the Governours owne hand". The work went "nimbly forward".

The Rev. Hughes compared Tucker's "large, hansome and well contrived house" with the "thacht hovell" of St Peter's Church, was disgusted, and said so. When Tucker next saw him he remarked: "Take you heed of and looke well to yourselfe: for if you serve me so but one more, I shall tie your neck and heeles together until your back crack, and so helpe you to repentance." Hughes was not intimidated, so Tucker turned on Rich, who decided it was time he returned to England to expose Tucker, especially the "overplus" scandal. The governor knew the repercussions would be some time coming and continued with plans to replace St George's Town with a new capital, on the opposite shore of Castle Harbour. He proposed to call it Tucker's Town.

Tucker had to be tricked into leaving Bermuda. Ensign Wood, whom Tucker had once wished to hang, made known the existence of a letter which purported to be from a friend in England saying that Tucker had better journey to England fast to defend his reputation. Tucker snatched the letter out of Wood's hands and

Richard Moore's departure in similar circumstances: a local man suddenly in charge preferred to ingratiate himself by throwing open the official drinks cabinet and inviting cronies to a non-stop party.

Order and witchcraft

Captain Nathaniel Butler, brought in to rescue the situation, was the most positive of Bermuda's governors (1619–22) under the Somers Island Company. He was not a man to be trifled with, a lesson driven home to one Henry Harriott who not only challenged Butler's authority but interrupted a sermon in

read it pensively. While making arrangements to leave, he was persuaded by Wood to let Miles Kendall take over as governor in his absence. The news of Tucker's impending departure came as such a relief that his broad hint about a farewell "present" produced an immediate donation of 1,500 lb (680 kg) of finest tobacco in case he changed his mind.

The man who deputised for Tucker was, a "good fellowe" and "conveniently manageable". According to his successor, however, he was "a man mainly marching downhill to all dunghill actions, senseless of reputation and utterly incapable of all noble respects". The situation was a repetition of Master

St Peter's to call The Rev. Hughes a fool. He was "to be conveyed manacled through the main to Southampton there to have one of his ears nailed to a post to be especially erected for him and to be named 'Harriott's Post' and so to remain for the space of one half hour". After which he was to be taken back to St George's, placed in the pillory, fined 1,000 lb (450 kg) of tobacco – and have his other ear cut off. When that was over, he was to remain a prisoner during the governor's pleasure.

Having made his point, however, Butler wished to show that he was not going to be another Tucker, and Harriott was allowed to keep one ear. Butler was generally scornful of

Tucker's methods, which he described as "dissonant from the laws of England... every petty larceny and two-penny pilfery being equally rated with the highest felonies and censured with death".

Harriott's fine in tobacco reflected the trend toward using tobacco as currency rather than Bermuda's distinctive Hog Money, which did not exist in sufficient quantity to cover everyday commerce. These coins, specially minted for Bermuda, were silver-plated copper; a hog and the value expressed in Roman numerals were shown on one side, a sailing ship on the other. The hog motif was undoubtedly a trib-

transactions did not depend on cash. In any case, the export of Hog Money was forbidden.

Workers were paid in tobacco. Craftsmen received two pounds (1 kg) a day, labourers one (0.5 kg). When the company shipped out boys (as labourers or apprentices) and young women (as wives), they were sold to the highest bidder in tobacco. Prices were expected to cover at least the cost of the passage. These human cargoes sometimes turned sour: one lot, drawn from English prisons, were found to be suffering from jail fever, wrongly diagnosed as plague. The men were isolated on Castle Island; the women, many of

ute to the wild pigs that dominated the diet of the grateful early settlers. Hog Money is highly prized by collectors today.

Tobacco road

The value of tobacco as currency was not based on a compulsion to smoke. Officially, the things money could buy were products delivered by the company's magazine ship, which called once or perhaps twice a year. The ship collected as much tobacco as it could carry for the return voyage to England, so

whom were pregnant when they arrived, were given to anyone willing to live with the risk.

In most respects, Butler was progressive: he organised the construction of bridges between the larger islands, introduced conservation measures to protect turtles, established regular Assizes and a legislative assembly (the second parliament in the New World), and replaced the old St Peter's Church, about which The Rev. Hughes had never stopped complaining, with a new one made of stone which still stands, and built the State House.

As a writer, especially of letters to the company defending his policies, Butler was capable of polished vitriol, but as a poet he left room for

LEFT: Governor Butler protected local turtles.
ABOVE: "plague" victims were put on Castle Island.

improvement. Discovering Somers' grave in a state of neglect, Butler mounted a slab of marble over it and was personally responsible for the inscription. He even moved the date of Somers' death, which was 1610, by a year, in order to achieve a desperate rhyme:

In the year 1611
Noble Sir George Somers went home
*   to heaven...*

He had other problems. One was Kendall, who feigned sickness to avoid coming to trial and slunk away to England. He later made an unwelcome return and so, too (after Butler had left), did ex-Governor Tucker, who modestly

demanded official status as one who was above the law, presumably answerable only to God. Tucker had managed to settle the "overplus" controversy so that he retained the house he had built there. In the event, he didn't need legal immunity because he was able to behave himself until his death in 1626, when he was buried in the graveyard of Southampton church.

A local dynasty

Tucker's property was inherited by two nephews, George and Henry, and down this line a local dynasty came into being, in the early days almost as notorious as the old man (for treachery during the American Revolution) but later respectably eclectic in good works, not least Mrs Terry Tucker from the Isle of Wight in England, who married into the family and turned out scores of books and papers about her adopted land. Mr Teddy Tucker is a distinguished underwater explorer.

Tobacco production soared under Butler, but hopes that it would underpin the economy were dashed as thoroughly as those attached to ambergris, whaling and semi-official piracy. Tobacco, which was not as good as that grown in Virginia and the Caribbean, was further knocked out of commercial contention by having to carry an additional tax by which the Somers Island Company hoped to recoup its losses in Bermuda.

The tobacco growers resorted to keeping the best of the crop for themselves and handing over to the company the dregs. The better tobacco was especially useful for black market dealings with passing ships. With the company officers concentrated in St George's, the bays and lagoons of the other islands made furtive contacts a fairly simple matter. The black marketeers matched tighter surveillance with ruses like stuffing tobacco into barrels of fish. Reviled company "searchers" sniffed out illicit tobacco stashed in, around and under houses, often in purpose-built vaults. On discovery, the culprits were imprisoned, soundly flogged or (the fate of Captain Kendall, among others) clamped into the stocks which bore the placard: "This for the concealing of tobacco."

The civil war over tobacco finally came to a head under one of Butler's successors, Captain Henry Woodhouse, a military man whose absolute faith in the efficacy of stern discipline almost rivalled that of Tucker's. A certain Mrs Margaret Heyling, convicted of stealing a turkey, was let off a penalty of 12 lashes across her naked back but was made instead to sit in church for six months, in the corner as it were, with a humiliating placard. Woodhouse lost the moral high ground when Heyling was later declared innocent of her crime – he had to compensate her with 100 lbs (45 kg) of tobacco – and with the embarrassing disclosure that he was leasing public lands and pocketing the proceeds. Forced to resign, he remained to torment his successors.

The list of company governors after Woodhouse includes household names in Bermuda: Roger Wood, progenitor of a famous family; John Trimingham, merchant; and Sir John

Heydon, commemorated in the Heydon Trust estate. Trimingham first won attention as the leader of a demonstration protesting at the beheading of King Charles I in England.

Bermuda was predominantly royalist in so far as the troubles "at home" were played out on its shores. It was caught up in the struggle between the established Church and the Puritans and suffered its own purge of alleged witches. The 22 witch trials over a period of 40 years were held in the State House built by Butler. The first victim was Jeane Gardiner, accused of bewitching a mulatto woman. She was stripped and searched for diabolical mark-

ducking. He, too, floated and was forced by his religious convictions to acknowledge that there could be only one answer: "I am a witch," he declared. He was hanged, followed by two women whose names he mentioned in connection with strange goings-on concerning cats.

Bermuda struggled to keep up with political and religious changes in England, but with poor communications it was all too easy to be caught on the wrong foot when the Navy called, like being a Papist when a Protestant had just ascended the throne (and vice versa), or a supporter of the Duke of Monmouth, not knowing that his rebellion had already been put down.

ings – a boil or mole was sufficient. In her case, a blue mark in the mouth was the evidence that led to her arms being crossed so that thumbs could be tied to opposite big toes. Thus trussed, she was thrown into the channel where *Deliverance* now stands. That she floated could only be attributed to the assistance of the devil; so, in accordance with the practice of the times, she was dragged out and hanged.

Men were not exempt. John Middleton, a devout Puritan, was found to have enough blue marks on his body to justify an investigative

In volatile times, the way company rule worked in Bermuda could be debilitating. The fundamental weakness, from the company's point of view, was that in spite of everything Bermuda was not making money for the Adventurers. The company's interests lay in monopoly, and what was good for the company was in this instance bad for the people. The original investors lost interest and were happy to sell off parcels of land. The new owners had their own ideas about their role in Bermuda, and how loyally to serve the company's best interests was not one of them.

The inevitable impasse led to the dissolution of the Somers Island Company in 1684 and the

LEFT AND ABOVE: profitable shipbuilding replaced agriculture as a main industry.

passing of its charter to the Crown. The changes were at first barely perceptible. Colonel Richard Coney, the last company governor, stayed on in the same capacity until the appointment of the first royal governor, Sir Robert Robinson, the following year, which also marked the death of King Charles II.

The Crown was no less keen than the company had been to maximise tax and other revenues from Bermuda, but the restraints on trade were relaxed. The proviso was that the colonists should not do business with the king's enemies, whoever they happened to be at any particular time.

The colonists took the opportunity to

abandon what had proved to be fruitless agriculture in favour of the sea and a promising ship-building industry. A ban on the construction of ships of more than five tons was rescinded. Before the end of the century, Bermuda's shipyards had built 76 ocean-going vessels of between 10 and 100 tons as well as hundreds of two-masted fishing boats.

In the following century, they were launched at the rate of a couple of dozen per year in sizes up to 200 tons. The local cedar was so fine-grained that it did not need seasoning. Ships made from it were relatively light and strong; they were accordingly very fast and, in light weather, could outsail most

naval vessels. Around two-thirds of Bermuda-built vessels were sold abroad.

Even before the dissolution of the company, Bermudians had been venturing to Turk's Island in the West Indies for salt, a valuable commodity especially in the American colonies. The salt was raked by slaves in winter, stored in Bermuda, and when the weather improved sold in American ports as far north as New England or exchanged for corn, bread, flour, meat and so forth. Trade with the West Indies produced rum, molasses and cotton.

The salt trade was so lucrative that there were attempts by both French and Spaniards to seize Turk's Island. At one point there were no fewer than 750 Bermudians engaged in the salt industry on the island, and rather naturally the thought crossed their minds formally to annex Turk's Island, which of course would have made it a colony of a colony.

They had similar ambitions with regard to the Bahamas, which a few Bermudians had originally colonised on behalf of the British government. Bermuda behaved like a precocious mother-hen and in 1713 went to the lengths of sending an expedition to the Bahamas to clear out a nest of pirates who were thought to be doing the place no good. The notion of a greater Bermuda came to nothing, however, and Turk's Island was eventually made over to the Bahamas.

A threat to trade

While Bermuda was exporting cabbages and onions profitably to the West Indies, the male colonists considered agriculture to be demeaning. Able-bodied slaves and slave-owners alike preferred to earn their living at sea, or at least in the ship-building business. As a result, farms were left in the hands of geriatric black residents, mostly women.

The lure of greater profits away from the land lulled Bermuda into an economic imbalance in that three-quarters of the supplies necessary for subsistence were being imported from the nearby American colonies. That might have been tolerable as matters were; but 1775 was approaching and, when it arrived, Bermuda was in league with the worst conceivable trading partner, a rebel against the Crown. ❑

LEFT: St Peter's cemetery contains graves of probable descendants of early settlers.

RIGHT: Bermuda's land brought little agricultural gain.

Military Band on the March, Bermuda

WARS AND EARLY TOURISTS

Involvement in conflict was at first motivated by self-preservation and opportunism,
but nothing could stop Bermuda's development as a holiday destination

"Our necessities in the articles of powder and lead are so great", General George Washington wrote on 4 August 1775, "as to require an immediate supply... No quantity, however small, is beneath notice... Among others, I have had one mentioned, which has some weight with me... One Harris has lately come from Bermuda, where there is a very considerable magazine in a remote part of the island; and the inhabitants well disposed not only to our cause in general, but to assist in this enterprise in particular".

Heinous crime

Washington outlined rough plans for acquiring the powder, but 10 days after the letter was written – long before his plan could have been implemented – a group of men arrived who had made a secretive night landing in whaleboats at Tobacco Bay on St George's north shore. They removed slates from the roof of Bermuda's powder magazine and dropped inside. While they were forcing a door, their look-outs were surprised by a man in uniform. He was quickly killed. With no better idea of what to do with the body, the look-outs buried it where they were, which happened to be in the garden of the sleeping governor, George James Bruere, "a man of unpleasant disposition, to characterise him mildly".

Around 100 barrels of gunpowder were duly removed from the magazine and rolled down the hill to the boats. The barrels were heaved aboard, whereupon the boats dissolved into the darkness to transfer their cargo to the waiting *Lady Catherine* of Virginia, under the command of Captain Ord. In due time, the powder reached Philadelphia and a grateful Continental Congress lifted the sanctions which had been imposed on Bermuda as a loyal colony of the English Crown.

The discovery of the theft the next morning caused outrage. A "most heinous... crime,"

PRECEDING PAGES: military band on the march.
LEFT: the American Revolution.
RIGHT: George Washington.

Governor Bruere called the deed, and offered £100 for information. None was forthcoming. If Bermudians had been involved, they would have been guilty at least of treason, and the punishment for treason was unequivocal.

The story was soon embellished. One version had the keys to the magazine being stolen

from beneath the governor's pillow while he slept. Another put the blame on a Captain Morgan, creating the legend of "Old Morgan", a raincloud which hangs over Bermuda at certain times of the year and is supposed to represent the captain's restless spirit awaiting the trial and execution of the descendants of the guilty parties.

As fellow colonials, Bermudians must have shared some of the resentment underlying the American Revolution, but inhabitants of an isolated group of islands in the mid-Atlantic were clearly not in a position to do much about it. A great many had families living in America, and not only was the economy critically dependent on American ties but they were also staring starvation in the face.

The Bermudian Legislature took the extraordinary step of writing to King George III explaining that it had asked the American Congress for help, without which "the people… must inevitably perish", hoping that he would understand and forgive. Congress's reply to this request for help was revealing: Bermuda would receive the needed supplies if it could provide arms, ammunition… and gunpowder.

In the course of time, interesting facts about the gunpowder theft were unearthed – literally so in the case of the man whom the look-outs

Collusion between Bermudians and American rebels over the gunpowder did not mean, however, that the islanders as a whole were bent on throwing in their lot with the Americans. Officially, which is to say in the person of Governor Bruere, Bermuda remained unambiguously loyal to the Crown and housed American prisoners (in appalling conditions) in what is now the St George's post office. The Americans were in no doubt that Bermuda was enemy territory and in December 1779 despatched an invasion force in four warships. Their plans were upset by the arrival of strong British reinforcements on the very day of the intended

killed and buried in the governor's garden. His bones were exhumed a century later during building excavations for the "Unfinished Church". In daylight, the skeleton was seen to be wearing a French uniform, the long-postponed explanation for the disappearance of a French officer who happened to be in Bermuda on the night of the theft and had presumably gone for a stroll. The minutes of the Pennsylvania Committee of Safety, dated 26 August 1775, reveal receipt of an invoice for "1,182 lb of gunpowder" in the amount of £161.14s.8d. The signatory awaiting payment was "Henry Tucker, chairman of the Deputies of the several parishes of Bermuda".

attack. The ships withdrew. The decisive Franco-American victory at Yorktown in 1781 removed the need to try again.

An independent and belligerent United States put Bermuda (and Canada) into the front line as far as Britain was concerned, and so began a process to turn Bermuda into the "Gibraltar of the West". The need to beef up defences was given greater urgency by war with France in 1793 and, as history shows, the troublesome Napoleon was soon to enter the equation. A pleasant cameo from the Royal Navy's thorough survey of the deep-water possibilities in and around Bermuda was the high opinion formed of a local pilot, Jemmy Darrell, who happened to be a slave. The Navy recommended his freedom as a tribute to outstanding services; Governor and Council complied.

The untested balance of power in the Atlantic created perfect conditions for privateers, and Bermudians were not slow to recognise the opportunities. Following the notable example of Hezekiah Frith, the Bermudian economy became dependent on the substantial proceeds of privateering. "A rude, desultory kind of life," sniffed Governor William Brown, lately of Salem, Massachusetts. He lifted the restrictions on whaling, but that was not enough to divert Bermudian eyes from far bigger prizes.

enemy. "We hear of frequent arrivals at Bermuda of provisions from the United States," a Baltimore newspaper reported. "The traitors may yet be caught. It is a desperate game."

Bermuda's privateers had to run risks and lost many ships. The port of Hamilton alone recorded the loss of 39 registered vessels with cargoes valued at £200,000, mostly to American privateers. By the end of the war, though, the balance sheet looked better: Bermuda had acquired 43 foreign vessels, putting the strength of its merchant navy above 70 ships.

The official record of Hamilton's losses during the war coincidentally reflected the town's

Britain and America were at war again in 1812. Bermuda's unscrupulous entrepreneurs, a classification that excluded almost nobody, had recognised during the American Revolution the possibility of profiting from business with both sides during a war. What followed in 1812 enabled them to refine their methods in unknowing preparation for the bonanza presented by the American Civil War. Bermuda was in the best possible position to benefit from the willingness of certain Americans to sell supplies to British squadrons, technically their

growing importance at the expense of St George's. Established in 1790 during Governor Henry Hamilton's term, Hamilton was both more central than the existing capital and a far more convenient place for shipping. The sea approaches were less treacherous and the off-loading facilities a greatly needed improvement. Clamours to have the capital transferred to Hamilton were first heard in 1811, and on 1 January 1815 the move became official.

The American Civil War

On 19 April 1861, President Abraham Lincoln proclaimed a blockade of the Confederate states from South Carolina to Texas. This was the

LEFT AND ABOVE: Edward James's watercolours of Bermudian military activities.

signal for a resumption of the cat-and-mouse game around Bermuda that had started with 16th-century pirates lying in wait for Spanish ships on their way home from the New World bulging with treasure and tobacco. The principles were unchanged, but there were naturally a few modern refinements. The Southern states had cotton, desirable in the mills of Lancashire. Britain had arms and munitions, desirable in the South. Steamships powered by coal had come into use. With finite resources, the Union was best able to enforce the blockade on the coastal approaches; there was not a great deal to be done about traffic in the North Atlantic. Con-

rency. These astronomical sums were possible because raw cotton costing between four and six cents a pound (0.5 kg) in Southern ports was fetching 60 cents in England. The speculators did some simple arithmetic which showed that the cost of building a ship, and paying the crew, could generally be recovered by just two trips.

Major Norman Walker co-ordinated the Confederate activities in Bermuda. He watched, and was watched by, Mr C.M. Allen, the Union's man. Britain maintained that there was nothing wrong in transhipping cargo and therefore felt no obligation to intervene. Allen alerted the blockade fleet to the arrival of a ship from Eng-

federate tactics were self-evident: big ships – no matter if they were rather slow – between English ports and Bermuda (as well as Nassau and Havana); smaller ships, with a premium on speed, for the dash in and out of Southern ports.

Lincoln had agents in Bermuda to keep him informed of what was happening. These agents duly reported that the island was "swarming with secessionists". They might have added that St George's was also swarming with sailors, who were intoxicated by the thought of the pay on offer for blockade running. Captains could earn $5,000 per round trip, senior officers $2,500, and ordinary seamen $250. The men were to be paid in gold, not Confederate cur-

land, and the runners would soon be setting off on the second leg. Walker's preoccupation was coal. In the interest of speed, the blockade runners needed high-grade coal, which would normally have been American anthracite. With those supplies cut off, Walker had to maintain adequate stocks of Welsh semi-bituminous coal.

The extra power of high-grade coal was not the only criterion. It also burnt more cleanly, a vital consideration when the ships were specially designed with the lowest possible profile. They were propelled either by screws or paddles and, in an emergency, the funnels could be telescoped out of sight. The steam was blown off through underwater exhaust pipes. As operations were usually at night, the hulls were painted a dull grey to render them almost invisible. Obviously, no lights were shown, and even the lamps on the binnacle were shrouded so that only the helmsman could see them. Cocks were excluded from the live poultry on board in case they crowed. The blockade runners, varying between 100 and 900 tons and drawing 9 or 10 ft (about 3 metres) of water, could achieve 14 knots – enough to outrun the fastest warships.

Excitement and, of course, the money attracted hundreds of adventurers, some of them senior Royal Navy officers on furlough. Assumed names were the order of the day:

Giraffe. It was re-fitted in Wilmington to emerge as the *Robert E. Lee*. Under the command of John Wilkinson, the *Lee* ran the blockade 26 times with cargoes of cotton to the value of $2 million in gold. Wilkinson was forced to undertake one of these runs from Wilmington – with a substantial quantity of Confederate gold – fuelled by an inferior type of North Carolina coal. The coal belched smoke but would not make steam. With an enemy ship closing fast, Wilkinson told his engineer to try burning cotton soaked in turpentine. The *Lee* accelerated to safety but was captured, without Wilkinson, on its next run.

"Captain Roberts" enjoyed the admiration even of his enemies, and when his legendary steamer *Don* was eventually captured, a Union officer leapt aboard with a cry of "Well, Captain Roberts, so we have caught you at last!" To the officer's disappointment, "Roberts" had taken the mail ship home to England for a spot of leave. He moved on to another romantic career after the war under his true name and a fancy title, Hobart Pasha of the Turkish Navy.

Better remembered than the *Don* was a ship bought in England for $32,000 and named

LEFT AND ABOVE: the island played a role in the American Civil War.

Germ warfare

Dr Luke P. Blackburn was in stark contrast to the colourful characters who had turned St George's into a cosmopolitan free-for-all. He purported to be a physician of New Orleans and an expert on the yellow fever that had reached epidemic proportions in Bermuda. He refused any kind of payment for treating scores of patients. One of Mr Allen's spies, however, exposed him: the saint-like doctor was in reality a Southern agent collecting bedclothes and handkerchiefs stained with the tell-tale "black vomit". He planned to give the infected articles as lethal presents to the poor of the North. Blackburn had already left for Halifax when the incriminating trunks were found, packed and ready to go. There are examples in ancient history of infected items being thrown over the walls of besieged cities, but Blackburn deserves an unworthy place in the more recent annals of germ warfare.

The merchants of Bermuda were making so much money out of the Civil War that the fall of Wilmington was devastating. It had not occurred to most of them that the Confederacy might actually lose the war, and they were left with enormous stocks for a market that vanished virtually overnight. There was no reversion to the *status quo ante*; the technological advances brought about in time of warfare had finished

Royal tourist

Princess Louise, the daughter of Queen Victoria but a resident of Canada by virtue of marriage to the Marquess of Lorne, the Governor General, alerted Bermudians to commercial possibilities that were to rescue the islands. Before air travel, North Americans seeking relief from bitter winters travelled as far as a slow steamer could carry them in the time available. The Caribbean was warm but out of reach of East Coast ports; Bermuda was an obvious alternative.

Princess Louise's "discovery" of Bermuda attracted considerable publicity throughout the United States and in Canada, and among the

off the wooden boat-building industry. As small islands with nothing in the way of natural resources once the cedar had gone, the economy of Bermuda was precariously hitched to windfalls. The cycle began with the discovery of a lump of ambergris and ended after several ups-and-downs with the American peace.

The hectic economic opportunities created by the American Civil War summarily ceased with the peace, and earning a living thereafter became a matter of cultivating potatoes, onions and arrowroot. This was altogether too humdrum an existence for some, and they were inclined to emigrate to the United States to renew more exciting business acquaintances.

many who were persuaded to emulate her royal example was the writer Mark Twain. His feelings on arrival after a turbulent voyage could not have been all that different from those of Sir George Somers': "Paradise, but you have to go through Hell to get to it."

Of course, the development of tourism was disrupted by wars, even by wars from which Bermuda could hardly have been more remote. Boers captured during the war in South Africa were imprisoned on some of the smaller islands. They recognised a market for souvenirs and set about making and selling them. World War I had a more direct bearing. Bermuda raised separate black and white

Spies at the Princess Hotel

Had anyone known, there was a clue to the super-secret intelligence work going on in Bermuda during World War II. It lay in the number of young English women who arrived with one feature in common: lovely legs. They were "trappers", the nickname given to codebreakers who could read and analyse enemy communications at high speed.

"It was fairly certain that a girl with unshapely legs would make a bad trapper," a medical report noted. "Nobody has discovered what part the leg plays. There is here the basis for some fundamental research." The motives of the doctor who wrote the report were considered suspect and he was not commissioned to investigate further.

The covert activities included ULTRA, the means by which British Military Intelligence was able to decipher enemy signals. All would have been lost if the enemy suspected that their codes, conceived by the supposedly infallible ENIGMA machine, had been broken. The women were necessarily tight-lipped, and that put a damper on their social lives.

In addition to the electronic interception and interpretation of signals sent by German submarines operating in the Atlantic, the Bermuda station was responsible for sifting through the mail carried in ships and aircraft between the US and Europe, especially Lisbon, a hotbed of spies. The targets of this surveillance were German agents in the US who were reporting on American arms shipments to Britain and other sensitive matters.

The trappers became so skilled that they could open, examine and re-seal without trace the 200,000 letters usually found in Pan American Flying Clippers on their stop-over in Bermuda.

The operations room of what was known as "Bletchley in the Tropics" (Bletchley Park, Oxfordshire, being the general headquarters) was in the basement of the Hamilton Princess Hotel.

Cut off by the U-boat offensive in 1942, Bermuda ran short of everything. The rationing authorities decided that people would eat less bread if it was not fresh; so it was aged for a day before being put on sale. Unfortunately, the flour which went into the bread was much older, and the freshest bread served to the trappers and their colleagues had mould running through it.

They put up with these privations in order to score many notable successes, not all military. The Vollard Collection of 270 Impressionist paintings was on its way by sea from France to New York to be sold and the proceeds of the sale would be valuable dollars for Hitler's war-chest. The search was concentrated on the ship *Excalibur*. When it called at Hamilton agents were ready, they cut open the ship's safe with oxyactylene and discovered the collection. The paintings, stored for a while in the Bank of Bermuda vaults, were sent to Canada. After the war they were returned to the

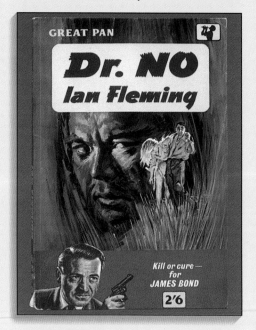

owners from whom they had been forcibly removed.

After the war, Ian Fleming, himself in naval intelligence, put James Bond on assignment in Bermuda. At the height of Bond's popularity, there were suggestions that he actually existed and still occupied in the Hamilton Princess a penthouse belonging to Sir William Stephenson, "A Man Called Intrepid". Fans combed the hotel for signs of the private lift and the gold-plated Cadillac which their fictional hero supposedly enjoyed.

When the results proved negative, they looked around for other clues. Their eyes were drawn to a giant fish tank in one of the hotel bars. Of course, declared the *cognoscenti*, the very tank which had once contained Dr No's ghastly sharks! ❑

LEFT: early visitors.
RIGHT: spies weren't fictional characters in Bermuda.

volunteer units, both of which found themselves in the thick of the trench warfare in France, taking heavy losses.

The impact of casualties in a small (albeit still divided) community were deeply felt, although once again it is Bermuda's strategic position in the Atlantic that history dwells on. The most famous running battle in this connection was probably that involving the German Admiral von Spee. The cruisers *Scharnhorst* and *Gneisenau* under his command struck an early blow in a devastating action against the Royal Navy's Bermuda-based Fourth Cruiser Squadron under Admiral

Sir Christopher Cradock. The Admiral and the crews of the cruisers *Monmouth* and *Good Hope* lost their lives. The defeat was avenged two months later (December 1914) at the Battle of the Falkland Islands when the battle-cruisers *Inflexible* and *Invincible* under Admiral Sturdee sank von Spee's squadron. Like Cradock, von Spee went down with his ship.

World War II

A pocket battleship named after the gallant admiral, the *Graf Spee*, was the focus of one of the epic sea battles of World War II, and once again Bermuda was involved through the locally based Royal Navy squadron and its commander,

Commodore Henry Harwood. The German battleships posed an enormous threat to Atlantic shipping and top priority was given to their destruction. Harwood's force, the cruisers *Exeter*, *Ajax* and *Achilles*, had no real answer to the *Graf Spee's* 11-inch guns, but on running into the battleship off the River Plate in Uruguay they engaged in a ferocious action which virtually destroyed *Exeter* within an hour. The *Graf Spee* was damaged too, however, and was forced to limp into the neutral port of Montevideo while the battered British ships kept vigil outside. On the third day, the *Graf Spee* re-emerged but, on the orders of Captain Hans Langsdorff, was scuttled before battle could be resumed. Langsdorff later shot himself.

Bermuda again contributed troops to the Allied effort, and as usual there were cat-and-mouse naval games in surrounding waters. But the colony's more important roles were in new areas: as an intelligence-gathering centre, and as a component in the Anglo-American lend-lease programme which provided Britain with badly needed destroyers when the US, as a neutral nation, was not supposed to sell them.

The US was given a 99-year lease to build a base in Bermuda. The construction of the base, and especially a large airport, changed the face of the islands. It encompassed most of St David's Island and all of Cooper's and other smaller islands; the channels in between were filled in to make a runway that took into account the prevailing, and strong, winds. Much of the labour was recruited locally, although, compared with the Americans involved, at discriminatory rates of pay which gave impetus to the trade union movement.

The number of American forces personnel in Bermuda increased sharply after Pearl Harbor in 1941. They had money to spend but little to spend it on because of the cordon thrown around the islands by German U-boats.

As in the previous three centuries, the threat of direct invasion never materialised and the island defences remained untested. The Atlantic fortress became gracefully obsolete in a new age of post-war weaponry. The enduring legacies of the war were the re-shaped geography of the islands and the irreversible presence of that hitherto alien object, the motor vehicle. ❑

LEFT: the Cenotaph commemorates both world wars.
RIGHT: the military marches on.

Two Natives, Bermuda

FROM SLAVERY TO HARMONY

Whatever their origins – colonists, slaves or indentured labourers –
early arrivals struggled to make a good life

Bermuda was uninhabited until the arrival of Europeans. There is nothing in the history of the islands to parallel the slaughter of an indigenous population as occurred in, for example, the Bahamas. The first black man known to have stepped ashore was probably not a slave but a sailor in a Spanish ship, the unfortunate fellow who was sent ashore with a lantern to look for a piece of wood and was terrified out of his wits when dive-bombed by cahows. He lost no time in leaving.

Nor were slaves, when eventually imported, necessarily black. Some of the earliest were Native Americans and Caribbean Indians who paddled their canoes unwisely far from shore and were picked up by privateers. These chattels were later joined in Bermuda by prisoners of the Pequod and Sachem Philip wars in New England. Others were Irish, a wildly unsuccessful experiment which caused the Assizes to rule that "it shall not be lawful for any inhabitant in these islands to buy or purchase any more of the Irish nation upon any pretence whatever".

"Accidental negroes"

Slavery was forever controversial in Bermuda, although not always for obvious reasons. The first consignment of 14 slaves in 1619 was in reality a bribe offered to the governor, the unworthy Miles Kendall, by a passing pirate who wished to enter the harbour so that his ship "might carine herselfe and take in some necessaries". Kendall had no qualms about accepting them; his concern was how to make them his own when, strictly speaking, they were the property of the Somers Island Company. The verdict on the proper ownership of these "accidental negroes" eventually went to neither Kendall nor the company but to the Earl of Warwick.

Slaves were not present in Bermuda in significant numbers until 1640, although the few who had preceded them were appearing in

court records as early as 1632, usually in the grim context of being hanged, drawn and quartered for theft. Most of the negroes were brought to the islands from the West Indies and arrived with Spanish names. The company regretted accepting some Indians presented by a pirate named Jackson and actually freed them.

Not all Native American or Caribbean Indians were so lucky. A gift of some "unruly" Mohicans from the Dutch governor of New York was accepted, as was another hapless wretch who was snatched from America while enfeebled by drink. By whatever means they reached Bermuda, there was enough Indian blood about to produce a distinctive sub-group in society which is still evident today, especially around St David's.

The principle of slavery was sometimes examined metaphysically. According to Theodore L. Godet, a 19th-century Bermudian doctor, his compatriots two centuries earlier were squeamish about enslaving poor Englishmen kidnapped from their villages by "monsters in

---

PRECEDING PAGES: island life around 1890.
LEFT: *The Bermudian* by Andrew Wyeth.
RIGHT: the well-known rubber tree in Hamilton.

human shape" and sold in the colonies. Their disgust at "buying and selling our fellow-creatures" was assuaged, in the case of black people, by the thought that they were "an intermediate race between man and monkey... half human" and therefore didn't count. The English who were shipped to Bermuda in circumstances which Godet would have deplored were technically indentured labour, although they might have been hard-pressed to notice the difference between that and outright slavery.

Godet, who seems to have regarded himself as something of a liberal in these matters, remarked in 1850 that nearly 20 years after their

tise. They were supported by at least one clergyman, The Rev. Sampson Bond, who agreed that "the breeding up of children in the Christian religion makes them stubborn".

If slaves belonging to different masters married, the children were born into slavery, the first going to the mother's household, the second to the father's, and so on. One piece of legislation exempted a master from prosecution if he accidentally killed a slave during the course of punishment. The deliberate killing of someone else's slave entailed compensation to the owner according to the slave's value.

The slaves did not always take this lying

formal liberation, the blacks were progressing well. "They undoubtedly possess organs peculiarly adapted to the science of music" and, if they were taught and practised, "become sufficiently expert to bear an inferior part in a private concert". He was optimistic about their future development generally: "...nothing but the want of intelligence can prevent them from assuming the rank of the labouring classes among the white population of the islands."

The early debate on the ethics of slavery foundered on whether a slave had a soul and, if so, whether baptism would render the holder unsuitable for servitude. The plantation owners problem was easily resolved – do not baptise. They were supported by at least one cler-

down. There were rumblings of discontent for some years before a revolt of free negroes and slaves in 1656, which resulted in the execution of three leaders and exile to the Bahamas for some of their supporters. Slaves (and at least a couple of white men) sentenced to death were occasionally offered a reprieve if they agreed to become executioners themselves.

Irish troubles

The rebellion of 1664 was a curious affair sparked off by the unwanted Irish slaves, who had arrived seven years earlier and been sold for £14 each – rather less than the going rate. They caused trouble from the moment they stepped ashore, and a warning was issued "that those that hath the Irish servants should take care that they straggle not night nor day as is too common with them".

The Irish seem to have got on quite well with the black slaves. One John Maclarie, given the job of delivering a cask of rum, opened it in the company of the governor's negroes. The party was broken up at an advanced stage by a marshal who then sold what little of the rum he was able to rescue. The Irish managed to persuade a number of black slaves to join an uprising for the specific purpose of exterminating non-Catholics. Just where unbaptised black

Local disturbances added to the unease caused by the atrocious slave rebellions in the French West Indies and resulted in extraordinary measures against Bermuda's slave population. A 1761 enactment, for example, declared "that any negro, who met a white person during the night, and was challenged, should fall on his knees; on failure of which, such offender was to receive 100 lashes". During another crisis, an Englishman who so much as saw a slave on the roads after curfew, which was half an hour after sunset, was obliged to kill him. If the slave managed to escape, the Englishman was liable to be fined up to 100 lb (45 kg) of tobacco.

slaves fitted into this scheme of things is unclear.

On learning of the plot, the governor banned gatherings of more than "two or three" Irish and/or negroes. Offenders would be "whipped from Constable to Constable whilst they run home to their masters' houses". It was then that the Assizes decreed no more buying or selling of the Irish nation. Owners seem to have offloaded their Irish slaves before the next rebellion in 1681 which was potentially more serious: five of the ringleaders were executed and two men, who had ridden from one settlement to another calling for support, were made to ride the gibbet.

LEFT AND RIGHT: black Bermudians *circa* 1890.

On the whole, the life of a slave in Bermuda was marginally better than in America or the West Indies. In the absence of large plantations, there were no chain gangs nor, for the men, much agricultural drudgery. "The most able of the male slaves were trained to the mechanical arts and to navigation, leaving only the most worthless of both sexes to be employed in the very inconsiderable tillage carried on."

The seafaring slaves, at least, seemed to enjoy a sense of freedom. A Bermudian privateer manned by 80 black men was once captured by an American privateer and taken to Boston where the slaves were offered their freedom. They unanimously preferred to return to their owners. As a neat counterpoint on a similar theme, an American brig carrying 78 slaves called at Hamilton in 1835, the year after slavery had been abolished in Bermuda. The slaves were brought before the Chief Justice "in the midst of such a scene of excitement as has seldom been witnessed in the town". They were offered their freedom in Bermuda and all accepted bar one woman named Ridgly, who chose to continue to the Carolinas with her five children.

Slavery, but not racial segregation, was abolished in 1834. Bermuda opted for total emancipation rather than an apprenticeship scheme. The owners were compensated to the sum of

£128,240 for 4,000 freed slaves (about 740 black people already being free). The Bermuda Parliament simultaneously passed an act increasing the franchise qualification from property worth £30 to £60, a condition not removed until 1965.

The racial prejudice prevalent in the 19th century is reflected in a book by "A Field Officer" who, perhaps sensibly, chose anonymity: "Although the coloured Mudians have almost all been taught to read and write, yet their memories are so defective, and their dispositions so idle, that, with few exceptions, they forget before they are twenty everything that they have learnt."

Although there was no overt race discrimination in the statute books, social, political and economic realities were in the mould of the segregated American South. The races attended separate schools, occupied different pews in church and didn't intermarry. Black people adopted a form of tactical voting which circumvented the colour prejudice in the prohibitive franchise property qualification and put a black carpenter, William Joell, into the colonial parliament in 1883. Others followed him, but slowly; it was not until the 1950s that black Bermudians were a significant political force.

Using the trade union movement as a power base, Dr Edgar Fitzgerald Gordon was able to force the pace. He died in 1955, but the momentum he created led to a successful boycott of segregated cinemas in 1959. Soon, black people started to appear in restaurants and theatres.

Party politics arrives

Until the 1960s Bermuda had no true political parties. The formation of the Progressive Labour Party (PLP)in 1963 set a precedent quickly followed by the United Bermuda Party (UBP), both multi-racial. The chosen leader of the UBP was – almost inevitably – a Tucker, in this case Sir Henry Tucker, banker. Under his influence, Bermuda's government was transformed into a modern a bi-cameral system.

The UBP dominated government for 30 years after the 1968 election. In 1971 Sir Henry made way for a black government leader, Sir Edward Richards. Sir John Swan was elected premier in 1982, and during his terms of office the black middle class flourished. In 1996, Bermudians had their first female premier, Pamela F. Gordon, appointed by the UBP mid-way through their term of office. But the times were changing; in 1998 the PLP assumed control of the government, and the leader of that party, Jennifer M. Smith, JP, became the first elected woman premier.

In 2003 the PLP won again, in the first election held under the new system based on the British model of one MP per seat. However, Jennifer Smith's leadership proved unpopular within her own party. Three days later, after being unable to form a cabinet, she resigned and was replaced by Alex Scott. December 2007 saw yet another PLP victory, this time under the leadership of Dr Ewart Brown, JP. ❑

LEFT: uniform harmony.
RIGHT: the scenic moongate attracts tourists.

MODERN BERMUDA

The world's top offshore financial centre has a reputation as a playground strictly for the well-heeled visitor. Here is an insider's view of contemporary society

The fact that Bermuda survives as a leading vacation destination for East Coast Americans is truly a credit to the natural assets of the island group itself. Seen as a chic and sophisticated paradise, the islands have recently suffered from a growing perception that they are old-fashioned and unfriendly. Bermuda is beautiful, but not perfect, and in the past an almost lackadaisical attitude to the tourist industry by some was nothing to be proud of. Nor is the fact that by the end of the 1990s annual air arrivals had dropped by nearly half since the early 1980s.

At first, it appeared that Bermudians were in denial of a problem – after all, the islands had been hosting visitors for more than a century. When visitors claimed the islands were getting too expensive, some so-called industry experts justified it by saying that the complainers were not rich enough to be there in the first place.

Even worse, there were quips that some of the older regular guests were dying off. The truth of the matter was that, with air travel becoming more affordable, other destinations, particularly those directly to the south, were developing industries of their own. They proved to be challenging competitors, with lower airfares, less expensive packages, good service and lots of island entertainment – and their people, new to the tourist dollar, seemed more appreciative of the business.

The number of North Americans visiting Bermuda declined following the terrorist attacks on the US in 2001. However, there are significant signs of improvement.

Luxury at a price

Value for money has been a big issue for a large number of visitors. The idea is that if they are paying a high price for a Bermuda holiday, they expect decent service. It is obviously up to the

individual restaurants, hotels and other businesses to ensure their own quality control, but the government is working on sprucing up the general morale in the industry. Incentives are offered to those who go above and beyond the call of duty. And now there is an annual black-tie gala event, modelled upon the music indus-

try's Grammy Awards, where managers and maids alike are honoured for their hard work, with a top prize valued at some US$20,000.

Icons of Bermuda culture such as the Gombeys (troupes of dancing drummers, *see page 156*) travel far and wide, promoting the islands. The Gombeys can even claim New York City's glamorous Waldorf Astoria Hotel as the venue of one of their gigs. As one can imagine, this attracted a lot of attention both on and off the island.

Meanwhile, there is a school of thought that believes the day of government-run tourism is over. David Dodwell, former Minister of Tourism and a successful hotelier, mooted the

PRECEDING PAGES: Hamilton's Front Street.
LEFT: a cruise ship and scooters, popular modes of transport around Bermuda.
RIGHT: doing Bermuda's business in shorts.

idea of a semi-private tourism authority with less red tape and more action. Developing hotel properties and updating existing stock is a priority. About 40 hotels and guesthouses have closed since the 1980s and few properties have replaced them.

While international business eclipses tourism as the dominant industry, former hotels are being developed as condominiums. Both government and private interests are exploring ways to encourage investment through improvements to the hotel stock, and also promoting the beauty and attractions of the island to the travelling public.

were making up more than 40 percent of the total number of visitors to Bermuda, compared to just 20 percent in 1990.

In the past, the value of cruise ship visitors was underestimated. It was a misconception that they did not spend much money on the island: they stayed on the ship while in port, did not do much shopping apart from buying small souvenirs and they even ate on the ship. The reality is, however, that cruise ship passengers travel by taxi, visit sights and pay hefty port charges directly to the government.

In an effort to encourage more cruise ships, the government has changed its policy to

Initiatives are aimed at attracting a more diverse blend of tourists to counteract the somewhat stuffy image the islands have acquired. However, the genteel, sophisticated image of the islands is maintained. In fact, Bermudian restraint in the limiting of cruise ship travel, the continued ban of hire cars and the protection of the reefs have all helped to make Bermuda's environment more attractive to visitors in a climate where ecotourism is becoming popular.

A cruise destination

While the air arrivals have proved challenging, Bermuda has become an attractive cruise ship destination. By 2003, cruise ship passengers

accommodate more of these visitors, allowing one weekend cruise ship – Bermuda had previously prohibited weekend stops of ships to give locals time off. Fortunately there is room to negotiate how many ships are allowed to dock, as Bermuda, with its close proximity to the US east coast, is in heavy demand by cruise lines.

Economic bedfellows

It was only natural for locals, who had spent a lifetime in the service industry, to want more for their children. With the wealth they had acquired through tourism, the next generation was sent to university abroad to study business. When those young professionals returned home, they gravitated towards the highly paid international finance industry, which was blossoming at that time. Bermuda now stands next to London and New York as a global insurance and reinsurance centre.

The tourism industry, by attracting airlines with regular flights from popular locations, enabled the development of international business. These businesses, primarily financial services, work to support the tourism initiatives as they know the degree to which it benefits them and the general standard of living.

Whether the two economic pillars are compatible is questionable. As the years rolled on

to $2,500 a month; two-bedrooms anything up to $4,500 and executive rentals from $13,000 all the way up to $20,000. In fact, at the start of the 21st century, some of the annual rents had begun to look more like a sale price elsewhere in the region.

The haves and have nots

For local families not employed in international business, times in the 1990s were tough, especially for many of the single-parent families. So while Bermuda was booming financially, socially there was some discontent, especially among the lower-income group.

there appeared to be a serious disparity in the levels of income – international versus local business. And rents, which compared to the rest of the world had always been considered high, skyrocketed. Landlords with family-sized properties or new apartments wanted the offshore executive tenants, whose companies often subsidised the rent.

The rental income became enough to easily pay off a high mortgage, effectively pushing prices even higher. The end result: renting a one-bedroom apartment ranges from US$1,500

LEFT: relaxing around Penno Wharf, St George.
ABOVE: fun on the water.

In November 1998, the general election produced a change. Out went the United Bermuda Party (UBP) and in came the Progressive Labour Party (PLP). For three decades the UBP, the political wing of the establishment, forged a pragmatic coalition of white and black residents which sought to bring a measure of social progress without scaring off Bermuda's conservative benefactors. And during all that time the PLP had to endure the humiliating reality that, as the only truly black party in a substantially black island, they just couldn't get themselves elected.

This was only partly due to some inconveniently drafted constituency boundaries. The deeper problem was that few people, black or white, trusted the PLP to run the island in an efficient, businesslike manner. The assumption that the PLP were bad for business was underlined by their consistently strong support of unionised labour. For decades, the UBP and their establishment mentors portrayed the PLP as menaces who, given half a chance, would wreck the economy with unjustified wage increases, unemployment pay – and income tax to make up the shortfall. However, at the beginning of the PLP's term of office only one relatively small international business pulled out, while several others arrived or expanded.

Most notably, the PLP put in place an Employment Act, legislated the CURE (Commission for Unity and Racial Equality) regulations to combat discrimination and added more teeth to the island's Human Rights Commission. They also brought into law more stringent guidelines for the employment of expats, and dealt confidently with OECD (Organization for Economic Cooperation and Development), European Union and British concerns over the island's low-tax status. However, critics argue that the PLP has reneged on its promise to be a people's government. Certainly escalating rents and real estate costs are widening the gap between the island's haves and have nots.

Independence

There are still political and social issues to deal with in the future, such as availability of affordable housing, rising crime rates, tackling drug abuse and attaining high educational standards, but stability has been Bermuda's byword.

For the most part, party unity has been maintained, but there have been some cracks. The issue of independence bubbles up regularly and could present a challenge for Bermuda. Independence was the downfall of one Premier, Sir John Swan, who resigned after a referendum showed Bermudians didn't want to cut ties with Britain. In political "retirement" Sir John emerged as a moderate voice for a progressive Bermuda and still made the news headlines on a regular basis.

Bermuda now lies in an interesting position. Its main industries – international business and tourism – are mature. With more than 100 years in tourism, it is likely that the islands will once again become a model to other destinations.

The islands are the first to go through the social ramifications of the resort industry. And perhaps this is an early example of what other destinations may face in years to come. Just as Bermuda led in the development of resort tourism, it now has another opportunity to lead the way again in the 21st century.

Future prospects

The people who come to the islands to enjoy a holiday or to work seek different things, but their very presence changes Bermudian society. In spite of high prices, these picturesque Atlantic islands are still an ideal spot to get away from it all and relax. The provision of a sophisticated business environment with comprehensive conference facilities and a wide range of accommodation makes it a desirable place for work and leisure.

The quality banking and investment management services, the communications links and the lack of income tax on the islands all continue to be a major draw, as do the general cleanliness and relatively low crime rate of the towns and beaches.

It now remains to be seen whether Bermuda can match or even surpass the popularity of its recent past.   ❏

LEFT: fresh fish for sale on Devonshire dock.
RIGHT: a beach beauty.

ISLAND ARCHITECTURE

The Bermudian landscape is rich with distinctive buildings – a permanent legacy of the resourceful pioneers who shaped the islands

Whether first seen from the air or from the sea, the feature that dominates the Bermuda landscape is not so much a vista of pretty beaches and tall palm trees – but something far less glamorous and more mundane: its roofs.

Pristine clean and glaringly white, their stepped form is so unmistakably Bermudian that photographers patiently spend hours lying in wait, propped at some awkward angle against a wall, trying to capture the right shadows cast across an obscure section of rooftop, hoping for the picture which will "say it all". Painters set easels to face inland, chanelling their vision away from turquoise seas and colourful sprays of hibiscus and oleander, looking upward, hoping that a few deft strokes on the white paper will magically capture the essence of the slopes.

The casual observer, of course, would be quite justified in wondering what this lofty obsession is all about. One may well wonder how it is that an island so generously endowed with natural beauty can be symbolised – rather accurately, as it so happens – by its roofs.

Artistically manipulated

Actually, Bermuda's rooftops are only one aspect of an entire style of architecture that is found nowhere else in the world. It is a distinctive style, a conglomeration of individual features that have been artistically manipulated into a pleasing, cohesive whole. Together, they also represent the complete embodiment of all those traits that make Bermuda so unusual. They reflect the convergence of climate and natural resources with the ingenuity of the local people.

Bermudian architecture is frequently referred to as being the country's sole truly indigenous art form; an authentic creation which only its people could have produced. Some maintain that the seeds for each feature were borrowed

from distant shores and then modified to suit local needs; another school of thought argues that it is entirely home-grown, pure, without the dubious benefits of external influences. Although neither may be absolutely correct, there is no doubt that Bermuda does have a style which is distinctively its own.

All architecture is blatantly influenced by the peculiarities of the building materials and by the specific characteristics of the climate that they will inevitably have to withstand. The difference with Bermuda, however, is that these technical considerations have been further inhibited by two additional restrictions. In the first place, when early settlers came to erect permanent buildings, the only suitable raw materials that could be found were corallian limestone and cedar. Imported alternatives were, and are, expensive, and awkward to acquire. Secondly, in the absence of any significant surface fresh water – there are no rivers and only a handful of small lakes – everything had to be designed around the absolute necessity for catching and storing rain water.

These early builders were well-versed in the potential severity of the weather; after all, their predecessors had been shipwrecked in Bermuda during the kind of ocean storm that Shakespeare immortalised as *The Tempest*. They were motivated less by aesthetics than by their own physical well-being, designing sturdy structures capable of withstanding the blustery torments of the Atlantic while capitalising on any shade and breezes in the hot and humid climate. Finally, they crowned their buildings with limestone roofs, an ingenious contrivance specifi-

open porches, to couple the refreshing benefits of outdoor living with the advantage of the shade.

The challenge was always to devise a roof that would allow the occupants to save and store the all-important rain water. Without the grey slates of Europe or the wooden shingles of North America, early Bermudians instinctively eyed the native limestone and the cedar.

A wooden superstructure was made for the roof using hand-hewn cedar logs for the rafters. Over these they laid carefully cut "slices" of limestone. Somewhat inaccurately, these pieces of over-lapping stone are still called "slates". The lower rows were fastened first and the oth-

cally designed to catch all the fresh rainfall needed for domestic consumption. Bermudian architecture successfully met these diverse requirements of function and comfort.

Practical designs

Basically, the houses consisted of thick walls generously breeched by windows, necessary for light and air. Shutters hang decoratively at either side, or dangle from above in the traditional *jalousie* style, always at the ready should an errant storm brew. The chimneys are square, solid and firmly capped by slabs of limestone, not the more vulnerable red, kiln-fired "pots" which are so typical elsewhere. Most homes have

ers added sequentially so that they ascended step-like to the crestline. To seal the roof against potential leakages, the finished surface was coated with a wash of lime.

The rain water was not gathered through conventional guttering; instead, it was corralled by a simple pattern of shallow walls which systematically directed each drop into downpipes located at strategic points along the roof edge. The water was then fed into a large storage tank dug into the solid bedrock adjacent to the main house. From this naturally cool, man-made cavern, it was carried by bucket into the house as required. This time-proven method for collecting fresh water is still practised today;

the only major modifications during the past four centuries have been to excavate a water tank directly beneath each dwelling and then electrically pump water up into the house.

At first glance, casual observers may feel the exteriors of Bermudian buildings are rather flat and bland, only enlivened by the practice of painting exterior walls in colours ranging from pastel pinks and blues through to the occasional outbursts of more vivid greens, tangerine and yellow. Likewise, shutters and wooden trimmings are also painted.

In truth, the fragile Bermuda limestone did indeed inhibit local architects and almost com-

Preserving the past

These houses incorporate a style of architecture that was meant to last, not something intended to survive just one lifetime before falling prey to the demolition ball.

The designated custodian of Bermuda's architecturally rich heritage is the Bermuda National Trust, a body comprised mainly of volunteers and relying heavily on public donations and bequests. The Trust, sometimes in conjunction with the local Audubon Society, manages various properties, which include buildings, open land and even fascinating cemeteries, whose headstones record many of

pletely denied them the opportunity to embellish outside surfaces with anything sculptural. There is nothing on the island remotely flamboyant or baroque. For better or worse, there are no cherubic angels swooping downward from corner clusters of acanthus leaves or any majestic neoclassical colonnades. Instead, Bermudians have opted for a more subtle decorative art form, one in which angular shadows emerge from each feature, moving continually like patterns of chiaroscuro along the walls, beneath the eaves and across the rooftops – decoration forever in motion as the sun progresses through the sky.

LEFT AND ABOVE: pastel-coloured island homes.

the less-known aspects of local history. The headquarters of this organisation are at Waterville, an architectural delight located on the edge of Hamilton harbour.

Of those buildings formally designated as historic properties, several are open to the public. Others are retained as museums or private residences, but the majority can be viewed by arrangement. Both Verdmont and Camden are referred to elsewhere in this guide, but there are also a great number of others that warrant a visit. St George's is a living monument to this island's fine architectural heritage, and it is difficult to imagine anyone being unable to enjoy a simple stroll through its winding streets.

Among the buildings that are of historic interest is Bridge House, located within sight of Kings Square in the heart of the town. Erected at the end of the 17th century, this former mansion has been the home of two governors by the name of Popple, as well as an enterprising Virginian privateer named Bridger Goodrich. The house was therefore once a focal point for considerable plotting and planning during earlier times. In the 19th century, a family of silversmiths named Rankin worked each day in the same downstairs rooms that now, appropriately, house an art gallery. The surrounding gardens, as with most National Trust properties on the

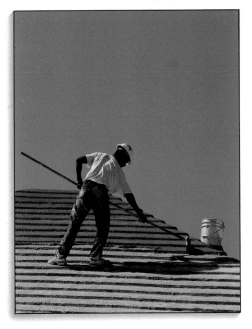

island, have been planted in a distinctive manner intended to reflect the original.

Nearby is Bermuda's oldest stone structure, the State House, which is open to the public. Built in 1620, it was originally the seat of local government. Today it is used by the Freemasons – rented for the exorbitant sum of one peppercorn, a princely due which is graciously handed over to the government during the annual Peppercorn Ceremony in Kings Square.

"Buckingham", "Casino" and "Reeve Court" are all in this same general vicinity. Each is a private residence, however, and so, unless a tenant is willing to give a private guided tour, these must be viewed from the outside. Collectively,

the grouping represents a characteristic neighbourhood from the 18th century, each with external watertanks clearly visible in the back garden.

On Water Street is the Tucker House. It was built as a private home in 1712 and is currently a museum, with a small bookshop below. The museum has been laid out in a way that enables the visitor to amble through each room and perhaps recapture a true feeling of what it would have been like to live in a old Bermudian home. It is well furnished with authentic pieces and decorated with incidental mementos and family pictures so as to recreate the domestic atmosphere of a previous era.

Designer air

One architectural feature worthy of particular note is the use of "tray" ceilings in the rooms. This was another Bermudian design that elevated the ceiling well up into the structural rafters, enabling warm air to rise while effectively leaving the lower section of the room cooler for the family. Evidently the Tuckers sought to enjoy the maximum in all home comforts.

At the opposite end of Bermuda, in Sandys Parish, is the magnificent estate called Springfield. Parts of the main building were constructed in the 17th century, so this property and its grounds certainly warrant a visit. In particular, attention should be drawn to the "buttery" which stands off the main courtyard.

A buttery is a small out-building specifically designed during those days prior to refrigeration as a place to store the spoilables from the kitchen pantry. It was said that items kept in the buttery – a shaded and well-ventilated structure – would be safe from insects, vermin and miscellaneous bacteria for days on end. Today, the distinctive pyramidal roof of the buttery remains a popular feature on the landscape.

Throughout the island, Bermuda's style of architecture embodies characteristics that make it quite distinctive from all others. Dominated by white roofs and sturdy walls, it survives as a permanent testimony to the ingenuity of those early settlers who exploited only two raw materials, but who successfully provided themselves with comfortable shelter in which to sit and enjoy the simple luxury of a goblet of fresh water. ❑

LEFT AND RIGHT: local architecture is distinguished by the roofs.

FESTIVAL FEVER

*Home-grown talent and international stars grace Bermudian stages every year
for spectacular performances in music, dance and drama*

Bermuda's theatrical scene builds to a peak in mid-winter with the Bermuda Festival. For six or seven weeks in January and February, residents and visitors can sample a fare of music, dance and drama, plus inspired foolery and magic by international talent.

The size of visiting companies and their productions is governed by the Bermuda-sized limits of island theatres and stages. The festival's programme folder notes: "The venues of the Bermuda Festival are all small halls. There are virtually no bad seats."

Festival events are held in the cosy 300-seat theatre in the Hamilton City Hall, in churches – the Bermuda Cathedral and St John's Church, near the capital – and in the 600-seat Ruth Seaton James Theatre in Cedarbridge Academy in Prospect.

Experimental theatre

The idea that tiny Bermuda could mount an arts festival was first tested in 1970, when the Arts Council sponsored an experimental but ambitious Summer Festival. It offered a play, a film, two dance companies, an abridged opera and a show of primitive art. The festival idea lapsed until it was resurrected in 1974, the result of a fortuitous circumstance: the friendship of a new governor with a celebrated violinist. In England Sir Edwin Leather, Governor of Bermuda, had been chairman of the Bath Festival, where he was associated with Sir Yehudi Menuhin. At the governor's suggestion the community created a winter arts festival that continues, well attended, to this day. Most performances are by overseas artists, though there is at least one local production.

Visiting troupes are impressed by the expertise and tireless work of backstage crews, mostly volunteers from the Bermuda Musical and Dramatic Society. These crews can spend half the night clearing the stage of one set and erecting another for the next performance on top of a full-time job.

LEFT: a souvenir festival programme.
RIGHT: City Hall is a favourite festival venue.

Over the years, many wonderful performers have delighted and sometimes surprised festival audiences. Dance companies have included stars of the Bolshoi, the Royal Winnipeg Ballet, the Alvin Ailey Dance Theater, the Dance Theater of Harlem, Momix and Break Urban Funk. African companies have also brought

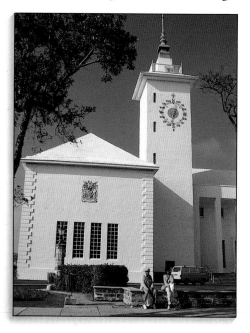

their colourful, high-energy programmes to the festival. Musical groups as diverse as the Canadian Brass, Moscow String Quartet, the King's Singers, Natalie Choquette/La Diva, Awadagan Pratt, Sweet Honey In The Rock, Branford Marsalis and ChuChu Valdez have graced the stages. Dramatic international as well as local productions always play a significant part.

International Film Festival

The Bermuda International Film Festival (BIFF) was established in 1997. It takes place in March and attracts an eclectic array of independent films from around the world. The Academy of Motion Picture Arts and Sciences has elected to recognise BIFF as a qualifying festival in the Short Films category for the Annual Academy Awards®.

Bermuda provides an intimate atmosphere for both the visiting filmmakers and the festival patrons. All this with just a handful of commercial theatres that, for practical reasons, usually only show Hollywood blockbusters. When BIFF rolls around, local people starved of more exotic fare flock to see the films. Screenings are followed by a chance to chat about the films with directors, producers, actors and others from the creative side of the production. And, since this is all happening in

George Benson, Diana Krall, Marcus Johnson, India Arie, Patti Labelle, Joss Stone, Arturo Sandoval, Lionel Richie, Smokey Robinson, Earth, Wind and Fire, and dozens of others. Local artists also get a chance to perform, often opening for the international acts.

Bermuda Guitar Festival

Great music is the goal of the Bermuda Guitar Festival, established in 2004 by local classical guitarist and popular teacher, Steve Crawford. He almost single-handedly, revived the popularity of the classical guitar in Bermuda. The four-day event, held in March,

Bermuda, there are dozens of lively parties associated with the film festival, where participants can see and be seen.

Bermuda Music Festival

Established in 1995 as the Bermuda Jazz Festival, this three-day music event now includes R&B and soul artists on its list of performers. While satellite or "fringe" events take place in clubs around the island, the main events take place at the Royal Naval Dockyard. The shows are performed on the water and the stage floats a few yards out from the water's edge; the music can be heard for miles.

Artists who have performed here include

allows guitarists to show off the rich quality and versatility of their instrument. Hungary's Katona Twins guitar duo were so impressed with the first festival and its appreciative audiences that they returned for the second, which signalled the green light for other top-tier artists, such as Michael Chapdelaine and guitarist, composer and Grammy Award-winner Andrew York.

Musical and Dramatic Society

Whether it's the British roots or the need for large numbers of actuaries, accountants and lawyers to express themselves outside of work, Bermuda has an astonishing amount of good live theatre, of which the Bermuda Musical and Dramatic Society (BMDS) is the heart. The group was founded in 1945 by theatre lovers who met in each other's homes to read plays. It soon began to mount productions of these plays in venues around the island. In 1972, it moved to its present location at the corner of Dundonald and Washington streets, which houses an intimate theatre, workshop space, a lively pub and also hosts a steady schedule of social events as well as dramatic productions.

Over the years the BMDS has presented such productions as *The Beauty Queen of Leeanne*, *Boston Marriage* and six 15-minute plays written and performed by local authors and actors. There is also a regular Christmas pantomime, with heroes and villains and men in dresses, in true British tradition.

Gilbert & Sullivan Society

Strangely, there is little Gilbert & Sullivan performed by the Gilbert & Sullivan Society, which presents a major musical play every year, as well as choral productions. In recent years, one of its most remarkable feats was presenting 14 performances of Bizet's opera, *Carmen* (in English) for the Bermuda Festival of the Arts, with overseas and local principals and local adult's and children's choruses. The society was the first non-professional company to secure the rights to and produce *Les Miserables* and in 2007 it staged a stunning production of *Dreamgirls*.

The G&S Society engages talented stage and musical directors, often from the UK, who work for months to shape dedicated local amateurs into professional-quality performers. To be in a Gilbert & Sullivan show requires participants to sacrifice almost everything for six months, except work or school, for rehearsals – but the result is always worth it, for performers and audiences alike.

Philharmonic Society

The Bermuda Philharmonic Society has a long tradition of providing orchestral music on the island. Music teachers, accomplished local musicians and visiting professionals flown in for special concerts make up the orchestra. With

LEFT: the late Yehudi Menuhin was indirectly responsible for the first Bermuda Festival.
RIGHT: an appropriate programme cover.

a mobile population, including guest workers who may only live on the island for a couple of years and young people prone to take off for education or job opportunities overseas, concerts need to be planned around available talent. If a piece requires a bassoon, and last year's bassoonist has moved back to Europe, the musical director has to rethink the idea or hire an overseas musician.

The choir, which, in recent years, has varied in number from 30 to over 100, presents less of a problem. The society generally performs an autumnal orchestral concert, a spring concert with orchestra and chorus, and another event

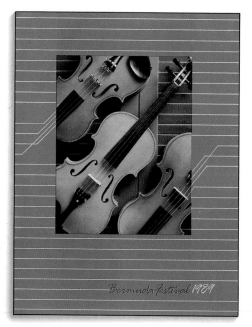

Bermuda Festival 1989

at Christmas. Its most popular appearances are the open-air "Pops" concerts which take place in June at St George's and Dockyard, for which the orchestra is often joined by the Band of the Bermuda Regiment.

Bermuda School of Music

While visiting Bermuda, you may see posters or advertisements for public concerts sponsored by the island's largest private music school, the Bermuda School of Music. In the spring, the school sponsors a chamber music concert, with international artists. It's also home to the Bermuda Chamber Choir, which performs classical works several times a year. ❑

SAILING THE SEAS

Both local and foreign sailors must be skilled in order to negotiate the reefs that surround Bermuda's islands, but help is never far away

There is something magical about the thought of sailing to Bermuda. It is as if an invisible lure is dangled in front of seafarers to tempt them into a hidden lair somewhere beyond the horizon.

In a far more practical sense, sailing to Bermuda from the American mainland can take upward of five days, and for those heading to the island from Europe, the passage will probably last at least two or three weeks.

If that seems a great deal of ocean swell, bear in mind that Bermuda is three-quarters of the way across the Atlantic. The island lies roughly 600 miles (960 km) due east of the Florida-Georgia boundary and is virtually on the same latitude as Casablanca, North Africa. It does indeed sit right out there, all alone.

Bermuda Harbour Radio

However, for those with sufficient skill and enough daring to make the ocean crossing, the rewards are worth the inconveniences of perpetually damp clothing, and staring at little on the horizon but waves while simultaneously swallowing handfuls of sea-sickness pills. These discomforts are soon forgotten when the low-lying form of the Bermudas is sighted deep along the brow of the waves. Soon one of two lighthouses will appear: St David's or Gibbs Hill. But there is another bonus in store, more subtle than any of the scenic preludes previously experienced, because at this stage yachts will have floated into the welcoming, warm and static domain of Bermuda Harbour Radio.

It is the general consensus among seasoned salts that Bermuda Harbour Radio is one of the friendliest, most helpful nautical stations in the world. The genial staff happily transmit 24 hours every day – dispensing navigational information to the lost and the weary, clarifying clearance procedures for the uninitiated and even arranging for messages of assurance

to be passed on to loved ones far away. This service is a fitting introduction to the courtesy and cordiality for which Bermuda has come to be known.

Most sailing vessels entering Bermudian waters head for St George's, to clear themselves straight away with local Immigration and Customs officials. Harbour Radio usually channels new arrivals in through The Cut and directs them across to the other side of the harbour to the quayside at Ordnance Island, opposite Kings Square. While awaiting clearance, all vessels must fly the familiar yellow "Q" flag.

Bermuda hosts thousands of transient yachts every year and has tried to ensure that entry procedures are basically uncomplicated and, on the whole, quite conventional. In short, there are no peculiar stipulations and there is certainly nothing sufficiently abnormal to cause last-minute panics or worried scurryings below deck. Furthermore, local officials tend to be polite and helpful – mercifully unlike their

PRECEDING PAGES: sailing from Newport to Bermuda.
LEFT: *Scaramouche.*
RIGHT: a little something for indoor sailors.

typically officious and detached counterparts in so many other seaports.

Each crew member must carry personal identification and the usual travel documents; before setting sail, foreign nationals should check for any visa requirements *(see Entry Regulations, page 283)*.

The yacht itself must have a valid Certificate of Registration and is presumed still to be carrying all of the relevant paperwork with which it was issued when clearing the last port-of-call. Any crew intending to leave the boat in Bermuda should be aware that a confirmed onward ticket is required before final landing

Once cleared, all sailors are free to travel throughout Bermuda as, how, when and where the proverbial spirit moves. There are innumerable bays and inlets to explore and seemingly endless miles of indented shoreline, all offering picturesque scenery.

Repairs and provisions

St George's is an ideal arrival and departure point. It is capable of satisfying all of the conventional requirements of seafarers, from laundry facilities through to specialist stores, such as sailmakers and chandlers. Repairs can be arranged (check the Yellow Pages or ask at

approval can be granted. Anyone arriving here for the first time would do well to note that Bermudians are diligent in their efforts to keep "undesirable" items away from their shores. The list includes the usual illegal drugs and guns, but also broadens to include large hunting knives, harpoons and spear-fishing paraphernalia. Anything that is deemed to be a weapon is promptly placed in bond and is returned only when the owner is about to cast off.

Visitors will be relieved to know that Bermuda is a relatively peaceful island; and unlike some parts of the Caribbean and South China Sea today, pirates have long since ceased to prowl.

any yacht club). In St George's and Hamilton boating supplies are available and some grocery stores will make dockside deliveries.

Although Bermuda's coastline is not cluttered by cove-bound fishing villages, a variety of convenient, temporary mooring is available. Harbour Radio or the Marine Police will suggest where the best anchorages can be found for overnight stays. Among the most popular spots in the East End are St George's Harbour, Ferry Reach, Shelly Bay, Castle Harbour and Great Bay, off St David's Island; off the West End, many sailors prefer to make for Ely's Harbour, the Great Sound, Riddells Bay and Dockyard. Private berthing privileges can be secured, by prior arrangement, with the yacht clubs in either Hamilton or St George's. (They may also know of boats that require casual crew for upcoming local races.)

Dockyard was developed by the British Royal Navy during that grand period when Victorian confidence seemed to acknowledge no boundaries. For decades, it served the expanding empire as the prime North Atlantic ship-building and re-supplying depot – becoming a bustling focal point of unprecedented nautical activity. Nowadays, the former boatyard is an ever-growing commercial development, with shops and restaurants, art galleries and studios, and

almost as challenging a mismatch as a grand prix engine on a roller skate. In the wrong hands, it threatens either to fly out of the water altogether or to nose-dive into the depths. There is a trophy awarded to the boat that does not sink during the race season – and, in many years, no team has been able to claim the prize.

Under certain conditions, it needs as many crew as can be crammed in – the rules of dinghy racing are relaxed on this point – with the interesting corollary that, if and when these conditions change, the surplus crew may be expected to jump overboard.

Bermudians grow up in small boats much as

marinas and watersports. Dockyard is home to one of Bermuda's most popular attractions, the Maritime Museum, with its wonderful exhibits of seagoing vessels and treasures rescued from the vast deep.

The Maritime Museum also highlights the colourful history of the Bermuda dinghy, the island's premier sailing vessel and one that is unique to this small group of islands. The Bermuda dinghy, just over 14 ft (4 metres) of open boat under monstrous sails, could be

LEFT: Bermuda fitted dinghy, *circa* 1900.
ABOVE: Hamilton in 1912, photographed by Walter White on his honeymoon.

French children learn to appreciate fine wines. In the absence of automobiles until after World War II, the small boat in Bermuda was traditionally the family transport and goods van rolled into one, so when it was wheeled out for fun a few sporting modifications were in order. Competitive sailing in Bermuda began in 1840 under the parallel auspices of the Royal Yacht Club (Royal Navy officers and nobs in sloops) and the Bermuda Native Yacht Club (black fishermen and boatmen in whatever was at their disposal, inevitably small open boats).

As the cost of ocean racing in sloops edged ever upward, the attraction of thrashing around Hamilton Harbour cheaply in the family banger broke down the racial bias. The quest for speed meant more and more sail and removable decking to reduce the amount of water taken aboard. The dinghy racing rules, deliberately kept minimal, permit a detachable iron fin 12 ft (3.6 metres) long as a keel and stays to support the mast. Special racing "fitted dinghies" were built from 1890s onward, the *Victory* on display in the Maritime Museum being one of the first.

Dinghy racing

Bermuda fitted dinghy racing, which is as exciting for spectators as it is for participants, is held every other Sunday from late May to Septem-

become accustomed to each other for the longer haul that lies ahead. Others, of course, have made Bermuda a specific destination and intend to stay for a while. Important yachting events such as the Newport-Bermuda race and the Marion-Bermuda race attract hundreds of sailors to the island. And visitors can often participate in local club races.

Whether cruising among the islands of Hamilton Harbour or simply relaxing with a leisurely sail up and down the coastline, sailing around Bermuda is not particularly hazardous. Pleasure trips must always be tempered with a regard for the conventional rules of safety. It is

ber in one or other of St George's Harbour, Hamilton Harbour, the Great Sound or Mangrove Bay.

Local racing is only one part of the story, however, as Bermuda becomes even more popular with foreign craft and crews. Some of the sailing boats that call into Bermuda are on a deliberately brief visit. They may have stopped off only to collect fresh water and food or to pick up a spare crew member; others come in to effect minor changes and repairs. Some American skippers use the relatively short hop to Bermuda as the "shake-down" leg of a major trip across the Atlantic or down to the Caribbean – a chance for crew and boat to

not uncommon to find a yacht embarrassingly perched atop some coral head in the centre of the harbour.

The number of seafarers who persist in using out-dated maps is astonishing; others chance their luck without any charts whatsoever. In recent memory, there was even one rather expensive yacht that came to grief while using the map depicted on a souvenir placemat. The simple reality is that Bermuda is encircled by a complicated network of reefs, banks and sandbars – many of which are hidden. Vessels sailing through these waters should carry a comprehensive set of up-to-date charts on board, at all times.

Another essential safety factor is the need to pay attention to local weather conditions. Conditions are subject not only to the prevailing systems of high and low pressure, but also to an untiring permutation of just about every other factor which might affect the weather. Fortunately, Bermuda's strategic position in the North Atlantic has made it a key location for professional meteorologists who devote their lives to plotting the movement of great winter storms.

There are all manner of government and quasi-government agencies that have invested millions in keeping their eyes on the ever-changing patterns of local weather. No sailor ever needs to find himself battling an unexpected squall simply because of a reluctance to telephone for a report. Harbour Radio puts out regular comprehensive broadcasts each day, and an instant update is never further away than the nearest handset.

For its own part, the Bermuda Government does its utmost to furnish conditions of safety and protection to all boats travelling in and through the country's waters. It uses various departments to ensure that marker-buoys, flashing beacons and suchlike are effectively maintained and functioning.

Any deviations to established patterns or procedures are very promptly reported to Harbour Radio, which, in turn, relays them to the public over the airwaves. Records are also kept of boat movements in and out of Bermudian territorial waters, so that a log is maintained for possible use with the Coast Guard in the event that a vessel should be overdue or go missing. Harbour Radio also serves as a clearing house for information about bulky and potentially dangerous flotsam and jetsam which may be a hazard to shipping in this part of the Atlantic.

Many magnetic myths

Much has been written both in jest and in myth about the curious magnetic variations which have been reported by sailors in boats which sail the Bermudian seas. Actually, the truth is both simple and entirely devoid of anything remotely mysterious.

As a point of instant clarification, two of the terms "deviation" and "variation" need to be defined. "Magnetic deviation" refers to the extent to which any individual compass deviates from the global norm or how inaccurate the manufacturers have made it. This should have been determined already, as automatically as adjusting the hands on a watch.

On the other hand, "magnetic variation" is that amount by which all compasses vary, according to where in the world they are being used. In and around Bermuda, the recognised variation between True North and Magnetic North is approximately 15 degrees to the west. All pertinent calculations on bearings should, therefore, incorporate this adjustment.

Anyone planning to charter a boat once they have arrived should contact the nearest Visitors' Service Bureau for up-to-date prices and information. Small craft such as sunfish, up to catamarans and yachts, are available. Detailed charts can be acquired overseas or through the Department of Marine & Ports, on Front Street in Hamilton, and the local Marine Police are always eager to give assistance and advice to anyone afloat. In addition, there is the comprehensive service of Harbour Radio.

The vastness and variety of Bermudian waters provides a unique opportunity for all types of sailors to experience enjoyment and adventure. In exchange, the seas demand respect. ❏

LEFT: a joyous celebration.
RIGHT: a coat of white paint to lighten up the day.

BERMUDA SPORTS

*Whether you visit Bermuda to work or play, there is a wide
variety of activities to enjoy – from sailing to soccer, golf to cricket*

A thletic pursuits are an integral part of island life. Not only do Bermudians play a great deal – there are more than 30 organised sports on the island – but sports also play a key role in Bermuda's tourism industry. Spectacular golf courses, natural sailing facilities and excellent fishing are among Bermuda's major tourist attractions, while the international events attract some of the world's top athletes in sailing, road running, triathlon and rugby.

The sports pages of the *The Royal Gazette* reflect this cosmopolitan interest in world sports and Bermudians themselves often compete at an international standard that belies the island's size and relative isolation.

Holiday match

Nothing illustrates the Bermudian passion for sport quite like Cup Match, an annual two-day cricket game. Played between the St George's and Somerset clubs on the Thursday and Friday before the first Monday of August, it may be one of the only sporting events in the world for which a public holiday was created. First played in 1902, the game attracted such crowds that by 1947 the government gave in to rife absenteeism at work and declared both days public holidays. Officially, the Thursday is the Cup Match holiday while Friday is Emancipation Day.

Some historians believe the match grew out of early black celebrations to mark Emancipation Day (1 August 1834) but to the majority of Bermudians the holiday is simply "Cup Match". It is not only the island's premier sporting event, it is also the holiday of the year and a major social gathering that attracts some 12,000 people, including the governor and premier. It is a carnival at which the cricket often seems incidental to chancing your luck at the Crown and Anchor tables or indulging in local delicacies such as curried mussel pie, shark hash or conch stew.

PRECEDING PAGES: Bermuda has more golf courses per square mile than any other nation.
LEFT AND RIGHT: two island pastimes.

Cricket and football (soccer) are Bermuda's national sports in terms of players and spectators. Cricket, played between April and September, has around 1,200 junior and senior players and 27 clubs, while football has almost 2,000 players and 30 clubs. Like most sports on the island, they were segregated until the early 1960s,

although both are now predominantly black and the leading teams remain those with origins as black working-men's or community clubs.

Internationally, Bermuda ranks among the best of the non-Test cricket nations, having advanced to the semi-finals and finals of the International Cricket Conference Trophy, the qualifier for the World Cup. Several Bermudian cricketers have played professionally, most notably all-rounder Alma (Champ) Hunt in the 1930s and bowler Clarence (Tuppence) Parfitt in the 1980s, both of whom played in Scotland. Bermuda also hosts first-class tours from England and the Caribbean.

The Somers Isles Cricket League runs games every Sunday but next to Cup Match the premier games are the Eastern, Central and Western Counties Cup competitions, which are actually area club tournaments.

International ball games

Football is the national winter sport and the Bermuda Football Association runs league and cup matches on most Sundays from October to April. Bermuda has a creditable international reputation, winning a bronze medal at the 1978 Central American and Caribbean Games. The island plays at all levels from the Olympics to regional youth tournaments; it is also a popular touring destination for English and European clubs.

On the water

The protected waters of the Great Sound, Hamilton Harbour and Harrington Sound make Bermuda a natural venue for international yachting regattas. Its position in the mid-Atlantic also makes it an ideal destination for long-distance races from the United States, such as the famous Newport-Bermuda Race, first sailed in 1906, and the more recent Marion-Bermuda Cruising Race, first held in 1975. Both are sailed in June of alternating years and the arrival of the boats at the Royal Bermuda Yacht Club and the Royal Hamilton Amateur Dinghy Club in Hamilton Harbour is one of the

Several Bermudians have played professionally in England and the United States, most notably Clyde Best, who starred for English First Division club West Ham United in the late 1960s and early 1970s, and Randy Horton, who played for the New York Cosmos in their 1970s heyday. Striker Shaun Goater MBE played in the UK for Southend United and Manchester City, and Kyle Lightbourne played for Coventry and Stoke City.

The top club competitions are the Dudley Eve Trophy, played over Christmas and New Year between the top four league teams at the halfway stage of the First Division season, and the FA Challenge Cup with its final each April.

colourful highlights of a Bermudian summer.

Bermudians have been yacht racing since the early 1800s when working dinghies were "fitted" for racing. Fitted dinghy racing in traditional 14-ft (4-metre) craft with vastly over-canvassed rigs remains the island's only original sport. International Race Week, an invitational regatta that attracts sailors from North America and Europe each April, has been an annual event since the late 1920s. The King Edward VII Gold Cup is the world's oldest match-racing trophy and is now contested each November by some of the world's leading skippers as part of the World Match Racing Conference "grand prix" series. In 2000 the island was a host to the Tall Ships race, and the harbour was full of vessels and their crews.

The Bermuda Yachting Association includes more than a dozen racing classes and Bermudian sailors compete regularly at regional, world and Olympic level. Sailing remains a predominantly white sport, though less so in the smaller dinghy classes.

Scuba-diving, water-skiing and para-sailing are among the other water sports enjoyed on the island. Powerboat racing is a popular summer spectator sport with races held on alternate Sundays from April to November at Ferry Reach, near the airport, the highlight being the annual Around the Island Race in July or August.

Fishing is virtually a year-round sport here, although the best time for deep sea quarry such as blue marlin is May to November. Offshore fishing also includes world-class blackfin and yellowfin tuna as well as wahoo, barracuda, dolphin (fish), amberjack and almaco jack. Commercial over-fishing, however, has greatly reduced reef and shore fish stocks in recent years.

Golfing paradise

Golf is another year-round sport but is better in the cooler winter months. The island has more golf courses per square mile than any other nation in the world: eight in just 22 sq. miles (57 sq. km). The limited size of the island means courses can be relatively short. The hilly terrain makes each of them a unique test and the sweeping ocean views ensure that Bermuda's courses are among the most spectacular in the world.

Bermuda's most famous course is at the Mid Ocean Club, a 6,547-yd (5,986-metre) course in the exclusive Tucker's Town area at the east end of the island. Designed by Charles Blair MacDonald in 1921, it was redesigned by Robert Trent Jones in 1953. Eisenhower and Churchill once met here and the fifth hole over Mangrove Lake is one of the best par fours in the world. The Bermuda Amateur Match Play Championship is held here each March. In 2007 and 2008 the Mid Ocean hosted the PGA Grand Slam. Mid Ocean, Tucker's Point, and Riddell's Bay, Bermuda's oldest course, in Warwick Parish, are all private clubs and require an introduction from a member or hotel; but there is easy access to the other five clubs.

Port Royal, a 6,425-yd (5,875-metre) public course overlooking Southampton's South Shore and designed by Trent Jones in 1972, is regarded as one of the best public courses anywhere and is the site of the Bermuda Open Championship each October. St George's Golf Club, a tight, unforgiving course, and nine-hole Ocean View in Devonshire are other excellent government-run courses.

Private Tucker's Point Golf Course stands on the former Castle Harbour course, it will be open to members only when the Tucker's Point Club, an exclusive resort and residential complex, is complete. The course at Belmont Hills

Golf Club in Warwick, formerly Belmont Golf and Country Club, is open to the public, as is a tricky par-54 course in the grounds of the Fairmont Southampton Hotel.

Year-round tennis

Bermuda is also a tennis player's paradise with more than 80 courts on the island, most of them either clay or cement surfaces. Play is possible year-round with the tournament season running from March to December. Some courts, such as those at the Pomander Gate Tennis Club and the exclusive Coral Beach and Tennis Club, require a member's introduction but most hotel courts are available to

LEFT: an equestrian event at Government House.
RIGHT: sports fans.

non-guests (at up to double the rate). There are public facilities at the Government Tennis stadium in Pembroke Parish and at the Port Royal Golf Club in Southampton.

Interestingly, Bermuda helped introduce lawn tennis to the United States. The first tennis equipment was brought to Bermuda by a local businessman, Thomas Middleton, in 1873. He passed the equipment on to the Chief Justice, Sir Brownlow Gray, who erected a court at his home in Paget where the game was played by an American visitor, Mary Outerbridge. The following year she laid out the first American courts at the Staten Island Cricket Club in

The most popular local race, however, is the Marathon Derby held on 24 May, a gruelling 13-miler (20-km) first run in 1910. Open to residents only, it is the unofficial road race championship of the island and attracts up to 500 runners, cheered on by huge crowds along the Somerset-to-Hamilton route on Bermuda Day.

Bermuda has a tradition of track and field excellence, competing regularly in Olympic, Commonwealth, Pan-American and regional games. As in football and other sports, many young Bermudian athletes win scholarships to American or Canadian schools and colleges, which further improves the overall standard.

New York. Sir Brownlow's original grass court still stands at Clermont on Harbour Road.

Track and field and other sports

Running has a strong following in Bermuda. Road and cross-country races occur in June, usually on Sunday mornings, over distances ranging from 3 miles (5 km) to a full marathon. The biggest event is International Race Weekend in mid-January which consists of races under floodlights on Front Street, Hamilton, on Friday night, a 6-mile (10-km) event on Saturday and a marathon on the Sunday. Grete Waitz, Joan Benoit Samuelson, Orlando Pizzolato and Rob de Castella have run in the events.

One of the most successful modern athletes is high jumper Nicky Saunders. A bronze medallist at the 1982 Commonwealth Games, he has held the Commonwealth record on several occasions and was placed fifth at both the 1987 World Athletics Championships in Rome and the 1988 Olympic Games in Seoul. In 1990 he won the gold medal in the Commonwealth Games which were held in Auckland, New Zealand.

Most major sporting events are held at the Bermuda National Stadium Complex, which includes the National Sports Centre, it is located in Prospect, on the outskirts of Hamilton.

Triathlon has been one of Bermuda's fastest-growing sports. Annual individual and team championships have been held each September since 1979, and in 1987 the island staged the first Bermuda International Triathlon in which the world's top professional triathletes competed for $100,000 in prize money.

Swimming and cycling are popular. The Bermuda Amateur Swimming Association runs a strong national programme and competes at Olympic, Commonwealth and regional level, while the Bermuda Bicycling Association stages regular road races, time trials and criteriums – all supposedly within the island's 20 mph (35 kph) speed limit! – as well as the international Grand Prix Aux Bermudes each April.

major rugby nations, are two of the international highlights on the island's sporting calendar.

The National Sports Centre is also the base for field hockey and squash, two other sports with strong expatriate followings. Teams from North America and Europe compete annually in the Bermuda Hockey Festival each September and the Bermuda Squash Open attracts world-ranked players in November.

Horse events

The island also has a thriving horse-riding community and three-day eventer Peter Gray, who won a bronze medal at the 1987 Pan-American

Rugby Union maintains a popular following in Bermuda, particularly among British expatriates, with four clubs fielding eight teams most weekends between October and April at the National Sports Centre. Bermuda has traditionally been regarded as one of the rugby powers in the region, having won three Caribbean Championships by 1981.

The Easter Classic, an annual Easter Sunday game involving star guest players from Britain, and November's World Rugby Classic, which attracts leading ex-internationals from the world's

Games, is still a well-known international sportsman. More recently M.J. Tumbridge took home a gold medal in the 1999 Pan Am Games. The major shows are at the Agricultural Show at the Botanical Gardens, Paget, in April and the Mini Grand Prix, at Government House, Pembroke, in November. The Bermuda Equestrian Federation runs the National Equestrian Centre in Devonshire as a venue for international events.

Outside of cricket and football, the two most popular "working-class" sports are softball and bowling. Bernard Park in Pembroke hosts league softball games six nights a week virtually year-round, while Warwick Lanes in Warwick Parish has 16 lanes open seven nights a week. ❑

LEFT: local football stars play in the English leagues.
ABOVE: hockey has a strong expatriate following.

THE VISUAL ARTS

Centuries-old paintings grace island galleries alongside the work of distinguished contemporary painters and sculptors

Bermuda's semi-tropical beauty and distinctive architecture have inspired artists for at least 150 years – ever since the pressures of turning an empty island into a homeland eased enough to allow the leisure to do so. In a romantic sense, the isolated island lay like an empty canvas awaiting the touch of paint and brush. No prehistoric paintings decorate Bermuda's caves as in so many civilisations, nor are there Old Masters or masterpieces.

The earliest surviving art took the form of portraits, as visiting painters were called upon to preserve the images of leading citizens rather than the beauty of their natural surroundings. Portraits by English artist Joseph Blackburn, who was in Bermuda from 1752 to 1753, hang in the Tucker House Museum in St George's. Others by American John Green, painted from 1765, are displayed in his one-time residence, Verdmont. Prized items for collectors are ship paintings by "Edward James" – suspected of being an alias for a remittance man who painted, among other subjects, Civil War blockade runners en route to southern Confederate ports.

Historic illustrations

Women watercolourists recorded local flora and fauna in attentive detail. Flower paintings by Lady Lefroy, whose husband was governor from 1871 to 1877, are preserved in the Bermuda Archives, and her fish paintings are in the main library. Both "Edward James's" and Lady Lefroy's works have been used to illustrate the history section of this book.

It wasn't until the early 20th century that more than a few Bermudians transferred pictorial impressions to paper. Since the 1950s visual art has blossomed, as local amateurs and a few professionals have embraced the styles and subject-matter of the rapidly changing art scene. There are now three flourishing

volunteer art groups, augmented by several private studios and commercial galleries.

In the forefront is the 500-member Bermuda Society of Artists, which evolved from the Bermuda Art Association. The Association held exhibitions from 1928 onward in the former Hamilton Hotel, where a number of paintings

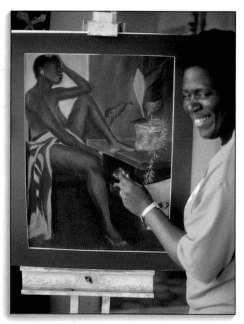

went up in flames when the building burned to the ground just before Christmas in 1955. The Society, in its gallery in City Hall, holds frequent exhibitions and events to coincide with the winter Bermuda Festival.

Bermudians are justifiably proud of the Bermuda National Gallery, which opened to great acclaim in 1992. Occupying the East Exhibition rooms of City Hall on Church Street, the two-storey facility is the island's only climate-controlled space. Given that the US Navy has used Bermuda to test the durability of paint – the theory being that if paint can stand up here, it can stand up anywhere – climate-control is a key factor.

PRECEDING PAGES: *Shinbone Alley, St George's* by Ogden Minton Pleissner.
LEFT: *St George's 1934* by Jack Bush.
RIGHT: Sharon Wilson continues to produce quality art.

The island's climate may be the worst in the world for the toll it takes on works of art, with three elements – humidity, salt and ultraviolet light – all playing a part. The humidity can be absorbed by the canvas and can be seen later as mildew coming through the oils; some very valuable prints have been destroyed in this way. The ultraviolet light is strong enough to fade the tops of red cars, and what it does to works of art is tragic.

In 1982, the long-standing dream of a National Gallery began to be realised with an Act of Parliament that established the Bermuda Fine Art Trust. A rich gift to "the people of

tional exhibits. The Gallery ushered in the 21st century with the first-ever exhibition of 20th-century Azorean art, examining the link between the Azores and Bermuda and celebrating the 150-year anniversary of Portuguese settlement on the island.

Regularly scheduled activities at the Gallery include Wednesday's lunchtime programmes and Saturday's focus on children, when "activity pages" stimulate learning by asking youngsters questions about the artworks they are viewing. (Adults are admitted free when accompanied by a child.) There is also a museum shop, selling a plethora of art-related gifts.

Bermuda" was a small collection of paintings by British and European masters from the 15th to the 19th centuries, which was bequeathed by painter and parliamentarian, The Hon. Hereward Watlington. The bequest carried provisos, one being that the collection should be housed in climatically controlled environs.

Happily, the Watlington Collection is now a part of the Gallery's permanent collection, along with works of art by Reynolds, Gainsborough, Romney and Murillo. In the late 1990s, the collection was augmented by the addition of sculptures from 11 different African countries. In addition to the permanent collections, the Gallery also shows changing interna-

Retrieved artworks

The prestigious Masterworks Foundation was established in 1987 for the purpose of "bringing home" works painted in Bermuda in decades past by visiting artists. The Foundation grew from a loan exhibition of "Masterworks Inspired by Bermuda". Volunteers, seeing a more lasting future for the concept, went on to organise and hunt for more pictures to return to Bermuda for display. Thus began an ambitious drive for funds to purchase works from owners and overseas museums. One of the organisers, Tom Butterfield, had the original idea of competing in a London marathon and getting his running sponsors to pledge their donations to the Masterworks Foundation. This scheme paid off to the tune of $17,000.

Some of the retrieved artworks, of which there are more than 700, are exhibited in the former Arrowroot Factory in the Botanical Gardens in Paget. They were finally displayed in a custom-built site in 2008. Sample works can be viewed on their website (www.bermuda masterworks.com). In addition to the collection, Foundation members support educational and cultural programmes such as "Artist Up Front Street", "Artist in Residence", "The Grand Festival by the Sea", community art days, after-school arts classes, Saturday-

American Winslow Homer is represented by a poster printed by arrangement with a Massachusetts museum. Titled *Bermuda Settlers*, it is a playful depiction of the wild hogs found by English settlers supposedly left behind by 16th-century Spanish expeditions. Among postcard reproductions at the gallery is Andrew Wyeth's poignant study of a black woman, *The Bermudian*, seated by a worn wall. The original was shown in a 1986 exhibition. Another wry view of a rundown area is American George Ault's 1922 watercolour *Behind the Bakery Shop*. An oil by Canadian Jack Bush incorporates the figure of a black woman carrying a bowl of fruit

morning artist encounters and a summer field trip camp for six- to 12-year-olds.

In 1989, two large local firms contributed substantial sums toward the purchase of particular works. One is a small painting of Government House or *La Maison du Gouverneur* by French artist Albert Gleizes, who moved from Impressionism through Cubism to a simplified linear style. The other firm helped with the purchase of American Ogden Minton Pleissner's oil *Shinbone Alley, St George's*.

LEFT: Bermuda inspires both painters and paintings.
ABOVE: *St George's Bermuda* by Ogden Minton Pleissner.

on her head. Most of the retrieved paintings celebrate the glories of island seas and greenery accented by pastel houses whose snow-white limestone roofs reminded Mark Twain of icing on a cake.

The West End acquired its own artistic showcase with the formation of the Bermuda Arts Centre at Dockyard. This small gallery has adjoining studio facilities where two or three artists may be working at the same time in different media.

Contemporary painters and sculptors now at work on the island form a changing line-up. Some show their work only sporadically, but there are certain undisputed leaders.

Bermuda's impressionist

For decades, the understated watercolours of the late Alfred Birdsey encapsulated the spirit of Bermuda. He was willing to be described as an impressionist, though not in the sense of the French pioneers whose aim, he said, was "painting with light". His scenic watercolours, deliberately lacking in depth, appear to have been dashed off at speed – as indeed they were.

Background areas are indicated by a swatch of colour rather than a solid ground; stick figures of people are sketched in quick dark outlines. The effect is as if a butterfly on the wing had lightly brushed the paper, and a spider had tracked it after wading through an inkwell. "Once over lightly" comes closest to describing this delicate technique. Birdsey produced memorable murals, one of which adorns the Bermuda Tourist Bureau in Boston; another is in the Bermuda Commercial Bank on Church Street, Hamilton. The artist's daughter, Jo Birdsey Linberg, also an artist, runs the Birdsey Studio in the back garden of Rosecote, the old family home in Paget.

Bermuda has two distinguished sculptors: Desmond Hale Fountain produces bronze statues, while Chesley Trott creates streamlined cedar carvings.

Fountain of youth

Although Fountain, a Fellow of the Royal Society of Sculptors, no longer has a gallery in Bermuda, visitors can see the artist's work all over the island. His memorial of Sir George Somers stands on Ordnance Island in St George's, while the *Spirit of Bermuda*, a statue of Johnny Barnes *(see page 171)*, is on Crow Lane not far from where the retired bus driver greets commuters every week-day morning. And in Butterfield Bank on Reid Street a lifelike bronze of Mark Twain sits on a bench. Desmond Fountain has described himself as a "Fountain of Youth" because he has created so many life-size figures of children caught in spontaneous poses. Some of his work can be seen outside the City Hall in Hamilton and in the grounds of hotels, including the Fairmont Princess. In addition to depicting humans, the artist creates animal sculptures; dogs, lizards and toads are all included in his menagerie of bronzes. ❑

RIGHT: Desmond Hale Fountain's *News Flash*.

CALYPSO CULTURE

Bermuda is increasingly influenced by North American music
but modern musicians are still performing old-time calypso and traditional tunes

Bermuda's musical landscape is a colourful and varied part of its culture. From classic sounds to calypso the island has a spicy mix of rhythmic beats closely linked to the Caribbean islands hundreds of miles away. The origins of calypso can be traced back to the 17th century when enslaved Africans cre-

Dorsey and Babe Ruth adorned the instrument with their signatures. In 1953 the Brothers toured the United States and a few years later appeared on the *Ed Sullivan Show*.

Following closely in their footsteps was Bermudian calypso singer Hubert Smith. It was thanks to one of the Talbot Brothers' tours that

ated work songs for the field and witty songs of commentary to spread news and gossip.

Calypso legends

During the 1940s and '50s the Talbot Brothers were ambassadors of calypso music for visitors to the island. Sporting colourful shirts and even more colourful straw hats, these six Bermudians, who grew up in Tucker's Town, before it was annexed for tourism, were known for their harmony and puckish sense of humour.

Just as well-known was Roy Talbot's "doghouse" or string bass fashioned out of a wooden meat packing crate with a single fishing line string. Celebrities such as Bing Crosby, Tommy

Smith got his first gig in the former Coral Island Hotel. The hotel needed a group to cover the Talbot Brothers' set in their absence. As Hubert told it, "The manager felt that we needed a name so he gave us the name of his hotel. That night we were born 'Hubert Smith and his Coral Islanders.'"

Proud moments followed: a private audience with Queen Elizabeth II, for whose first official visit to the island he was asked to compose a song. When Prince Charles came calling he was again given the honour of composing an official welcoming tune. Smith took up his pen

ABOVE: veteran entertainer, the late Hubert Smith.

again for Princess Margaret's visit, and over the years serenaded Churchill, Eisenhower, Kennedy, Johnson and French Premier Laniel – not to mention a host of celebrities.

The Queen awarded him an honour and a private tour of the royal yacht *Britannia*. He was most famous for his composition, *Bermuda is Another World*, which became Bermuda's unofficial national song.

Keeping the music alive

At a time of life when most working men retire, Hubert Smith demonstrated no such inclination. He spent a few days each week getting local musicians on a better footing in the island's entertainment business, and he was constantly lobbying hoteliers to showcase island talent. His legacy was simple: "I would want to see more Bermudian musicians playing good music for locals and visitors alike – even if they only have half the fun I had."

For the last 10 years of his life (he died in 2002 at the age of 81) Smith was concerned about a decreasing demand for his kind of Caribbean-influenced calypso music. Prominent in his thoughts was the future of local music – especially since the demise of his own Coral Islanders – as hotels were choosing small combos and soloists over the larger bands.

"I'm afraid calypso in Bermuda is going the way of the dinosaur unless the young musicians make it a part of their repertoire and demand to be heard," he said, sadly. When the musical entertainment was mixed – a combination of popular music and calypso – he recalled packed houses. "There was even calypso for dancing."

BERMUDA MUSIC FESTIVAL

The Bermuda Music Festival, held in October, takes place at the Royal Naval Dockyard, where artists perform on a floating stage. Originally a jazz event, it includes R&B and soul artists. Stars who have performed at this annual three-day event include Diana Krall, George Benson, India Arie, Arturo Sandoval, Cassandra Wilson, SpyroGyra, Patti Labelle and Joss Stone.

In addition, local jazz artists perform at clubs and restaurants across the island at festival time.

Special packages include flights from the US, hotel accommodation and festival tickets. For more information visit: www.bermudatourism.com/MusicFest/.

Today only a few of the old-time calypso singers and musicians are left. One is Stan "Lord Necktie" Seymour, who began his career in 1955, with Hubert Smith, as one of the Coral Islanders. His nickname hails back to the calypso carnival competitions held in Bermuda throughout the 1960s, which he won three times. "As a calypsonian singer you have to have a fictional name and I chose mine because I wore a long necktie with my costume."

In 1963 Seymour left the Coral Islanders to form his own trio and then went solo in the 1980s. His main instrument is the guitar but he also plays harmonica, bass, drum and tambourine. Seymour composed many songs, including his most famous, *The Diddlybops and the Gooseneck Handlebars*, recorded in 1962.

While "Lord Necktie" continues to serenade diners in a variety of restaurants and hotels on the island, he realises no calypso artist can perform in only one musical style. He's the first to suggest that contemporary musicians must be versatile.

Changing tunes

Modern-day exponents of calypso agree. Randy Lambert, guitarist and leader of TEMPO, says that while they do play calypso, they also perform pop, R & B, soca, reggae, jazz and Latin music. Sean Tucker, the keyboard player with Legacy, reveals that their repertoire also includes a bit of everything, because modern audiences want variety.

It is a commonly held belief that there is an abundance of talent to be found in Bermuda but limited opportunity, especially since the number of hotels with a resident band is decreasing. Most musicians are part-time performers. Tucker, for example, is an attorney, while Ron Lightbourne is a teacher and Tom Ray works in the insurance industry.

Proof that the music is still alive and well and living in Bermuda can be found in Hubie's Bar on Angle Street in Hamilton (see *Travel Tips page 301*). The bar has the smoky, vibrant atmosphere of an old 1930s speakeasy and from 6 to 10pm the alcohol flows and music from the band, Jaz, keeps pace. Visiting musicians, from keyboard players to saxophonists, who are interested in a jam session are welcome to join in. So the musical offering is never predictable. One thing is certain – the small dance floor is always full. ❏

TREASURE ISLAND

*The early colonists landed on Bermuda in search of bountiful booty
that they believed would bring them quick and easy riches*

Bermuda was settled by the early colonists with the expectation of making money, preferably easy money. But as one bright scheme after another came to nothing and ruin stared everyone in the face, there were always two straws to cling to: the possibility of unearthing treasure or of slipping away for a spot of profitable piracy.

Hopes of finding treasure were not unreasonable. Spanish treasure ships returning from the New World passed right by Bermuda and, as the settlers knew only too well, ships regularly fell victim to the reefs. Treasure might even have been buried on the islands by pirates who were forever lurking around Bermuda with a view to seizing Spanish prizes. Behind the romance of buried treasure was the simple expedient that pirates taking up offers of amnesty to fight a war for King and Country, a potentially lucrative activity in its own right, needed a safe place to deposit their booty for the duration. Pirates who went down with their ships took with them the vital secret, the proverbial "X marks the spot".

The search for treasure began almost from the moment passengers and crew from the shipwrecked *Sea Venture* stepped ashore. One who chose to spend the rest of his life on the islands, Christopher Carter, turned down the offer of St David's Island in favour of the much smaller Cooper's Island because he believed it concealed a hoard. He spent years fruitlessly looking for it.

Bermuda's treasure, as it turned out, generally got no closer to shore than the reefs. Modern diving equipment has greatly facilitated the search. A local diver, Teddy Tucker, has produced a chart (on display in the Maritime Museum, with reproductions on sale locally) which pinpoints an astounding number of wrecks in local waters. Tucker himself hit the jackpot in 1955, bringing up a collection of Spanish gold bars and ornaments that were sub-

sequently bought by the Bermuda government and put on display in the museum. The prize piece in the Tucker Treasure was a gold cross mounted with seven emeralds. As the collection was being laid out for Queen Elizabeth's royal opening of the museum in 1975, it was found that the cross had been stolen. What was supposed to be the cross was a plastic replica. The real one has never been recovered.

Scenting success

The "Adventurers" of the Somers Island Company who financed the settlement of Bermuda were as optimistic as the settlers. Their hopes soared with the finding of a washed-up lump of ambergris, an evil-smelling substance produced in the stomach of a sick whale but nevertheless a priceless ingredient in the manufacture of scent. The discovery was not to be repeated, however, and their hopes turned to pearls. Richard Norwood, who had made a name for himself in England with the construction of a

---

PRECEDING PAGES: sunken treasure.
LEFT: a permanent shipwreck lies off Spanish Point.
RIGHT: Teddy Tucker, treasure retriever.

crude diving bell made out of a hogshead, was sent out in 1613 to search but drew a blank.

The clarity and relatively even temperature of the water around Bermuda – its incomparable cleanliness in the Atlantic is a scientific fact – was always a powerful inducement for underwater experimentation. A Bermudian invented a "diving bell" at the beginning of the 17th century. It was little more than an ordinary barrel but it contained enough air to enable him to remain underwater for 45 minutes.

Less intrepid Bermudians resorted to plucking their treasure off the reefs while it was still warm, so to speak. A Dutch ship that ran aground off

that a ship was in trouble. Tearing off his surplice, the priest led the charge down the hill.

"Legal" piracy

Official policy with regard to islanders doing business with pirates or going into the business themselves was negative, but it rang hollow because some of the big names behind the Somers Island Company were deeply, and not always discreetly, involved. In practice, a hair's breadth separated privateering, which was legal, and piracy, which wasn't. Privateers were licensed to seize ships belonging to the King's enemies but were required to deliver their prizes intact so

Somerset in 1618 without sustaining serious damage was typical of how the system worked. Sympathetic islanders comforted the captain by saying that the ship could easily be freed in a day or two. The captain repaired to the village to relax. When he returned to his ship after the agreed interval, only a bare shell remained. He could hardly have been consoled by the suggestion that a second storm must have been responsible, nor by the fact that he was stuck in Bermuda for a year before he could arrange a passage home.

The parishioners of St Ann's church, still standing near Gibbs Hill lighthouse, were by all accounts keen "wreckers". They are said to have interrupted a service with the news

that the proceeds of ship and cargo could be split between the privateers and the tax collector.

Pirates were pirates because they skipped that particular formality and kept the lot for themselves. In Bermuda, there were always eager hands waiting in small bays to off-load interesting items of cargo at night before the ship put in an appearance at the customs shed in St George's the following morning.

Trading with pirates was forbidden because the company had a monopoly both on buying Bermuda's produce, especially tobacco, as well as in supplying the colony with goods from a company ship which called once or twice a year. Pirates might offer better prices both ways, but trading with them was a mixed blessing. Dealings with one pirate, Daniel Elfrith, master of *Treasurer*, invariably turned sour. A shipload of grain Elfrith delivered was infested with rats that virtually devastated the islands.

On another occasion, he persuaded the governor to give him 100,000 ears of corn, almost as much as the colony had been able to save, in exchange for "windie promises" and eight negroes. The promises in question were a slice of the profits of some piratical enterprise he had concocted. The corn was lost forever; the scheme flopped. "Probably nothing", a historian sighed, "during the first 20 years of the

and he had to swim back to Madagascar, a distance of some 12 miles (20 km). The locals appear to have received him with good grace, and he devoted the rest of his life to "presiding over his colony, settling disputes among native tribes, and directing a little traffic in slaves or an occasional trading voyage to Mauritius... until at last he fell a victim in a native squabble".

Good and bad luck

Falling victim in a native squabble was not the only danger. A Bermudian privateer crew captured by an American pirate were hoisted to the top of the mast and bounced on the deck;

'MARK ANTONIE'
Wrecked 1777

BERMUDA

E II R

50c

Colony stirred as much trouble as the *Treasurer*".

Bermuda produced two pirates rated "first class" by their peers. John Bowen, "an educated fellow" who was probably a grandson of Richard Norwood, took 20 men ashore in Mauritius for a "hilarious" party that lasted six months. It killed him in the end. When the priests denied his body holy ground, he was buried in the highway.

Nathaniel North, regarded as Bowen's equal, might seem to have blotted his copybook in Madagascar by capturing a local chief and ransoming him for $1,000. His boat capsized

LEFT AND ABOVE: treasure hunting is part of Bermuda's colourful history.

another luckless captive was "made to talk" by being tied to the bowspit "with burning matches to his eyes and a loaded pistol at his mouth".

Such misfortunes apart, there were sufficient strokes of good fortune to keep Bermudians' faith in treasure and piracy alive. Thomas Tew set sail from Bermuda in 1691 and set a course for the Red Sea, where he bagged an Arab vessel that netted the crew £3,000 each. He operated out of Madagascar until he had accumulated booty worth £100,000. Bermudians who had financed his expedition got their money back 14 times over and "Arabian gold showed its face on the island for a while, notwithstanding the efforts of its first recipients to be discreet." ❑

FOOD FOR THOUGHT

There's no lack of choice in Bermuda's restaurants: from fresh fish caught
by a local fisherman to island specialities, from Italian staples to Japanese noodles

One of the great dining mysteries of the island is that there is not a single restaurant that could rest on its laurels as serving an entirely Bermudian menu. Bermuda offers a pot-pourri of eating places, including Italian, Danish and Japanese. But to find those honest-to-goodness, rib-cleaving dishes such as peas 'n' rice, johnny cakes and paw-paw casserole the visitor is entering the realm of the endangered species, for these uniquely delicious dishes adopted by Bermudian cooks from West Indian influences are not always readily available.

All-island spread

The Black Horse Tavern on St David's Island serves up generous portions of turtle steak, mussel pie, fish and conch chowder and myriad seafood delicacies. But receiving a good recommendation for an all-island spread is as unlikely as being asked to take tea at Government House.

There are a few restaurants, however, that approximate this experience. Cheap and cheerful Woody's in Somerset is considered more of a saving than a source of the elusive local cuisine. For dining *sans* frills, meander through the back of town to the Ex-Artillerymen's Club on Victoria Street and discover Grannie Mack's, which serves up goodly portions of local dishes, all of which can be washed down with home-made rootbeer. If something stronger is required, repair to the club bar, where veterans regale anyone willing to listen with old war stories. Lunches are inexpensive and one may well be enough for two people.

On Burnaby Street, down the hill from the bus terminal in Hamilton, The Spot is a casual lunch place that's been "on the spot" for a long while. Moderately priced lunches, burgers and sandwiches are served to a seemingly endless flow of businesspeople, and sometimes it's necessary to queue up for a table during peak times.

Hotels and restaurants carry a selection of local dishes – usually fish. Succulent Bermuda lobster (in season), garden-fresh vegetables, tangy citrus and fresh fruits are all part of the Bermudian fare. Their enemy is supply-and-demand, with

local fishermen hard-pressed to provide for all hotel, restaurant and local tables. As a result, these foods are imported when supplies diminish.

When ordering fish do specify the local catch of the day, which may be red snapper, red hind, yellowtail, wahoo, rockfish – the choices are endless. Don't, for goodness sake, pass up the fish chowder and don't be put off by the knowledge that this dish actually uses as its base rejected fish heads. When the post-filleted fish is thrown into a pot with spices and slow-boiled for at least two days (for that authentic Bermuda taste), the result is a very tangy blend. Add black rum and local sherry peppers and your taste buds will thank you for the experience.

PRECEDING PAGES: island eating.
LEFT: service in the sun.
RIGHT: visitors and locals alike buy fresh fruit from mobile stands like this one in Southampton.

Sunday breakfast

Any local cook will readily attest to the fact that the traditional Bermuda Sunday morning breakfast of cod fish and potatoes is well worth whatever it takes to get the real thing. Restaurants such as the Green Lantern on Serpentine Road in Hamilton and the Paraquet, in Paget, to name a couple, serve this speciality every Sunday morning. But, if possible, wangle an invitation to have breakfast in a Bermudian home.

Be aware that there is a different recipe for almost every adult Bermudian, but the one favoured by those who can trace their ancestry back to the English colonists tends to be boiled

wash it down with strident belts of "dark and stormies" – black rum and ginger beer.

Bermudians favour fish which is simply prepared and tend to avoid any that is smothered in sauce, as sauce can often hide a multitude of sins of the grill. Fresh fish with squeezed locally grown lime or lemon and a touch of butter is delicious. Imported fish need not be frowned upon, since the secret is in the preparation, not necessarily the length of time since it was caught. Keep in mind that asparagus grown in up-state New York may reach local tables in less time by air than by a lumbering lorry en route to a Manhattan restaurant.

cod served with olive oil and egg sauce and garnished with tomato and onion sauce. This calls for a different treatment of the cod, hence the result is rather chewy with a residual salt content that creates a tremendous, potentially alcoholic, thirst. It might therefore be wise to call a taxi for the trip back to the hotel.

For a really exotic recipe, try the cod (soaked overnight in cold water) sautéed in onions, garlic, green and red peppers, fresh tomatoes and thyme. Let this languish for a while in heated olive oil until it becomes rather like a loose casserole, then serve with buttered new potatoes (the local variety, if in season), hard-boiled eggs, sliced avocado pear and ripe bananas, and

One native dish that stands out from many is cassava pie, which Bermudians include in Christmas dinners. Made from the root of a cassava, it is grated, ground, squeezed, dried and then baked (with chicken or port) to a golden brown. Its cousin, the farine pie, is another Christmas delicacy, and can be found in speciality stores throughout the year. Bermudians eat heartily at Christmas. A typical Yuletide dinner would consist of turkey, ham, mashed potatoes, pumpkin, sweet potatoes, peas 'n' rice, cassava pie, Christmas pudding for dessert – and lots to drink.

As for dining out at night, Bermudians take the view that there is a restaurant for most tastes and pockets. Tom Moore's Tavern has a lineage dating back to the 1600s and, together with the Waterlot Inn (300 years old) and Fourways (*circa* 1727), is a formidable challenge in the realm of *haute cuisine*. For informal lunch or dinner try the Lobster Pot, with a nautical decor and great fish chowder, plus superb escargots served with a pernod sauce. The Swizzle Inn, a stone's throw from the airport, is very casual. In the old days clientele were coaxed to "fly on a swizzle", the house concoction consisting of a variety of rums and fruit juices. At Dockyard in the West End, the Frog & Onion is an utterly charming place, wildly popular with Bermudians, with both indoor and terrace dining. It's in one of the great

out is restricted to "typically Bermudian" restaurants, pubs or seafood places. A great number of restaurateurs are able to satisfy palates with a taste for international cuisines.

International cuisine

The island is awash with Italian restaurants such as Little Venice and Portofino (both on Bermudiana Road in Hamilton), Tio Pepe on South Shore Road, Southampton and La Trattoria in Washington Lane, Hamilton. Ristorante Primavera is an elegant eating place on Pitts Bay Road in Hamilton, near the Ferry Terminal. At Collector's Hill in Smith's Parish, the

limestone buildings that once housed a warehouse, and specialises in seafood and steaks.

For an English pub atmosphere, try the Hog Penny on Burnaby Hill, featuring typical pub fare and the occasional curried lamb. Upstairs is the Barracuda Grill, another seafood house. For white-gloved service, try the nautical, hushed atmosphere of the Newport Room in the Fairmont Southampton Hotel. The theme highlights famous vessels that took part in the historic Newport to Bermuda yacht races.

None of the foregoing is to imply that dining

LEFT: casual dining often involves fish chowder.
ABOVE: Fourways dates from around 1727.

Specialty Inn is a great stopping-off place after a visit to Verdmont or Spittal Pond.

Rosa's Cantina has a good Tex-Mex menu, as well as Mexican beers, while the House of India and East Meets West restaurants serve traditional Indian fare. Both are in Hamilton. To satisfy the yen for Chinese food, dine in Hamilton at Chopsticks on Reid Street for Szechuan, Hunan and Cantonese dishes.

For charm and elegance, head for Ascots, in the Royal Palms Hotel, or the Carriage House in St George's. Be sure to allow space for a taste of Bermuda's great dessert, the sweet-sweet syllabub, made of guava and sherry – the perfect end to a meal. ❑

Front Street — Hamilton — Bermuda

LIFE ON THE DOCKS

Navigating the future of Bermuda's docks is as tricky as negotiating the island's intricate channels

Apart from the lovely scenery and the ingenuity of its people, Bermuda has no natural resources. There is little agriculture, a small fishery, and virtually no manufacturing. The island relies on the outside world for everything from food to fuel, to construction materials. Sometimes even fresh water has to be imported, since there is no natural source other than rainfall. As a consequence, the country's port system is a critical component of its economic engine, handling most of the $5.5-billion worth of imported goods received on the island each year.

Visitor or local, most people are aware of the activity surrounding the gleaming cruise ships that moor along Hamilton's Front Street, or in St George's and the Dockyard; however, the activity at the container-ship terminal, although less visible, has a greater impact on people's lives. Here, week after week, almost everything they consume lands on the island.

Bermuda's main cargo-ship terminal is in Hamilton, at the eastern end of Front Street. This is the home of the container ships *Oleander*, *Somers Isles* and *Bermuda Islander* that ply the waters between Bermuda and eastern US ports. Occasionally a huge, hulking box of a car ship, such as the amusingly named *Melbourne Highway*, will berth and disgorge a fleet of vehicles.

The Hamilton cargo facility is far from hideous or noisy when compared to other ports. Nevertheless, many people argue that it is unattractive to visitors, disruptive to traffic, and an inappropriate use of the city's prime waterfront land. Various plans exist to move the cargo port to St. George's, St. David's, or elsewhere, away from the city centre. However, the terminal remains, since commerce began in Hamilton and goods were offloaded and carted to the merchants, many of whom established themselves on Front Street to be near the wharves.

As well as importing, Bermuda has exported agricultural products to cities across the US Eastern Seaboard, but today ships arrive fully loaded and leave almost empty – 98 per cent of the cargo they carry is on the eastbound leg of the trip. Every week ships set sail from North America for Bermuda: *Oleander* leaves Port Elizabeth in New Jersey on Friday and arrives in Bermuda in the early hours of Monday; *Bermuda Islander* sails from New York, making as stop in Salem, New Jersey, every Monday, arriving at its namesake destination early on Thursday; and *Somers Isles* travels the 800 nautical miles (1,483 km) from Fernandia Beach, Florida, three times a month, leaving on Friday and arriving the following Tuesday.

A tricky passage

Arriving in Bermuda by sea is complicated by the reefs and narrow passages, particularly when the weather is stormy. Ships can often be spotted on the horizon in the early morning, just outside the ring of reefs that surround the island. They're not just waiting until it's light enough to see what they're doing; they're waiting for the pilot. Whether laden with cruise ship passengers or cargo, all large ships, even those whose captains know the waters as well as they know their own names, must have a local pilot on board as they wend their way through the intricate channels. Insurance policies mandate this to ensure the safe berthing of the ship. Also, an extra pair of eyes and local knowledge of the waters can be welcome at the end of a long journey, especially if the sea and conditions are challenging – heavy rain, poor visibility, large waves or heavy wind in the narrow channels.

Stately procession

With the pilot aboard, a visiting ship moves out of Five Fathom Hole and heads towards Hamilton Harbour on a trip that will take about 90 minutes. It turns right along The Narrows, a 38-ft (12-metre) channel cut through coral beds. On the left is St Catherine's beach where *Sea Venture*'s exhausted crew stumbled ashore so long ago *(see page 33)*. Beside it are the

---

PRECEDING PAGES: Hamilton Harbour around 1935.
LEFT: Brian Richardson, a pilot of the *Oleander*.

massive stone walls of St Catherine's fort, which at one time welcomed cruise ship visitors with a shot from its formidable cannons. Just beyond the fort, the ship turns left and heads down the long South Channel running the length of Bermuda's North Shore.

About 10 miles (16 km) down, the North Shore ends, giving way to a large inland body of water, the Great Sound. It is here that the full spread of Bermuda can best be seen. The Dockyard is over the right shoulder of the skipper as he turns his ship into the Sound. At the far end of the Sound lies Gibbs Hill lighthouse. Skippers say the night-time glow from its rotating lamp

can be seen on the horizon 50 miles (80 km) away. The ship picks its way along Dundonald Channel and then bears left into an area of small islands. It passes through narrow Two Rock Passage and continues on into the enclosed Hamilton Harbour in the geographical heart of the island. It's a clean, quaint-looking harbour.

The ship steams quietly to the docks to berth at the far end, where it is met by a gang of dockworkers, or stevedores for unloading.

When the stevedores swing into action, it's very easy to see the docks as the hub of Bermuda life. Huge, imposing cranes huff and lift massive containers from the hulls of ships on to the docks. Strange-looking trucks called

toploaders pick them up and lug them to storage areas. Trucks arrive. Toploaders load the trucks up solidly and the containers are on their way to the importers. The container ships are the island's lifelines and the docks its great clearing house.

Every year, the docks handle about 140,000 tons of general cargo. That compares with just 7,500 tons of air freight – excluding mail – handled at the airport. Recent import statistics show heavy reliance on the United States: 73 percent of all goods passing through the docks come from America. The remainder arrive from Europe, Canada and Japan.

With all that business, one might think that the docks would appear disorganised. But it is striking how clean and efficient they look – a result of the containerisation of the cargo business. Containers revolutionised the port, changing it from a labour-intensive business to a fully mechanised industry. Until the 1950s, rope-slings were used to load the cargo into ships; this work is now carried out by machine.

The container revolution

Containers also prompted a complete upgrade of the docks labour scene. It used to be considered demeaning labour. Men were hired on a casual basis and they only worked when the ships were in. Bermuda was one of the first ports in the world to regularly employ dock workers – decasualisation, they called it. Before it, a gang of men was 21 to 22 strong. When the old ships came in to port, the gang could move about 7 tons of cargo an hour. Now, with containers, more than 35 tons can be moved each gang hour.

In the old days, the docks were congested with traffic. There were no warehouses, and importers used transit sheds to sort their goods. People would come to the sheds to take advantage of goods sold at "ex-dock" prices. Today, there may still be confusion along the docks – but at least now it is organised confusion.

One of the main reasons for the reduced chaos is that few containers are stripped of their cargo on the docks. About 80 percent of the containers disembarked are put directly on to the backs of trucks for delivery to grocery stores or general importers who personally strip them for delivery to their customers. Containers remaining on the docks are stripped and their cargo is stored in sheds for pick-up.

It is the job of the shed managers to ensure

that the right goods reach the correct person – to make certain that everyone receives exactly what they want and that everyone is satisfied. When shipping is on schedule, the sheds are in great demand. Sometimes the shed managers have to chase the importers by telephone to have items moved out; they have only five days to pick up their goods, otherwise a demoorage charge is imposed.

Most importers pick up their goods promptly, since customers are waiting. It's not unusual for shop owners to know precisely where merchandise is. "It will be on the dock Monday, so you'll have it Wednesday," is welcome news

island's power supply. And items such as cement and fresh water occasionally arrive in special tankers.

One regular sight at Dockyard is a cable repair ship, which maintains Bermuda's important "real time" connections with the rest of the world. Occasionally a foreign cargo ship or trawler will limp into Bermuda for repairs and tie up there. And, at the beginning of the 21st century, the cruise ship *Pacific Princess* (which was used in the popular 1970s US TV series *The Love Boat*) was mothballed on the wharf at Dockyard, for a year or so, while her owners determined her future.

to clients, who may have been waiting weeks for a special order.

The Hamilton container facility is not the only spot cargo ships appear on the island. Tankers and other cargo vessels arrive regularly at both ends of the island. There are frequent deliveries of oil to service the island's motorised vehicles and boats, as well as providing the fuel the Bermuda Electric Light Company (BELCO) burns to maintain the

LEFT: brightly coloured buoys embellish the view across the harbour.
ABOVE: an ambitious young man fishes hopefully for a large cruise ship at the docks.

A challenging future

Bermudians work hard to maintain and improve their shipping industry. As cargo and cruise ships grow larger, developing facilities that can accommodate modern vessels is a challenge on an island with little land to spare. Add to that a fragile marine ecology and a tourism industry predicated on a beautiful natural environment and the challenge is amplified. Negotiating the future of the docks is as tricky as navigating the intricate sea channels. Bermuda's commercial and government planners know they must carefully develop shipping and ship transportation – their survival depends on it. ❑

WILD BIRDS AND GENTEEL FLOWERS

Bermuda has a natural environment rich with rare flora and fauna,
and a vibrant but fragile marine life

Bermuda had enjoyed at least 70 million years of intensely private evolution when its tiny world was turned upside down. The harbingers were a boatload of 16th-century pigs deposited on the islands by Spanish sailors with the idea that they would multiply as a source of fresh meat for future voyages to and from the newly discovered Americas. The pigs, or hogs, multiplied so efficiently that in no time their paths were as wide as roads, the palmetto palms on either side deeply scarred by the pleasure derived from scratching their backs.

Privacy lost, an ecology which had so patiently developed its own checks and balances was defenceless. One of the notable victims was the cahow, a sea bird no larger than a pigeon but with a three-foot wingspan and a large, curved beak with saw teeth. The cahow might have survived the pigs, which dug up its burrowed eggs, but its fate was compounded by men, who ate the birds in prodigious quantities, and sealed by voracious rats. Within 30 years of the arrival of the rats, the cahow was presumed to be extinct and was forgotten, an immense evolutionary process terminated as abruptly and ingloriously as that of the dodo on Mauritius.

Environmental triumph

The rest of endemic Bermudian wildlife fared no better, and in the bat of an evolutionary eyelid, the face of the islands changed beyond recognition. The manner in which the cahow somehow clung on unseen to emerge as recently as 1951 – an absence of more than three centuries – as a defiant symbol of pristine Bermuda would not be out of place as the climax of some rousing environmental anthem.

The background to this drama (to summarise other parts of this book) was a volcanic rumbling on the floor of the Atlantic Ocean where it

is at its deepest, about 3 miles (5 km). The eruption propelled a finger of rock to the surface at a point where the water was just warm enough to sustain the growth of coral. Life, such as it was, depended on the flotsam of the Gulf

Stream. Migratory land birds, blown off course during what would normally have been a nonstop flight, landed gratefully on this unexpected refuge off the American coast. These intruders left their mark with parasites and droppings, but in every other respect Bermuda was left to its own devices. It somehow acquired a resident lizard, the skink, which shared its domain only with nomadic sea birds when they were on the nest. Bermuda was never touched by the intercontinental migrations of men; none spilled over as they did to the Caribbean islands in the south.

It was an early settler who was inspired to establish a pig colony in mid-Atlantic. The pigs were prospering when Captain Diego Ramirez

---

PRECEDING PAGES: harvesting Easter lilies.
LEFT: palms and evergreens populate island gardens.
RIGHT: the elusive cahow.

landed in 1603 and noticed the roads they had made. "The islands were covered with cedar, palmetto palms and other evergreens," he wrote. There was underbrush but little grass. If there were any flowers, he did not mention them. He applauded the absence of mosquitoes but complained about flies. Ramirez noted both sparrowhawks and herons but was impressed most of all by some wild birds reminiscent of the crows he had recently seen in Havana.

"When we landed", he wrote, "they came to us, perched on our heads, uttering a multitudinous chorus of cries". They burrowed in the headlands at water level, he said, emerging at

wrote William Strachey, chronicler of the Jamestown settlers shipwrecked on Bermuda five years after Ramirez's visit, "which was by hollowing and laughing. With the noyse thereof, the birds would come flocking and settle upon the very arms of him that so cryed: by which our men would weigh them and which weighest heaviest they tooke, twentie dozen in two hours". Bermuda's first settlers dined on cahows that they could catch "faster than they could be killed". Henry C. Wilkinson, Bermuda's outstanding historian, notes that "these silly birds were unable to learn the ways of man and soon succumbed".

The last straw was the invasion of rats con-

night to feed in a tremendous cacophony that terrified his crew. He described the birds in detail, so there is no doubt they were cahows.

His crew gathered their wits to discover that the birds were really harmless, not the diabolical creatures that had persuaded their predecessors to call Bermuda the Isle of Devils. "The birds were so plentiful", he wrote, " that 4,000 could be taken in a single bag. The men relished them enough to eat them all the time, and when we left we brought away more than 1,000 well dried and salted for the voyage".

The cahow startled other visitors until they, too, realised that the birds were just being friendly. "Our men found a prettie way to take them",

tained in a shipload of maize supplied by a pirate. As soon as they had devastated one island, they swam en masse to the next. The cahow, we now know, retreated to the safety of rocky islets, but there proved to be insufficient soil in which to burrow. They tried nesting in natural crevices, but that put them in unequal competition with the long-tail, another sea bird, which drove them out to rule the roost.

Protecting the wildlife

The settlers were not as mindlessly destructive as one might think. Setting fire to the vegetation was a desperate measure to contain the rats; the sacrifice of valuable cedar was not an easy decision. Daniel Tucker, the governor who ordered the burning, tried to safeguard the cahow by decree, and one of his successors introduced formal protection for the island's turtles.

Bermuda's varied and lush vegetation is a tribute to the settlers' attempts to make amends. Driving along any road is to unravel a chain of bright flowers and berries in hedgerows, tropical hibiscus and dusty pink oleander, virtually all imports which subsequently went wild. The fragrance in the air in spring is from citrus blossom and freesias, the latter a member of the lily family with white, purple and yellow blossoms.

The Bermuda Easter lily has a large white

the bay bean, fennel, a seaside morning glory with a distinctive heart-shaped leaf, golden rod, sea ox-eye, bay lavender, buttonwood and seaside evening primrose. The inland area has caves filled with ferns that are endemic and rare.

The whole of Bermuda has now taken on the appearance of a botanical garden. The official Botanical Gardens in Paget are the logical starting point for interested visitors, who would also enjoy the flora of Par-la-Ville Park in the centre of Hamilton, Fort Hamilton on the outskirts, the premier's official residence, Camden House, and Walsingham in Hamilton Parish. Bermudians have created many superb private gardens;

flower much like a trumpet and was until recently Bermuda's major, and at times only, export. Although the Easter lily enjoyed the fame, the island's national flower is actually the tiny, lavender-blue Bermudiana, which grows wild among the freesias.

The flora on a wild hillside include fiddlewood, allspice, Brazil pepper and Surinam cherry. The sage bush, also known as *lantana*, adds its pretty, multi-coloured bloom; the morning glory its blue, bell-shaped flower. Examples of coastal flora are to be found among the dunes above Warwick Long Bay and Horseshoe Bay:

LEFT AND RIGHT: not-so-wild life.

though these are not readily accessible to all.

Cedars which survived Governor Tucker's torch and the demands of Bermuda's later shipbuilding industry were blighted once more by a scale insect epidemic in the 1940s. While the cedar struggles to regain its regal position among Bermuda's flora, the little skink lizard hangs on tenaciously to its illustrious status as the only native creature. It leads a reclusive existence in quarries and cliff faces, reluctant to show its face unless tempted by a pungent bait, preferably tinned tuna fish.

The skink lost its monopoly to the pigs and later domestic animals, the most celebrated being a dog that was travelling with the ill-fated

Jamestown settlers of 1609. This dog has a documented place in history: as an expert hog-catcher (it is depicted in full cry on Sir George Somers' map), as a companion to the "three kings", and as a participant in a brawl over the fabulous ambergris.

Less has been written about later dogs than Bermuda's frogs, in particular the whistling frog imported from the West Indies in the 19th century and its deep-throated cousin, the giant toad *(Bufo marinas)*, a native of the same islands which was brought in to deal with cockroaches. The little frog, no bigger than a thumb-nail and rarely seen, sings melodiously, almost like a bird. The toads

is on the visitors – as many as 200 unpredictable species every year. "We lie under a major fly way," says Dr Wingate. Bermuda is on the regular migration route of about 60 species. They would not normally stop in Bermuda but will seek temporary refuge if the weather is bad. Other species will have drifted off course. "An exciting place", he says, "because you never know what will turn up next. Every year we get vagrants from Europe and Asia". Some arrivals are hard to believe – the Siberian fly catcher, for example, "from the opposite side of the planet". The comings and goings take place all year long bar the summer.

greet heavy rainfall with a lusty chorus and often exercise on roads on cool nights.

Dominant wildlife

The dominant aspect of Bermuda's wildlife has been the birds. With the unfortunate demise of the cahow and the exception of the longtail, Bermuda's resident bird population is, even to its great champion, the highly distinguished ornithologist Dr David Wingate, "poor and undramatic". He makes allowances for the European goldfinch and kiskadee fly catcher, as well as a small blue bird which seems to have formed an interest in golf, or at least golf courses. The focus of birdwatchers, however,

Dr Wingate was made a Member of the British Empire in 1975 and soon afterward was awarded the Order of the Golden Ark, the equivalent of a knighthood, by Prince Bernhard of the Netherlands. These honours were the culmination of dramatic developments, the first hint of which occurred on 22 February 1906 when Louis Mowbray, a Bermudian naturalist, found an unusual bird in a nest in rocks in Castle Harbour. He thought it was some kind of petrel but sent it off, preserved, to the American Museum of Natural History for identification. Comparison with bones found in caves opened up the possibility that it was a cahow.

In 1935 a young bird collided with St David's lighthouse; 10 years later, a similar bird was washed up on Cooper's Island. They fitted the description of cahows but were dead. The prospects of finding one alive looked unpromising because of the upheaval caused by the construction of the wartime US Navy base and airport where the cahow, according to historical references, had traditionally nested.

Although still a schoolboy, David Wingate was invited to join a search by Mowbray's son, "Louis S.", and Dr Robert Cushman Murphy. He describes a moment after painstaking work, usually at night, among islets and rocks. Dr

more numerous longtails. The urgent remedy was to secure a larger island for the cahow and build artificial nest sites with baffles that would keep out the longtails. The government declared Nonsuch Island a cahow sanctuary.

The process was nevertheless agonisingly slow: cahows take between 8 and 10 years to reach breeding age and they then produce just one egg a year, only half of which actually hatch. In 1965, Wingate became aware of another threat. "There were new and ominous signs that the breeding success was declining even further. After long and tedious research the problem was identified as DDT poison." The

Murphy had spotted something deep in a nesting crevice. He lowered a noose and gingerly lifted the bird out. He held it up to the light and drew in his breath: "By Gad, the cahow!"

Wingate completed his studies and returned to lead a full-scale conservation programme, becoming Chief Conservation Officer until 2000, when Jeremy Madeiros took over. It took Wingate 10 years to determine that there were 18 pairs alive. The survivors were living precariously on rocks in the natural crevices from which they might be driven at any time by the

LEFT AND RIGHT: the entire island looks like a brightly coloured garden.

cahow was getting enough in its food chain to weaken the egg shells and make them increasingly prone to breakages in the nest.

The ban on DDT in the US pulled the cahow yet again back from the brink, only for danger to reappear in 1987 in the wholly unpredictable form of a snow owl that had wandered from its normal Arctic home. The owl killed five young birds, but by then the population was large and resilient enough to absorb the loss.

In 2007 there were 80 breeding pairs, producing 39 chicks. This increase is encouraging but the cahow's survival will depend on protecting the privacy which was disrupted, in the first instance, by the snout of a peckish pig. ❑

THE BERMUDA TRIANGLE

*Ships and aircraft are reported to have disappeared without trace
around the islands. Is this a case for "The X Files"?*

The Bermuda Triangle, whose points are Florida, Puerto Rico and Bermuda, is remarkably in-grained in the popular imagination for something that became common currency only in 1964. In February of that year, *Argosy* magazine carried an article by a Vincent Gaddis about the inexplicable disappearance of

a significant number of ships and aircraft in a triangle of the Atlantic between Bermuda, Florida and Puerto Rico. The phenomenon of fully manned ships vanishing in perfectly calm weather had been well known to mariners since Christopher Columbus, he said, but it was kept a dark secret among themselves.

Paranormal pantheon

Vincent Gaddis's revelations were taken up by other writers, and the rapidly growing snowball produced more magazine articles, books and films. In no time the Bermuda Triangle had joined the Loch Ness monster, the *Marie Celeste* and UFOs in the pantheon of the paranormal.

The follow-ups borrowed freely from Gaddis's original article without looking too critically at his factual sources; the cult of the Triangle gaining credibility from reports that the US Navy, Coast Guard, Lloyd's of London and "top scientists" had investigated the matter and confessed to being completely baffled. Several sleuths latched on to the discovery that an area around Bermuda had long been noted in Royal Navy charts as one of magnetic aberration. One of the staple stories in the dossier was the case of the *Ellen Austin*. Gaddis had mentioned the ship, possibly as the result of coming across it in *The Stargazer Talks*, a book by Rupert Gould, which had been published in 1914 without attracting the same sort of attention as the more recent *Argosy* magazine article.

According to Gould, *Ellen Austin* was a British ship that in 1881 encountered an abandoned but still seaworthy ship "in mid-Atlantic". Some of the crew, he wrote, boarded the ship with orders to make for St John's, Newfoundland. The two ships parted "in foggy weather" but met up again a few days later. To the consternation of the crew, the shipmates who had transferred to the *Ellen Austin* had also vanished.

Gould did not say how or where he learned of this strange episode, nor did other writers who incorporated it in their work. The story was modified and embellished with almost every retelling. The location was apt to wander from "mid-Atlantic" to "West of the Azores"; some versions had signs of a struggle on the mystery ship, others had a second rescue crew put on board – only to have them vanish as well.

By the time a certain Richard Winer got round to writing *The Devil's Triangle* in 1974, the captain of the *Ellen Austin* had acquired a name, "Captain Baker", and the author a considerable amount of closely observed detail. Baker "looked back over his right shoulder" and waved a Colt revolver while urging his men aboard the derelict ship. At the height of the action, Captain Baker accidentally steps on a thumb-sized cockroach, not that it makes the slightest bit of difference to him or what happens next. When the mystery ship eventually disappears after accounting for two prize crews, it is engulfed in a watery haze.

These alarming goings-on were brought up to date with tales about the fate of aircraft. Bruce Gernon, an American pilot flying a light plane, was reported as being sucked into a greenish tunnel in the middle of a cloud. All his instruments malfunctioned as he went "weightless". The startled pilot managed to land safely at Palm Beach and did some calculations based on elapsed flying time, distance covered and so forth. His figures indicated that his aircraft, with a normal top speed of 195 mph (314 kph), must have been

them – and disappeared. A five-day search for the six missing aircraft produced nothing.

It was inevitable that the experts would start coming up with explanatory theories. The historically minded inclined toward the lost continent of Atlantis whose population, 10,000 years ago, developed a form of energy so powerful that they blew themselves to bits. The strange forces at work in the Triangle were the result of the Atlantis generators – whatever form they took – relentlessly churning out energy. A clairvoyant named Edgar Cayce confidently predicted that Atlantis would resurface in either 1968 or 1969.

Charles Berlitz, pronouncing with the author-

travelling at an astounding 1,180 mph (1,900 kph). The crew and passengers of an Eastern Airlines flight felt a powerful jolt that caused all their watches to stop, someone else noted.

Perhaps the most famous mystery concerning aircraft is said to have occurred on 5 December 1945. Five US Navy Avenger torpedo bombers took off from Fort Lauderdale on a routine patrol. The Flight Leader radioed that he was lost before communication with the ground ended. A rescue plane was sent up to look for

PRECEDING PAGES: a spooky view.
LEFT: a rum business.
ABOVE: a plane about to enter the Triangle.

ity of one who is "fluent in 27 languages", wrote the best-selling *The Bermuda Triangle*, in which he picked up where Einstein left off in developing the theory of relativity. He speculated about a time anomaly in the Triangle "as if time at certain moments could project individuals from the present into the past or otherwise bend the continuum of time in a manner blending the past and the present – and perhaps the future as well". If the forces of gravity, energy and mass in a ship or aircraft met their equal in anti-matter – whoosh, they would vanish.

The pastor of the Cathedral of Life Church in Torrance, California, The Rev. George Johnson, teamed up with Don Tanner, the religion editor

of *The Daily Breeze*, to study the Book of Revelations, which they believed might provide a simple answer. The book, they pointed out, "tells where the redeemed go after death and shows the significance of water in the kingdom of God in contrast to its present role as a destructive and captive force".

Entrance to Hell

After painstaking research, they held up their verdict: the Bermuda Triangle was one of two entrances to Hell, the other being the Devil's Sea between Japan and the Philippines.

Larry Kusche, a librarian at Arizona State University, turned not to the Bible but to naval records and newspapers to track down as much as was reliably known about incidents attributed to the Triangle. In contemporary records that he thought would have carried full reports of the *Ellen Austin* mystery, he could find no mention. Disappearances attributed to the Triangle might actually have taken place as far away as the Pacific, Ireland, Africa or not at all. He dug out a transcript of the radio traffic between ground control and the doomed US Navy torpedo bombers and concluded that, hopelessly lost, they had flown in formation for four hours until their fuel ran out. The plane sent to look for them evidently exploded in an accidental fire 23 minutes after take-off.

Kusche's list of verifiable facts at the end of the day should have put a wet blanket over the Bermuda Triangle for all time. The percentage of aircraft and ships lost in the busy Triangle was no higher than anywhere else; the Triangle was only exceptional in the number of reported incidents that, on investigation, proved to be false. When ships or aircraft were lost, the weather was invariably bad.

His summary left no doubt about his position. "The Triangle is the ultimate example of the paranormal, pseudo-science, fictional science and media run amok. It is the epitome of false reporting; deletion of pertinent information; twisted values among writers, publishers and the media; mangling of scientific principles; and the often deliberate deception of a trusting public." He was content to let it pass as a "manufactured mystery" but could not bring himself to condemn others who called it "an outright fraud or a rip-off". ❑

RIGHT: a painted ship in distress.

S. S. "Carribeau", Nearing Bermuda.

A WINTER'S TALE

Bermuda has evolved into a year-round resort blessed with mild winters when the pace of life is less hurried than in spring and summer

Mark Twain did it. So did Queen Victoria's daughter, Princess Louise. And US President Woodrow Wilson, not to mention Eleanor Roosevelt and literary types like Rudyard Kipling, Sinclair Lewis, Noel Coward and James Thurber.

What did they have in common? They wintered in Bermuda – despite the fact that today Bermuda is known primarily as a summer resort. In the days before the island became pre-eminently known for its pristine, eggshell-pink beaches and water sports, summer was the "off season", when hotels shuttered up and visitors headed home like the swallows to Capistrano.

Year-round resort

All that changed after World War II, when Bermuda evolved into a year-round resort with an emphasis on the spring and summer seasons. Now visitors, (holiday-makers are invariably known as "visitors" in genteel Bermuda, rather than as the crassly commercial "tourists"), are rediscovering winter in Bermuda, and, like that earlier genre of winter traveller, finding that Bermuda is more than sun, sand and sea.

In truth, winter in this tiny country tucked away in "the ocean's bosom, unespied", as 17th-century English poet Andrew Marvell put it, is more like spring in other parts of the world. Visitors are invited to come to Bermuda for "our springtime festival", or "our extended season", which knowledgeable travellers realise is packed with complimentary attractions and activities, not to mention significantly reduced hotel and restaurant prices and a lack of crowds.

The impressive sight of the first longtail bird catching an upper air current off the South Shore beaches is, to those Bermudians who catch a glimpse of this national symbol, the heart-warming signal that spring is at hand. And more often than not, the sighting is in February. Spring arrives early in this, the world's second most isolated archipelago (and that's official – the only other place farther from any other scrap of land is St Helena, west of Angola, which undoubtedly explains why the British sent Napoleon into exile there).

Yet due west, the United States' eastern seaboard is still in the snowy grip of winter. In

Mark Twain's day, the author had to make the tortuous winter journey to Bermuda through storm-tossed seas that pitched the puny passenger ships about like matchsticks, moving Twain to comment acidly that "Bermuda may be paradise but you have to go through Hell to get there."

The primary joy of winter in Bermuda is that it is another way of life from the hectic summer season. The tempo eases back to half-time and the days are filled with languid walks on deserted beaches or inland nature trails. There's browsing through the unhurried streets of villages like St George's and Somerset. And evenings lingering over succulent Bermuda

---

PRECEDING PAGES: Hamilton Harbour in the 1980s.
LEFT: the island was a winter haven in the 1930s.
RIGHT: hanging around for a haircut.

Dancin' in the Street

A drumroll, loud as thunder. Far down the road they appear: young men in bright capes and masks, dancing a wild acrobatic step. There is a hypnotic swirl of sound and colour. Costumes are a combination of African tribal and Native American; the headdresses are crowned with peacock feathers. Children fall into line behind the procession, and the Gombeys roll on, dancin' in the street.

The Bermuda Gombey, or Masquerade, is the island's premier folk art. The troupe, always male, traditionally consisted of males from the same fam-

ily who passed on the techniques from one generation to the next. The Gombeys' noisy, always rhythmic presence personifies the winter season in Bermuda, for they perform most often around the Christmas season. During other cool months, the Department of Tourism organises regular indoor demonstrations for visitors. Troupes perform at cultural events in the US, Canada and elsewhere; they were a huge hit at the Edinburgh Tattoo in 2002.

The dance is West African in origin, but the unlikely combination of military music, British Mummers (who used song and mime to entertain), slavery rites, West Indians and Native Americans, not to mention a touch of Mardi Gras, contribute to the distinctive Gombey heritage.

The word "Gombey" has a dual meaning: it describes a type of African drum, and in Bantu it means, literally, "rhythm". Louise A. Jackson, director of the Jackson School of Performing Arts and someone who has "observed, studied and travelled abroad with Gombey 'crowds' for close to 30 years", has written a book which traces the roots of the dance through its different cultural influences. In *Gombey* she writes: "African dancers have been known to use sculptured objects such as houses or boats on their heads, and all this has been seen in the Bermuda Gombey... American Indian influence on the Gombey dance is seen in the costume, character roles in the Gombey folk drama and use of Indian symbols." A tomahawk often rests near a dancer's shoulder during certain selected numbers.

In the past, the Gombey acted not only as entertainment, but also as social commentary. It was common for one "crowd" to travel to another's "territory", a Christmas tradition adapted from the Mummers, and to make sardonic observations. Jackson cites a few lines of a song as an example:

> ... All 'de way to Paget side
> Nothing 'dere but foolish pride
> All 'de way to Brackish Pon'
> Cow-heel soup an' damaged corn.

Biblical rituals have also been re-enacted in dance and mime, which possibly relate to the conversion of slaves to Christianity. The British, too, were responsible for a bit of cultural integration, for Gombey musicians use not the traditional tribal hand drum employed by other ethnic groups but a snare drum played with sticks which was used by British soldiers when they were stationed in Bermuda. The triangle, fife and whistle are additional military instruments played.

The strongest influence on the contemporary Gombey is, however, from the West Indies. The Caribbean has its own "Goombay" dancers, and slaves or convicts imported from other islands to work at Dockyard brought their own traditions. Only the Bermudian Gombey plays the drums with sticks, however, which reinforces its unique status.

The Gombey tradition is, unfortunately, a diminishing art form, for the intricate rhythms and acrobatic dance steps require peak physical condition and tireless practice. In the past Bermuda had several regional troupes, but economic pressures have meant that many dancers and musicians can only rehearse part-time. During the winter, should a Gombey troupe come your way, it would be fitting to continue a time-honoured custom by offering a few coins as a "Christmas present" in return. ❏

lobster (a large, warm-water crayfish that can only be caught and served between September and March), watching the Bermuda Regiment band, resplendent in scarlet and gold uniforms, recreate the martial splendour of the Old Empire under floodlights on Hamilton's Front Street, or simply warming the feet in front of a toasty log fire while enjoying that distinctively Bermudian hotel experience, the cottage colony.

Warm weather buffer

Only a geographical and geological accident makes any of this possible. Bermuda stands alone as the world's northernmost coral island

The lanes and byways of the Bermudian countryside are already ablaze with flowers, and that choicest of Bermuda fruits, the loquat, is at its prime in February, when a golden hoard loads down countless trees. The ever-so-slightly tart loquat is an instant roadside feast and one which Bermudians delight in transforming into jams, chutneys and a warming liqueur commonly known as Bermuda Gold.

Nature walks are at their best in winter, whether tramping the old Bermuda Railway, meandering through the backwoods and between sawn-away coral limestone cliffs, or on undeveloped country roads like Orange Valley

group, situated on the same latitude as Savannah, Georgia, but on average 10 degrees warmer, thanks to the benevolent intervention of the Gulf Stream, which surges northeastward between the southeastern US coast and Bermuda, acting as an effective buffer between these sub-tropical islands and the frigid North American continent.

Day-time winter temperatures can reach 23°C (73°F), with the average around 20°C (68°F). Golf and tennis addicts can exhilaratingly perfect their games without risking the heat prostration of hotter climes.

LEFT: a Gombey dancer in traditional dress.
ABOVE: national kite-flying day is Good Friday.

in Devonshire, Greenfield Lane in Somerset, the western stretch of Spice Hill Road in Warwick or Ferry Reach Road in St George's. Many of the more "countrified" roads are exploratory pathways to all-weather attractions, ranging from antique-crammed mansions and museums to enormous subterranean caverns and formidable fortresses that once made these islands the "Gibraltar of the West".

Richard Hansen, at the time an associate director of public affairs at the White House, Washington D.C., put it rather well when he said: "In winter, Bermuda appears to be a dream come true for the bird-watcher – observing the flight of the longtail from the cliff above Spanish Rock is worth nearly the cost of the trip, even for a non-bird-watcher like me – as well as the plant lover, those interested in the study of marine life, and the artist. The opportunities for enjoyment in these areas seem endless, and do not require summer temperatures. In fact, spring-like weather is more desirable." The Spanish Rock that Hansen talks about is the oldest surviving physical evidence of human presence in Bermuda. Spanish Rock is now part of the Spittal Pond Nature Sanctuary, one of a number of charming preserves protected by the Bermuda National Trust.

Just a few minutes away, up another wooded

hillside, is Verdmont, a fine Georgian mansion typical of the museum homes that provide such pleasant explorations in winter. Another National Trust property, Verdmont's interior walls and typically Bermudian tray ceilings are sheathed in pickled pine and its wide, pegged floorboards are designed like those of a ship's deck. Indeed, much of the building done in Bermuda in centuries past was by trained shipwrights – witness, for example, the beauty of the Old Devonshire Church.

Verdmont is notable for its large-hearthed kitchen, where many a Bermudian delicacy of old was cooked up. Some are still features of winter and spring holidays in Bermuda, notably the cassava pie, dating from earliest settler days, when it was created from ground cassava root flour, wild bird eggs and the pork from the wild hogs the Spanish left behind. Today it is Bermudians' traditional Christmas and Easter dish. The Gombey dancers perfom on New Year's Day in a characteristically Bermudian rite.

Good Friday is Bermuda's national kite-flying day, when thousands of colourful creations of every size and shape take to the air. Most notable is the classic Bermuda kite, with a long mast and buzzers, which purists make in part from wild Bermuda sagebrush sticks. According to tradition, the cross-shaped kites are supposed to be a reminder of the resurrected Christ rising to Heaven.

Easter Sunday is another day to savour off-season scenic splendour, particularly at dawn services which are conducted on tops of cliffs and in other spectacular settings. These are followed by the traditional serving of hot-cross buns and coffee. Guy Fawkes' Day celebrations in early November reveal British roots, but fireworks are now banned – something that does not apply to the serving of the Bermuda sweet potato pudding, traditionally eaten for dinner at this same time of year.

These customs tend to highlight the increased folksiness of the island in winter, when Bermudians, always friendly and solicitous (start a conversation at your peril without declaring "Good Morning!" or "Good Afternoon!"), have time to be especially out-going.

High-pressure hosts

Indeed, many Bermudians believe that the present-day decline in the number of winter visitors is necessary to provide an opportunity for a "recharging of batteries" after having played high-pressure host throughout the summer.

Winter is a time of replenishment – part of the rhythm of a seasonal cycle that more tropical climes are denied. It's a time for painting the house and enjoying showers that top up the depleted underground water tanks essential to Bermudian homes; a time for scraping down the multi-hued boat hulls on the slipways on inlets and bays; and a time to wait for the first, inevitable sighting of the longtail returned. ❑

LEFT: Bermudians wear winter clothes while visitors dress in summer outfits.
RIGHT: skirling ceremony during the winter season.

PLACES

*A detailed guide to Bermuda, with principal sites
clearly cross-referenced by number to the maps*

Bermuda's landscape is enormously varied. The popular image is, of course, of the island's pastel beaches and turquoise water. But there is more: from sophisticated towns to subterranean caverns. This scenic variety makes Bermuda interesting. What makes Bermuda fascinating is that it is all contained within just a few square miles. In context, the island's diminutive proportions are exceptional: 50 times smaller than Rhode Island, America's tiniest state, and 561 times smaller than Belgium, one of Europe's most compact countries.

This mix in landscape extends throughout the island. Above ground, there are fields of flowers, some cultivated, some wild, and botanical gardens with exotic, mysterious trees. Below ground are the caves, rich in stalagmites and drippy stones which configure into a range of shapes, from Buddha to the Manhattan skyline. Into the sea, deeper still, the variety continues: Bermuda's crystal waters attract divers from all over the world, who study the fish and submarine flora.

Trails, both man-made and natural, are other distinguishing features, along with shapely domestic architecture, beautifully maintained nature reserves and fields used exclusively for agriculture. Just when it seems safe to assume the island consists mainly of beaches and countryside, it throws up a surprise, like an exclusive clothing store surrounded by trees and offering top-quality goods.

Quality shops are something the island knows about, shops that are found, for the most part, in Bermuda's quality towns. The capital, Hamilton, is home to a handsome cathedral, dignified municipal buildings and a range of businesses, often family-owned, that can trace their origins as far back as 1844. St George's, on the other side of the island, is older still; it was Bermuda's first village and sports a colourful local town crier. The island has more golf courses per square mile than any nation in the world, and has one of the highest per capita incomes.

History, architecture, flowers and fine shopping – all contained in an area 14 times smaller than New York City. Coupled with some of the best beaches in the world, what more could a visitor ask for? ❏

PRECEDING PAGES: a Gombey dance troupe; artful houses; snorkellers on a South Shore beach.
LEFT: Hamilton's Front Street is lined with pastel-coloured buildings.

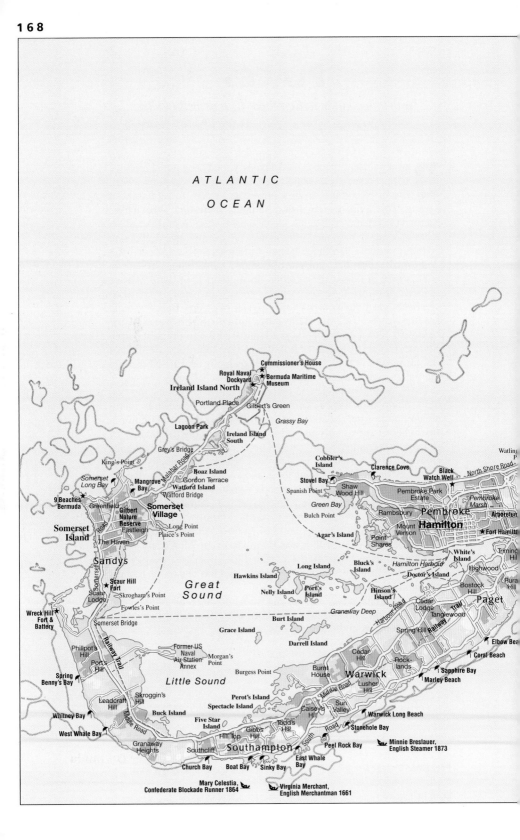

ATLANTIC

OCEAN

Commissioner's House
Royal Naval
Dockyard ★ ★ Bermuda Maritime
Museum
Ireland Island North
Portland Place
Gilbert's Green
Lagoon Park *Grassy Bay*
**Ireland Island
South**
Grey's Bridge
King's Point
Cobbler's
Island Clarence Cove
**Black
Watch Well**
Stovel Bay North Shore Road
Watling
P
Boaz Island Shaw
Wood Hill
*Somerset
Long Bay* Gordon Terrace
**Mangrove
Bay** Watford Island Spanish Point Pembroke Park
Estate
Watford Bridge *Pembroke
Marsh*
9 Beaches
Bermuda *Green Bay* Rambsbury Arboretum
Greenfield Bulch Point **Pembroke
Hamilton**
**Gilbert
Nature
Reserve** **Somerset
Village** Mount
Vernon Fort Hamilton ★
Eastleigh Agar's Island Point
Shares
**Somerset
Island** Long Point
Place's Point *White's
Island* Triming
Hill
The Haven *Hamilton Harbour* Highwood
Sandys Long Island **Bluck's
Island** Doctor's Island Rura
Hill
Hawkins Island Bostock
Hill **Paget**
★ Scaur Hill
Fort Nelly Island **Fort's
Island** **Hinson's
Island** Cedar
Lodge
Scaur
Lodge Skrogham's Point *Great
Sound* Tanglewood
Fowles's Point *Granaway Deep* Spring Hill
Wreck Hill
Fort &
Battery ★ Burt Island Elbow Bea
Somerset Bridge Grace Island Coral Beach
Phillpot's
Hill Darrell Island Cedar
Hill Rock-
lands Sapphire Bay
Former US
Naval
Air Station
Annex Morgan's
Point Burnt
House **Warwick** Marley Beach
Port's
Hill Burgess Point Lusher
Hill
**Spring
Benny's Bay** *Little Sound* Perot's Island Sun
Valley Warwick Long Beach
Leadcraft
Hill Skroggin's
Hill Spectacle Island Caisey's
Hill Stonehole Bay
Whitney Bay Buck Island Todd's
Hill
West Whale Bay Five Star
Island Gibbs
Hill Peel Rock Bay Minnie Breslauer,
English Steamer 1873
Granaway
Heights Hill Top **Southampton** East Whale
Bay
Southcliff
Church Bay Boat Bay Sinky Bay
Mary Celestia,
Confederate Blockade Runner 1864 Virginia Merchant,
English Merchantman 1661

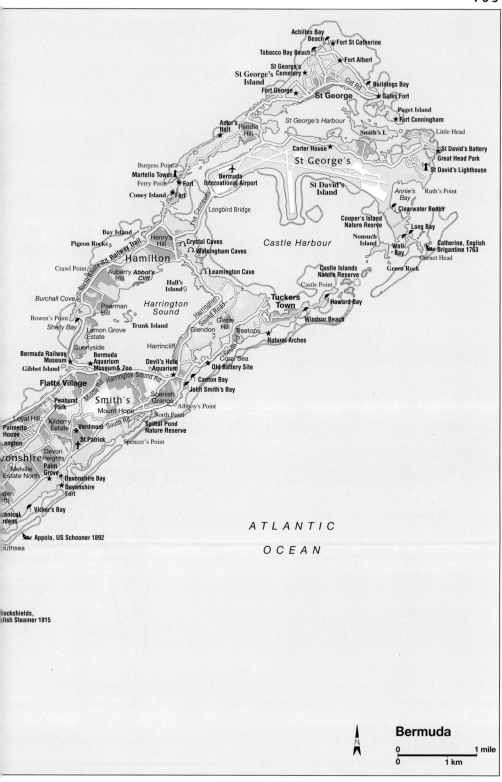

Achilles Bay Beach
★ Fort St Catherine
Tobacco Bay Beach
★ Fort Albert
St George's Cemetery ★
St George's Island
Cut Rd
★ Buildings Bay
Fort George ★
St George
★ Gates Fort
St George's Harbour
Paget Island
★ Fort Cunningham
Astor's Halt
Pendle Hill
Smith's I.
Little Head
Burgess Point
Carter House ★
St David's Battery
Great Head Park
Martello Tower
★ Fort
Ferry Point
Coney Island ★ Fort
Bermuda International Airport
St George's
St David's Island
St David's Lighthouse
Longbird Bridge
Annie's Bay
Ruth's Point
Clearwater Beach
The Causeway
Cooper's Island Nature Resrve
Long Bay
Bay Island
Henry's Hill
Crystal Caves
Walsingham Caves
Castle Harbour
Nonsuch Island
Well Bay
Catherine, English Brigantine 1763
Pigeon Rocks
Gurnet Head
Crawl Point
Leamington Cave
Green Rock
Auberry Hill
Abbot's Cliff
Castle Islands Nature Reserve
Castle Point
Burchall Cove
Hall's Island
Harrington Sound
Pearman Hill
Harrington Sound Road
Tuckers Town
Howard Bay
Bowen's Point
Shelly Bay
Lemon Grove Estate
Trunk Island
Glebe Hill
Glendon
Treetops
Windsor Beach
Natural Arches
Sunnyside
Harrincliff
Bermuda Railway Museum
Bermuda Aquarium Museum & Zoo
Devil's Hole Aquarium
Coral Sea
Old Battery Site
Gibbet Island
Flatts Village
Middle Rd
Harrington Sound Rd
Canton Bay
John Smith's Bay
Penhurst Park
Smith's
Spanish Grange
Albuoy's Point
Mount Hope
North Point
Loyal Hill
Kilderry Estate
Verdmont
South Rd
Spittal Pond Nature Reserve
Palmetto House
angton
St Patrick
Spencer's Point
Devon Heights
onshire
Melville Estate North
Palm Grove
Devonshire Bay
Devonshire Fort
den
anical rdens
Vicker's Bay
Appola, US Schooner 1892
outhsea

ATLANTIC

OCEAN

Rockshields, lish Steamer 1915

North Shore Rd Railway Trail

N

Bermuda

0 ——— 1 mile
0 ——— 1 km

Map on page 172

HAMILTON

*Bermuda's capital and business centre bustles with activity,
while the colonial architecture hides a colourful history
within the town's fascinating nooks and alleyways*

The city of Hamilton is changing as old buildings are torn down to make way for sleek, modern towers. The skyline, which was once dominated by the Cathedral, is taking on a more contemporary appearance. Legal restrictions that limited the height of buildings have been lifted resulting in an increase in the number of high-rise apartments, offices and stores. Critics argue that the city is losing its essential Bermudian character and is beginning to resemble any North American city, but architects have, in many cases, retained the clean lines of Bermuda's architectural heritage. The main thoroughfare, Front Street *(see page 175)*, is undergoing major development but thankfully the pastel and verandah effect is being safeguarded.

The capital is the nearest Bermuda achieves to a bustling metropolis. The narrow streets beyond the harbour usually teem with shoppers and office workers, and there is a busy, urban ambience during the daytime and things remain lively in the restaurants and nightclubs all evening long.

Around town

Hamilton covers an area of 177 acres (70 hectares), with a resident population of only 2,000. Because the town blends seamlessly into its parish, Pembroke, it seems larger than it is. This deceptive appearance is enhanced by the many interior arcades that meander off Hamilton's principal shopping streets. Turn a corner into what appears to be an alleyway, and find, instead, multi-levelled tiers of shops, restaurants and chic boutiques.

The unofficial boundaries might well be the Fairmont Hamilton Princess hotel on the west. Then extending all along Front Street and the waterfront to the roundabout on the east, which serves as the gateway to Paget parish.

This roundabout is known to all Hamiltonians as the place to wave "hello" to Johnny Barnes. Mr Barnes is a retired bus driver, sound of mind and sociable in spirit, who stands in the middle of the roundabout each morning to greet commuters on their way into work.

Barnes is a notable Bermudian figure, whose radiant eccentricity and loyal presence at the roundabout, come rain or shine, says a great deal about the island and its people. In 1999 Barnes posed for his statue – entitled *Spirit of Bermuda* – which was sculpted by Desmond Fountain and stands near the place where he waves each morning.

At the other end of town, the **Fairmont Hamilton Princess** has played host to

EFT: Johnny Barnes greets ach ommuter, rain shine.
IGHT: the ip-clop of orses' ooves.

royalty, movie stars and charity events. It was also the scene of stirring espionage during World War II *(see Spies at the Princess Hotel, page 63)*. Today, although life at the Princess is calmer, its ground-floor bar stays open late at night and is a local rendezvous for residents and visitors. Earlier in the day, the same bar is the setting for afternoon tea.

The large structure next to the Princess Hotel on Pitt's Bay Road is the **Waterfront**, a development that contains upmarket townhouses and offices. Opened in late 1999, most of the shops that originally moved in at the Waterfront have now moved on. However, there is a good grocery store, Miles, and the Bank of Butterfield maintains a small office with an ATM. Opposite the Waterfront is **Rosedon**, a small elegant hotel. The main building is a beautiful old colonial house dating from 1906.

Nearby is the headquarters of Bacardi. This modern glass-fronted structure with a spectacular fountain out front is hard to miss, though none of the famous liquor is produced on the island.

Diagonally across Pitt's Bay Road lies what was once the capital's finest smaller hotel, **Waterloo House Ⓐ**. Built on a series of terraces, accented with flowers and borders, planters and hanging baskets, it is now closed and its fate is uncertain.

Farther still is one of the island's distinctive **moongates**, the round, limestone gates through which honeymooners are meant to walk to ensure good luck. This particular moongate leads to a parking lot for the bakery, so dedicated romantics are urged to try elsewhere for their luck.

The colour of money

Between 1999 and 2002, Pitt's Bay Road underwent a dramatic transformation. First came the **Zurich Centre** by the waterfront, which houses international reinsurance companies. And next, rising from the ashes of the old Bermudiana Hotel, came two new edifices, the headquarters of reinsurance/insurance companies, ACE and

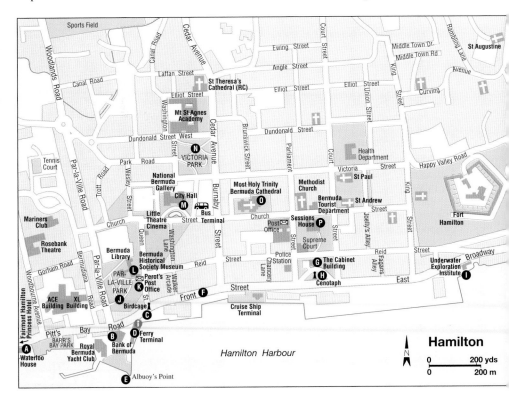

Hamilton

Map
on page
172

XL. The ACE building's exterior is pastel shades of pink, while XL House, through its play of white solids, windows and roof decks, evokes traditional Bermudian architecture in an abstract way. Across the street a stone staircase leads to the harbour and pretty **Barr's Bay Park**, which might be considered a bit of the front yard of the **Royal Bermuda Yacht Club**. Members' boats dominate the landscape, and the view to the other side of the harbour is lovely, glimpsed through the silhouettes of tall masts. (This on a cloudy day, of course. On sunny days and weekends, sensible members have jumped on their yachts and sailed away.)

The **Bank of Bermuda ⓑ**, owned by financial giant HSBC, was founded in 1890 by a group of prominent merchants. Its head office is located in a utilitarian building right on the waterfront near Barr's Bay Park. Approaching the bank, even on days without a breeze, means a brief encounter with a wind tunnel. A local ruling states that buildings cannot exceed the height of the cathedral, although at seven storeys high the bank headquarters must come close.

If you are not in a hurry, you can brave the queues at the bank branch and catch some of the local gossip, while cashing your traveller's cheques. For those less inclined to wait, numerous ATMs around the island accept international bank cards, dispensing Bermuda currency.

To the city centre

From the Bank of Bermuda building travel east along Pitt's Bay Road until you reach Queen Street on the left, the site of several historic buildings. At this junction, Pitt's Bay Road becomes Front Street, the premier shopping thoroughfare and "main drag" of Hamilton. Monitoring the ebb and flow of traffic is Bermuda's most famous moving postcard: the **birdcage ⓒ**, where a shorts-clad police officer can be seen directing traffic during the busy summer months.

BELOW:
Waterloo
House, once
Hamilton's
finest small
hotel.

Ferries and ocean liners

The **ferry terminal** ❶ is a pink building on Pitt's Bay Road, where you can buy a token from one of the machines inside, or from the receptionist. Bermuda's ferries are clean, efficient and run to schedule. If it's raining, a local passenger might well wipe your seat with her hankie before allowing you to sit down. It is from here, too, that glass-bottomed boats depart for short sightseeing cruises.

When the cruise ships disgorge passengers only a few hundred yards away, and hundreds of people pour into Front Street, the low-key island atmosphere turns to "big town". During high season, Wednesday nights are given over to "harbour nights", when sleek ocean liners lie at anchor in the harbour. Shops stay open until later than usual, and the whole of Front Street swarms with street musicians and food vendors.

Refuge is only a few steps away. Down the lane past the Bank of Bermuda is a small promontory jutting out to sea. This is

Albuoy's Point ❺ (also spelt Albouy's Point), a grassy park popular with office workers with their lunchtime sandwiches. The point is said to have been named after a "professor of physick" who fought courageously against an outbreak of yellow fever which was overtaking the island in the 17th century. At dusk, this peninsula is probably the best place in downtown Hamilton to watch the sun as it sets over the water.

Albuoy's Point is one of the main tourist stops for the shiny black-and-red sightseeing locomotive operated by the **Bermuda Train Company**. In 1999, more than half a century after the closure and sale of the Bermuda Railway, which ran from East End to West End and right down busy Front Street, the 60-seat train began tooling passengers around the capital during spring and summer. (Another train operates at Dockyard.) Other stops on the Hamilton route are at the National Gallery, Bermuda Cathedral, St Andrew's Church and the Bermuda Underwater Exploration Institute.

BELOW: the ferry is clean and efficient.

Map on page 172

A shoppers delight

Front Street ⓕ follows the line of the harbour all the way from here to beyond the docks. The south side is a series of warehouses and terminals used by the cruise ships that steam directly into Hamilton. When not in use for their original purposes, these buildings often serve as entertainment centres in the winter months, for lively events such as Gombey dance displays.

The other side, **Front Street West**, has a series of two-tiered pastel-coloured buildings. Walking on the brick pavement between these shops and their stocky, colonial columns, the pedestrian traffic divides into two lanes, for the regular pavement continues alongside. For such an apparently orderly island, it seems logical that strollers would divide into two lanes as well, one heading west and one east. No such division occurs, and a fair amount of jostling takes place, reassuringly confirming that Bermuda's formality throughout the island is self-imposed, rather than regimented.

This area signals the island's finest collection of shops. Many date from the 19th century, and family-owned businesses tend to remain in the family; it's not uncommon to be waited on by a Cooper in Cooper's. Goods are often British, and can offer big savings on similar items bought in the US, although canny shoppers check current prices before stepping on the aeroplane.

Front Street's retail scene is undergoing changes since its most famous department store, Trimingham Brothers, closed after more than 160 years in business. Also gone is Smith's, which had been purchased by Trimingham's shortly before it closed. The Trimingham's building is no more and is to be replaced by a high-rise, albeit in Bermudian architectural style, owned by Bank of Bermuda, HSBC. The Smith's building has survived and is now home to Brown & Co, part of the Phoenix Stores group. Here you'll find the Bookmart, great greeting cards and toys. A third department store, Cooper's, which has

BELOW: Front Street provides the island's best shopping.

several other island locations, remodelled its Front Street building. Despite the loss of these former shopping institutions, there are still stores where the keynote is quality and service is a way of life: **Bluck's**, established in 1844, offers an unusual array of china and crystal, and Bermuda's oldest wine and spirits merchants, **Gosling's**, which dates from 1806. The **Irish Linen Shop** is recommended for fine tablecloths, napkins and mats. A selection of Bermudian goods is also mentioned in *Travel Tips (see page 301)* at the back of this book.

Further along Front Street is **Walker Arcade**, one of Hamilton's prettiest enclosed shopping areas. Lined with shops and offices, it widens into a courtyard, complete with Spanish-style birdbath and terracotta tiles. It's a pleasant place to pause during a shopping spree.

The arcade is one of several rather labyrinthine alleyways that thread through to Reid and Church streets, leading to enclosed malls where businesses run the gamut from quaint to utilitarian. These interconnected passageways make for delightful exploring, and the visitor who sticks strictly to the "main drags" will miss out on a real treat.

Edible goodies will be missed too – the Paradiso Café, with its food and drink, is tucked away in Washington Mall, accessible via **Washington Lane**, which runs between Reid and Church streets.

While still inside Walker Arcade, walk through the iron gates to **Old Cellar Lane**. Before 1900 this alleyway was one of many stables, sheltering horses and carriages for patrons of local businesses in a sort of municipal "parking lot". Now, its whitewashed walls encompass several interesting small shops. **Sail On** stocks a variety of souvenir Bermuda T-Shirts and beachwear, and it also has a section for those in search of risqué gifts for birthdays or other occasions. In contrast, the **Gem Cellar** is the place for hand-made Bermudian jewellery. Particularly popular are hogpenny, hibiscus and longtail

BELOW: a sample of locally produced goods.

Map on page 172

charms for bracelets and pendants. In the same lane is the **Bermuda National Trust** shop, good for unusual Christmas decorations and unique gifts.

Horses and courses

Exiting onto Front Street again, horses (the likely descendants of those that were once housed in the stables in Cellar Lane) can be found tethered by the waterfront opposite. Visitors love to hire these horses and carriages by the hour and at night the clip-clop of horses' hooves on the pavement makes a pleasant sound.

Time was, it was difficult in Hamilton to find places serving casual meals, because a great deal of dining on the island was undertaken in the larger hotels. Nowadays, the capital's eateries offering a range of cuisines from Bermudian to Chinese to Indian to classic British pub grub. The **Hog Penny** on Burnaby Street is one of the latter, with its renditions of steak-and-kidney pie, bangers-and-mash, nightly entertainment and a friendly crowd. The

Pickled Onion restaurant and bar is worth a try, with terrace seating overlooking the harbour on Front Street. Indoors, there's live entertainment, which can be twinned with sampling the relatively inexpensive menu that includes a version of the local fish chowder.

Smack in the middle of the **Emporium Arcade** is a **bronze sculpture** by local artist Desmond Fountain. Appropriately, the sculpture is itself a fountain, crowned by the sylph-like figure of the former Miss World, Gina Swainson. This is one of two statues of Miss Bermuda 1979. The Emporium is also the location of the Visitor Information Centre (69 Front Street).

Chancery Lane lies tucked behind a series of offices – a steep, brick corridor that links Front Street to Reid Street. Here are several popular places to grab a meal. The huge tubs of plants, and wrought-iron canopies with motifs of grapes supporting glass hurricane lamps, lend an atmosphere that is vaguely Spanish. In contrast, **True Reflections** is an Aladdin's cave of

RIGHT: walking to school.

THE BACK OF TOWN

If among the resorts, Bermuda shorts, beaches and businessmen, the local culture still eludes, you should consider checking out the "Back of Town". Traditionally North Hamilton is not featured in travel brochures. In fact, in the past, visitors were advised not to stroll down the northern end of Court Street.

But the area is in line for regeneration, including plans for an outdoor market, and there are efforts to increase trade. The Back of Town, in contrast with Front Street, has been a predominantly poor, black area with a reputation for drug dealing and crime. But North Hamilton is also home to a number of law-abiding residents, Bermudian entrepreneurs, the headquarters for the Progressive Labour Party, and bars and restaurants.

The Corporation of Hamilton has committed to installing CCTV monitors and the Police Service has agreed to create a substation – welcome news for businesses in the area, who complained for years about the lack of attention, compared with other areas of the city.

Visitors must bear in mind that this is the rougher side of town – by Bermuda standards – and take a reasonable amount of care. You are, however, more than likely to have a good time and be spoilt for choice for local entertainment.

African treasures, with black literature and books on history and philosophy.

Wrought-iron gates lead to the headquarters of the United Bermuda Party; swap differences of opinion or champion the politics of your choice at **Dorothy's Coffee Shop**, a funky Bermudian café serving, among other things, the improbable combination of peanut-butter and bacon sandwiches. Dorothy's also has great coffee and is considered by many local people to be the best place in Hamilton to go for a hamburger.

The "grapes motif" of Chancery Lane extends to Front Street balconies, and buildings along here have some of the most elaborate exteriors in town; the filigree wrought-iron balconies could have arrived by ship straight from New Orleans' French Quarter.

The seat of government

The immaculate lawns in front of the two-storey **Cabinet Building** ⓖ (open Mon–Fri 9am–5pm) are extremely pleasant, especially at twilight, when tree frogs make their chirpy sound and scent is heavy in the air. This land has always been reserved for the public, a right that came about when the building was constructed around 1840.

At the tip of the lawns is the stately **Cenotaph** ⓗ, constructed using native stone, and which flies Royal Navy, Air Force and British Army flags commemorating locals who served in the British armed forces in World War I (1914–18) and World War II (1939–45). The Cenotaph is modelled on the memorial in London's Whitehall. In many ways, Bermuda is more British than Britain: Remembrance Day is a public holiday on the island, whereas in Britain it is not. On that day, 11 November, wreaths are laid at the Cenotaph in honour of the brave Bermudians who died in the world wars.

The legislature of Bermuda was first established in 1620 to make laws for "the peace, order and good government" of the island. It is based on the British system and consists of Her Majesty the Queen,

BELOW: a filigree balcony on Front Street.

Map on page 172

a Senate and a House of Assembly. In 1995, the then-Premier, Sir John Swan, called a referendum asking whether Bermuda should secede from the British Commonwealth. When the motion was rejected, Swan resigned. Sir John subsequently carved out a role for himself as a spokesman for moderation and modernisation in government.

Entrance to the **Senate Chamber** is up the green stairs of the Cabinet Building, which is lined with portraits. The 11 members are appointed by the Queen's representative in Bermuda (the Governor) in consultation with the Premier and the Leader of the Opposition. The Senate elects its own President.

Each Wednesday, from November until June, the Senate meets to consider the legislation initiated in the House of Assembly. Visitors are allowed in to the Public Gallery to watch the proceedings, which take place under a colonial-era ceiling with the ubiquitous wooden fans.

Many famous world leaders have met around the round table in the House of Assembly, from former US presidents Dwight Eisenhower and John F. Kennedy to Sir Winston Churchill and Lady Margaret Thatcher.

Black Rod, the silver-headed rod made by the Crown Jewellers, lies in a glass case. The rod represents the symbol of authority of the Head of State (the Governor). It is carried by an official (also called Black Rod) at the Convening of Parliament, which takes place in late autumn. Black Rod leads the procession of Members of Parliament to the Senate Chamber for the reading of the Throne Speech by the Governor.

The long, low waterfront building on the corner of Front and Court streets was once the Town Hall. In 1795 the first municipal elections were held here, at the extremely reasonable hour of 9pm. In the early 19th century it was the temporary home of the House of Assembly, shortly after the Bermudian Government was moved from St George's to Hamilton. The

BELOW: two views of the Senate.

Town Hall shared its premises with the customs warehouse. Today, the building is a government information office.

Submarine experience

Opposite the docks, Front Street turns into East Broadway. Before you reach the *Spirit of Bermuda* statue of the official greeter, Johnny Barnes is the site of the state-of-the-art **Bermuda Underwater Exploration Institute** ❶ (open daily 9am–5pm; entrance fee; tel: 297 7314), a large white structure on the harbour.

The Institute contains a plethora of hands-on interactive exhibits, including a simulated dive 12,000 ft (3,660 metres) to the ocean floor – plus the Harbourfront Restaurant, where you can enjoy a French meal along with splendid views of the busy harbour.

Bermuda's birdcage marks the junction of Front and Queen streets. If the first is noted for shopping, the latter is known for history, since it is graced with several buildings of particular historical impor-tance. One of the first shops on Queen Street proper is the highly recommended **Bermuda Book Store Ltd**, which contains the most comprehensive selection of books on Bermuda to be found on the island. It also has a great selection of crime fiction, ideal holiday reading.

Plants and stamps

Par-la-Ville Park ❷ is Hamilton's larg-est, most central public garden. Its gently undulating slopes provide a variety of plants out of all proportion to its modest size: there are palm trees, bird baths and flower beds containing plants with exotic-sounding names, such as "Flame of the Woods". The gardens were laid out *circa* 1850 as part of the estate of William B. Perot, and there is a personal, almost cosy air about the grounds which belies their municipal status.

The park's original owner, William Perot, created a famous postage stamp, for which collectors will now pay a fabulous sum (only 12 are still known to exist).

BELOW: the Bermuda Underwater Exploration Institute.

Map on page 172

Perot was Bermuda's first postmaster, appointed in 1821. He was a highly visible character on the island, collecting mail from the docks, storing it under his top hat, and making personal deliveries "at the drop of a hat".

Mail was taken on horseback from Hamilton to St George's on Mondays and Thursdays and made the return journey on alternate days. Somerset Bridge received letters on Wednesdays and Saturdays. Although a daily postal delivery commenced in 1842, just six years before Perot's stamp, some Bermudians feel that the efficiency of the mail service has declined since the days of horse-drawn deliveries; hence the high proportion of mail boxes, which are used for personal collection.

The room in which the postmaster worked has been restored and is now called **Perot's Post Office Ⓚ**. An authentic feel prevails, from the brass candlesticks to the wooden counter, where simple postal business is still carried out.

In fact, the well-proportioned interior is a modern invention, for in Perot's day the premises were shared with an apothecary shop. Still, to sit on one of the tall wooden stools and write a letter at the old-fashioned desks is delightful. It's worth taking time out to do this at the old post office, even if you don't usually write letters on holiday.

William Perot lived in the property next door in Par-la-Ville House, which is now the Bermuda Library and Historical Society Museum. The postmaster's passion for collecting exotic plants from all over the world led him to import from Demerara a rubber tree seed, and to plant it in front of the house. The seed grew to the massive tree under which local residents now take refuge from the heat, but the tree hasn't always been a favourite. Mark Twain, on visiting the island, is said to have been disappointed in this exotic specimen, for in his view a "rubber tree" would surely bear a crop of hot water bottles and rubber over-soles.

BELOW: a short walk past Perot's Post Office.

Bermuda Shorts

Knowing full well what Bermuda shorts are may not prevent visitors from being taken slightly aback on first spotting the things in the full glory of their natural habitat, which is to say terminating at the regulation four inches above the knee of a bank manager or business executive who is otherwise at his desk conventionally turned out in jacket, collar and tie.

The slim fit of the celebrated shorts as they are now worn obscures their baggy antecedents. The inspiration was the tropical kit issued to British troops stationed in Bermuda. Soldiers did not start wearing shorts until the 20th century, so the history of the Bermuda derivatives cannot be equated with the Scottish kilt, which was adopted by an eccentric Viking, known thereafter as Magnus Bareleg.

Stylish shorts bought as souvenirs in Bermuda in the latter half of the 20th century were transported to the American mainland where they were subjected to local imposi-

tions such as ostentatious check patterns. However, the sober, plain colours of the classical design are closer in spirit to the original.

In Bermuda, these relatively austere shorts are not meant merely for leisure. They are considered equally suitable for a defendant in court, whose shorts may even be seen to lend dignity to the proceedings. The official position is summed up in the booklet *Bermuda: As a Matter of Fact*, which pronounces authoritatively on local etiquette: "Bermuda shorts are an acceptable mode of dress in the most conservative areas of Bermuda life (for men)."

The sting is in the parentheses: the circumstances in which Bermuda shorts may respectably be worn by women are much narrower. On the beach, certainly; while shopping, on condition that they are not significantly higher than four inches above the knee; on other occasions, only with circumspection. Bermuda still has firm ideas about female decorum. Locally written tips for tourists invariably sound a splenetic note on one particular solecism, and that is women who wear hair curlers in public.

With the agitation caused by exposed hair curlers, it is not surprising that toplessness is entirely out of order. Club Méditerrannée went to extraordinary lengths to find suitably discreet corners of Bermuda. To no avail; vigilantes gave them no quarter and eventually, perhaps for other reasons too, the hotel closed down.

It was seemingly ever thus, because in 1816 the *Bermuda Gazette* wrote of "an elderly gentleman of venerable appearance and correct manners" who took exception to women who wore dresses "extremely low in the back and bosom or off the shoulder". He sidled up beside them and stamped the exposed flesh with an indictment: "Naked but not ashamed."

It was actually the longer-suffering women of 18th-century Bermuda who first put local fashion on the international map. While the men were mainly interested in the palmetto tree for its heady juice, women plaited the leaves into hats. The most famous was Mrs Martha Hayward, who was a descendant of Christopher Carter, one of the "three kings". One of her hats was sent to Queen Anne as a present and sparked off a fashion trend among Englishwomen.

LEFT: traditional ❑ business attire

Map
on page
172

The entrance hall of Par-la-Ville House contains antique furniture and framed portraits of Sir George and Lady Somers, plus pictures of the principal investors in the Bermuda Company after whom the island's parishes are named. The **Bermuda Library** (13 Queen Street), founded in 1839, contains an excellent reference division on the upper floor, including some rare books on Bermuda and colonial America, although permission must be obtained to see them. Of particular interest on the ground floor is a complete set of the island's first newspaper, from the inaugural issue printed on 17 January 1784, when the paper was known as the *Bermuda Gazette*, through to the daily edition of today's *Royal Gazette*. The lending library upstairs receives newspapers from the US, Britain and Canada.

The **Historical Society Museum** ❶ is a series of small rooms decorated in original style with hurricane lamps, cedar furniture and English china. The old pitch-pine flooring is authentically uneven; these planks were thought to have been imported by the Perots from the east coast of America. Pieces to note are the dazzling Waterford chandelier, dating to around 1840, a letter from George Washington "to the inhabitants of Bermuda", the Hog Money, and a cedar table which dates from 1680. Donations can be placed in the box on top.

The **Lemon Tree** restaurant stands at the entrance to Par-La-Ville Park. A favourite choice for breakfast and lunch, the restaurant's head chef, Jean Claude García, has been honoured for his cooking in his native France. Visitors can take out a homemade beef or fish pie onto the terrace and enjoy the park, which was once postmaster Perot's *(see page 181)* garden escape.

Eagerly awaited news

Near the corner of **Reid Street** is the **Phoenix drugstore** – "drugstore" in the American sense because pharmaceuticals

are only a part of the story. The Phoenix is the place to buy magazines, cosmetics, scissors, cigarettes and all other holiday supplies. It's in the Phoenix, too, that a time-honoured ritual is played out. Around 3pm the daily papers arrive from America. There is a flurry of activity as visitors and locals hurry to buy their copy of the *New York Times* or *USA Today*. Two and a half hours later, just before closing, the same flurry occurs, but this time for the British newspapers which are flown in direct from London – if you're lucky. Otherwise the papers arrive the next day.

A maze of walkways connects the Phoenix with **Windsor Place**, on Queen Street, and Washington Mall, on Reid Street – two enclosed malls, which, like Walker Arcade, are lined with boutiques and pastry shops.

Nightlife

Back on Queen Street, young people mill around the KFC (Kentucky Fried Chicken) emporium, and into Casey's, a haunt for locals where tourists are welcome. The former is one of the few fast-food take-away restaurants on the island, and always does a roaring trade, as does the nearby Mr Chicken, also well known for its fried chicken. Casey's serves inexpensive beer.

This area tends to be the only street life downtown Hamilton offers in the evening. If teenagers aren't eating fried chicken, chances are they're queuing at the **Little Theatre Cinema** across the street, which shows American releases shortly after they premiere in the US. As the programme changes weekly, there's usually a queue.

Church Street, which stands at the head of Queen Street, was named after the only church in town – in 1844. This Methodist Chapel was torn down to make way for an addition to the imposing Hamilton Hotel, which was destroyed by fire several decades ago. The loss of the Hamilton Hotel was a blow to the history of an island where tourism is a primary

BELOW: the Hamilton Hotel was the first on the island.

Hamilton Hotel, Bermuda. Bedroom and private bath

Map
on page
172

concern: the Hamilton was the first hotel to be built on the island. Opened in 1863 to attract wealthy winter cruise passengers, it experienced both exceptional popularity and huge losses before finally closing in 1945.

In and around City Hall

The place where the hotel stood is occupied by the car park of **City Hall** ⓜ, a grand building with a profusion of wind-divining instruments on top. The fountain pond outside hold goldfish, and the low stone walls surrounding the grounds are rarely empty of loungers. The lobby is rather austere, but upstairs there is an airy room, like a New York loft, that is the perfect place for the art exhibitions held here.

City Hall is also a venue for the annual Bermuda Festival and its East Exhibition Room is the site of the **National Gallery** (open Mon–Sat 10am–4pm; entrance fee; tours). This climate-controlled room houses a collection of Bermuda's best works of art as well as presenting a variety of exhibits from around the world. Space is limited, making it impossible to show the entire permanent collection. Precious items include Bermudian furniture and paintings, such as the Watlington Collection which was bequeathed to the people of Bermuda in 1992. It has works by Gainsborough and Raeburn.

Beside City Hall is the main **bus terminal**. It is possible to travel to almost anywhere on the island on the efficient pink public buses, all of which originate and terminate at this terminal. The fare structure is slightly complicated, however, as the island is divided into different "zones". You must have the exact fare in order to board a Bermuda bus, and it is therefore helpful to buy a booklet of pre-paid tickets or a transport pass from the terminal office near City Hall. This not only saves fumbling for coins in a queue of people, but proves less costly than paying for journeys individually.

Victoria Park ⓝ, which is situated directly behind City Hall, has a sunken

Victoria Park, Bermuda.

garden. Open-air concerts are held in the ornate bandstand, which was built to commemorate Queen Victoria's Golden Jubilee, in 1887.

Hamilton's cathedral

Church Street has had a chequered time with its religious centres. The Methodist Chapel notwithstanding, more than 100 years ago an arsonist burned not only the Anglican but also the Roman Catholic church. The present **Cathedral of the Most Holy Trinity** , also known as **Bermuda Cathedral**, on the site of the original Anglican church, was consecrated in 1911.

A mix of Gothic and Middle English architecture, Bermuda Cathedral is constructed using limestone quarried solely from William Perot's Par-La-Ville estate. The cathedral's interior is lined with characteristic arches and cloisters. The stone figures that run along the rear wall were created by the late Byllee Lang (1909–66), a Canadian-born sculptor who

taught on the island and influenced a generation of local artists.

Hamilton's main **Post Office** (56 Church Street) sits on the corner of Church and Parliament streets. Whereas postcards and letters can be mailed from the more exciting Old Post Office on Queen Street, this is the place for the serious business of sending home packages and island souvenirs. The Post Office has a couple of telephones from which long-distance calls can be made without incurring the heavy surcharge levied by many of the island's luxury hotels.

Honouring Victoria's jubilee

The **Sessions House** was built on the highest hill in Hamilton. It is a conspicuous, dignified edifice, with a clock-tower boasting a 6-ft (1.8-metre) pendulum weighing just under 100 lb (45 kg). This handsome tower was erected to commemorate the Golden Jubilee of Queen Victoria in 1887; a terracotta medallion of the Queen's profile can be seen under an

LEFT: fragrant flowers can be found all over the island. **BELOW:** Bermuda Cathedral.

Map on page 172

arch on the southern side. The large chamber in the House's upper storey is reserved for the use of the House of Assembly. In the chamber immediately below it, the Supreme Court holds its sessions.

The House of Assembly

The Bermuda Parliament first met on 1 August 1620. It is the oldest of all the parliaments of the British Commonwealth countries, and the third oldest in the world, after Iceland and Great Britain. Parliament meets on Fridays from late October through July. On other days the public can view the **House of Assembly chamber** if the Sergeant-at-Arms is free to unlock the door.

Entry to the chamber is via a massive oak staircase. On either side are **sculptures**, carved in 1840 and originally part of the exterior of the Palace of Westminster in London. London's legendary fog proved to be too damaging to the limestone figures, so they were removed to the gentler surroundings of Bermuda

around 1930. The figure on the left is of King William II holding a model of Westminster Hall; the one on the right once accompanied another figure that was of King John.

The arrangement of the chairs in the chamber follows the pattern in Westminster's House of Commons: double rows facing each other with a central gangway between. On the wall flanking the Speaker's Chair hang two enormous portraits, one of King George III and the other his consort, Queen Charlotte.

The Visitors' Gallery spans the back of the room. Visitors are encouraged to attend sessions, but sun-worshippers should heed this warning posted on each public bench: "At the opening of each sitting, when the speaker enters, and on the motion to adjoin when the House rises, visitors are requested to stand. The Sergeant-at-Arms is empowered to maintain order and decorum in the galleries and may refuse admission to persons improperly clad." ❑

BELOW: the Sessions House is a Hamilton landmark.

Sun and Savings

U nless you are aware that Bermuda is one of the world's premier offshore financial services centres, it might come as a surprise to see so many people in business attire in the streets of Hamilton. After New York and London, Bermuda is the most important insurance centre in the world. Sea, sun, sand – and savings?

The value of goods and services provided in Bermuda, the gross domestic product, now exceeds $5 billion, giving the 65,000 Bermuda residents one of the highest standards of living in the world.

Attracted by the Island's convenient location at the crossroads between the Americas and Europe, international business services – insurance, banking, trust and mutual funds – have become Bermuda's main source of income. More than 15,000 companies are registered in Bermuda, although no more than 400 maintain a physical presence.

Investors come in search of a sensible regulatory environment, professionals with expertise dating back three generations, world-class telecommunications and a neutral tax environment. Bermuda does not levy income or corporation taxes, although all imported goods are taxed at rates as high as 33 percent. There is little unemployment: any Bermudian who wants a job has one, and many have more – Bermudians are famous for moonlighting. The supply of suitably qualified locals falls short of demand, so the Island is the temporary home of an imported workforce of some 9,000 "guest workers". The most visible are in the international business sector.

Bermuda has just four banks: foreign-owned Bermuda Commercial Bank, which caters exclusively to corporations, the Bank of Bermuda (owned by HSBC), the Butterfield Bank and Capital G Bank Limited. After World War II, they began offering trust services for the wealthy. In 1956, David Graham, a Bermuda attorney, wrote a letter to *The Times* of London, pointing out that British shipping operations, then taxed to the hilt, could be managed tax-free from Bermuda. It didn't take long for some of the world's largest fleets to move their registrations to Bermuda. International business was off and running.

In 1962, Philadelphia businessman Fred Reiss pioneered the concept of "captive" insurance. A captive insurer is a company that insures its parent company's risks. Large international companies insure themselves against danger, and Reiss argued that, instead of paying a broker and an unknown insurance company, companies could insure themselves and make the profit that their brokers and insurers would have made. In a tax-free environment, those profits could grow exponentially, Reiss argued. Today, more than 4,500 captive insurance companies operate around the world and Bermuda is home to more than 30 percent of them.

Meanwhile, the banks began offering their services to a wider swathe of well-heeled individuals and corporations. Bermuda had developed a reputation for probity and exclusivity that other island economies could not match. The banks' habit of accepting deposits and making only the very safest loans – and few of them – has earned them the reputation of

LEFT: Bank of Bermuda crest

being "piggy banks". Until the 21st century, laws required all Bermudian businesses to be at least 60 percent owned by locals and, arguably, have protected banks from competition and saved Bermuda from the scandals that have engulfed some offshore banks. However, that requirement has been lifted for the Butterfield Bank and the Bank of Bermuda.

In the mid-1980s, a shortage of available coverage for high-level insurance led Robert Clements of Marsh & MacLennan, one of the world's largest insurance brokers, to persuade 35 banks and insurance companies to put together a pool of $500 million to allow a new company, ACE Ltd, to provide top-level coverage. Shortly afterwards, Clements found nearly 80 more investors who anted up $250 million for a second company, which is today called XL Capital. Both companies are headquartered in Bermuda.

Today, ACE and XL are two of the world's largest insurance and reinsurance companies (who jointly share insurance risk with other companies), with assets between them in excess of $48 billion. Their advent invigorated the Bermuda insurance market, and in 1993 eight companies that provided catastrophe insurance – against events like earthquakes, hurricanes and floods – joined them. In the 12 months following the 9/11 terrorist attacks on the US in 2001, almost 100 new reinsurance and insurance companies started up in Bermuda. Bermuda has never looked back. Its banks have grown in line with its insurance sector, as have the law firms, accountants and other professional firms.

The government monitors the island's economic growth, which, if it continues at the rate achieved in the 1990s – 3.5 percent a year, in real terms – will place greater stress on the infrastructure, roads, schools and citizens.

One growth area is electronic commerce. Bermuda was one of the first jurisdictions in the world to introduce legislation specific to e-commerce and to appoint a Cabinet-level Minister to look after it.

As many as 25 percent of Bermuda's visitors travel to the island on business, although the tourism and financial services industries are so closely interwoven that it is hard to separate them. When a business executive travels to the island for a series of meetings and then spends the weekend playing golf, is that tourism or international business? The cash register cannot tell.

The Bermuda Stock Exchange (symbol: BSX) is the world's leading fully electronic, offshore securities market. More than 200 equities, funds and debt issues currently list on the exchange, with a total market capitalisation or value (excluding investment funds) in excess of $210 billion. Bermuda is already home to hundreds of mutual funds, with assets in excess of $30 billion.

Just how much of the world's capital is resident in Bermuda is hard to pinpoint, but a conservative estimate suggests that the insurance, banking and mutual fund industries probably manage half a trillion dollars. Bermuda trusts, arrangements by which individuals and companies discreetly transfer their wealth to independent agents, add perhaps another $200 billion to the pool.

Bermuda's continued success is evident throughout the land, in the buildings under construction, in the expensive cars on the roads and the even more expensive boats moored around the islands'. ❑

RIGHT: the banking and finance industry has as many branches as a tree.

Bermuda, Tom Moore's Calabash Tree.

Map on page 198

HAMILTON ENVIRONS

*Outside the confines of Bermuda's capital lie suburban homes,
lush botanical gardens and pretty parks, historic houses and
the South Shore beaches – just the place to sit back and relax*

"The government uses kilometres; we use miles," explained a taxi-driver on the route out of Hamilton. Five parishes surround the capital, none more than a few minutes away by taxi, bus or motorbike, and all roads do indeed sport signs giving distances in kilometres.

The five parishes are as different from one another as common practice is from official thought, and each one provides an enjoyable day out of town. Pembroke parish is domestic; Devonshire deep country. Paget has both the Botanical Gardens and Camden, the official residence of the Premier. Warwick has the island's most spectacular beaches, although Southampton, far to the west, has Horseshoe Bay Beach and is perfect for walkers. All roads, whether travelled by miles or kilometres, lead back to Hamilton.

North Hamilton

The parish in which the capital resides, **Pembroke**, is primarily residential, its suburbs providing accommodation for the people who work in Hamilton. From Victoria Park north to the seacoast, houses tend to be small and rather tightly packed; the streets, too, are unkempt. On any other part of the island, this might be considered a slum, but Bermuda's high standard of living means that this "slum" consists of tidy two- and three-bedroomed houses which are given a seasonal coat of paint.

Walking the streets of Pembroke, especially on a Sunday afternoon, shows a completely different side of life to the upscale cuteness of Hamilton's waterfront area. The scene is suburban and peaceful, warm weather ensuring a constant flutter of domestic activity, from washing cars to painting houses, to children playing games in streets that are devoid of traffic.

Located behind Victoria Park, on Cedar Avenue is the pretty **St Theresa's Cathedral** ❶ (open daily 7.30am–6pm).

This cathedral, with its notable Spanish flavour and decorative tower, is one of six Roman Catholic churches in Bermuda. It opened its doors around 1930 and was visited by the Pope at the end of the 1960s. His Holiness (Pope Paul VI) presented a beautiful chalice to the local diocese, which can be viewed.

Beyond the cathedral lies a mosque. Here too are the town's **tennis courts**, where matches are frequently held and where locals stay trim in order to present a pleasing picture in lightweight summer clothes. Black Watch Pass and Black Watch Well, although often shown on maps as part of Hamilton, are best reached from the north, by following the North Shore Road and turning inland near

PRECEDING PAGES:
Harmony Hall in Paget; Horseshoe Bay beach.
LEFT: Camden.
RIGHT: a very attractive tower.

Government House. The importance of these sites is historical, rather than contemporary, and are only worth visiting if you happen to be in the area. The **Black Watch Well**, at the foot of Langton Hill, was dug by the Black Watch Regiment in order to replenish fresh drinking water during the great drought of 1849.

The well is close to the site of an old ducking stool, used to quiet women charged with gossiping and spreading false rumours. Though not in use today, the ducking stool scenario is reenacted in St George's several times per week.

Black Watch Pass ❷ was built for a different reason. The steep cliffs of the North Shore were so impregnable that horses, carriages and carts full of supplies used to make the tortuous trip from Hamilton to the North Shore over the hills, adding hours and danger to any journey. In a remarkable feat of engineering of the time, a pass was constructed in 1934, tunnelled through solid limestone. Although the pass is visually unremark-able, it is possible, just for a moment, to feel that you are not in balmy Bermuda but in some high mountain area. The air turns chill, and the steep stone walls with their tufts of spiky undergrowth are fleetingly impressive.

Government House, the governor's official residence, is not open to the public, but its lawns are often meaningfully employed. It's not uncommon to see the grounds festooned with marquees, tables and even equestrian hurdles, as local sporting events are frequently staged here. There is also an annual New Year's Party where Bermudians are honoured by the governor.

This was also the scene of a violent episode in Bermuda's history – the assassination of the country's then Governor, Sir Richard Sharples and his aide, Hugh Sayers, in 1973. The men convicted of the murders were later hanged and the country experienced some unrest.

The North Shore Road, which extends through the parishes of Pembroke, Devon-

BELOW: sporting events are held on the lawns of Government House.

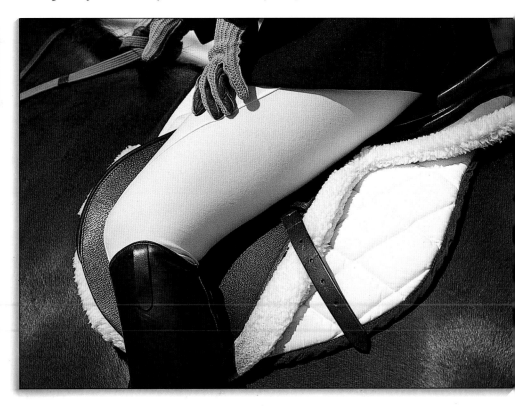

Map on page 198

shire, Smiths and Hamilton, concludes at its most westerly tip at **Spanish Point ❸**. The early Bermudian settlers found the remains of a Spanish encampment on this spot, and the site takes its name from that incident. The Point can clearly be seen all the way from the West End of the island, but was primarily noted for the ships that crashed into it in the dark. Pocket-sized **Spanish Point Park** offers wonderful views out to sea. To the west is the curve of Southampton and Sandy's parishes and a view of the Commissioner's House *(see page 231)*, perched on a hill in Dockyard. St Georges *(see page 255)* lies to the east. Modern boats in the bay contrast with the rusting **floating dock**, transported from Dockyard. It was the first to be towed across the Atlantic in 1869, when it was the largest dock of its kind.

East of Hamilton

Bermuda's isolated position in the Atlantic made the island particularly vulnerable to invasion and no fewer than 55 forts were built at various times. **Fort Hamilton ❹** (Happy Valley Road; open daily 9.30am–5pm; free), looming above the eastern edge of the capital, was built by the British to protect the approach roads into the city and to defend Spanish Point from attacks by sea. It is the finest example on the island of the mid-Victorian polygonal fort. In the 19th century, entrance was by a drawbridge, with another drawbridge linking the galleries to the main ditch. Today, the large 18-ton guns look out not at the advancing enemy but over flowering, well-manicured gardens. The ramparts afford a spectacular view over Hamilton and the harbour area.

The moat has been landscaped to provide an exotic tangle of flora and is reached through a labyrinth of underground passages cut from solid rock.

During the winter season, at noon on Monday the Bermuda Islands Pipe Band gives a colourful **skirling** performance, featuring Scottish bagpipes, drummers

BELOW: the communal tombs of Old Devonshire Church.

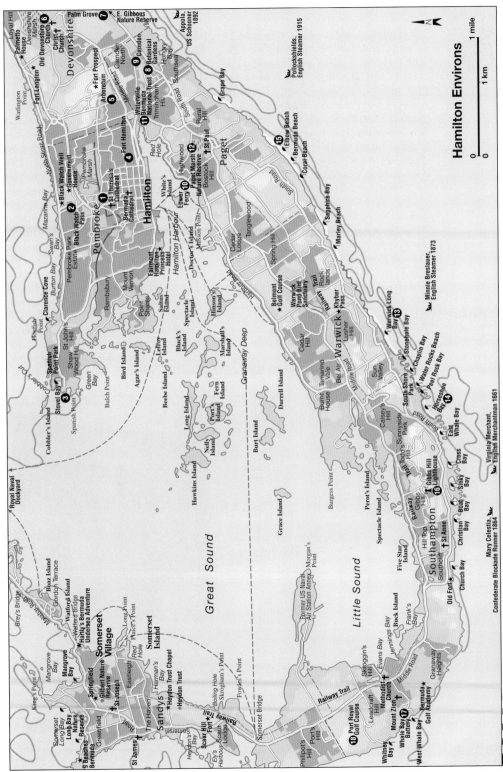

Hamilton Environs

Map
on page
198

and dancers. In the summer, the tearoom is open for tasty refreshments.

Not far from Fort Hamilton is the **Arboretum ❺** (open dawn to dusk), a 20-acre (8-hectare) oasis. Most of the trees planted here are for educational or scientific purposes, but this academic background does nothing to detract from its pleasing aspect. Bamboo or split-wood fences are used for protection around some of the trees, which gives an old-fashioned, rural flavour to the grounds.

The parish of **Devonshire** has rolling hills and touches of green, but the graceful name is a new addition: the parish was once known by the less attractive moniker "Brackish Pond". This was because of the large marsh that virtually covered it.

Bermudians are always keen to point out a landmark, the **Old Devonshire Church ❻** (open daily 9am–5.30pm; free; tel: 236 3671), which lies just south of Middle Road, the thoroughfare which bisects the parish. The original church was constructed in 1716, on the site of an even earlier church, but the stark and rather plain exterior that visitors see today was reconstructed in 1970, after an explosion. Many valuable items were destroyed, but a few were salvaged and can still be seen inside. Some pieces of the church silver are said to date from the 16th century, which makes them among the oldest pieces in Bermuda.

The earlier church was apparently just as popular as this reconstruction is now. A reprint in a local brochure gives this "thumbs-up" review from a guest staying with the Archdeacon in 1830: "In the afternoon we went to Devonshire Church which lies in a romantic valley near a large marsh, whence its name Brackish Pond. In front of the church is a venerable cedar, the largest I have yet seen and the church not having belfry the bell is suspended from a branch of this ancient tree.

"The Churchyard with its white-washed tombstones glistening amid the sombre foliage of the cedar, and the numerous winding paths, which all meet at the foot of the primeval tree that summons the natives to one loved spot, were scattered with groups of people. I remarked many

more aged persons than I have seen elsewhere in Bermuda..."

The island's "white-washed tombstones" are a notable feature on the landscape. At first glance Bermuda's **cemeteries**, with their massive vaults, appear to be similar to the above-ground funeral memorials found in marshy areas such as America's New Orleans. But in fact, these tombs recede deep into the ground, reaching, in some instances, to a depth of 10 ft (3 metres). The vaults can be family affairs, and what began as tradition has become a way of saving space.

Bermudians are buried in cedar caskets shaped like Egyptian mummy cases; this replaces an even older type of coffin which was unique to the island. A year and a day must pass before a vault can be opened after a funeral.

North of the Old Devonshire Church lies **Palmetto House**, a National Trust property occasionally open to the public. It is an example of a cruciform house, the architectural term for a house whose

Banana Tree and Fruit - Bermuda

RIGHT: tropical resources.

Hurricanes

A storm called Fabian struck Bermuda in September 2003 with a ferocity not seen since 1953. The Category 3 hurricane lashed the island with winds of up to 120 mph (193 kph) felling trees, ripping the roofs off homes and devastating the spectacular rock formations known as the Natural Arches, near Tucker's Town. Four people were killed when they were swept off the Causeway connecting Hamilton parish to the airport and St George's. Thousands of islanders were left without electricity for several days but a repair operation was soon underway.

Hurricane Fabian was even more powerful than the last big storm, Hurricane Emily, which caused $50 million worth of damage when it hit in 1987. Packing maximum gusts of 116 mph (185 kph), the gale hit Bermuda with a forward speed of 45 mph (70 kph), three times that of a normal hurricane.

The island's isolated position means that it is often on "hurricane-alert". In 1995 there

were not one but two tropical storms which caused havoc in the Caribbean, Hurricanes Felix and Luis, but both passed by Bermuda. Normally, hoteliers have plenty of warning over approaching storms, but Hurricane Emily hit with such force that little could be done.

Remarkably, there were no deaths and only minor injuries. The cruise ship *Atlantic*, carrying 825 passengers, broke its moorings at Hamilton docks, but the captain, Mario Palombo, said his crew never lost control of the 672-ft (204-metre) vessel.

The Royal Gazette put out a special edition to keep residents informed of damage. Many were without electricity or water, and stores quickly sold out of candles. The stores themselves use reserve generators in the case of power cuts, a practice that has now spread to the homes of private individuals.

According to the *Gazette*, the storm's sudden intensification into a Category 2 hurricane from a waning tropical storm wasn't detected until four hours before Emily struck Bermuda. Bob Case, of the Miami-based National Hurricane Center, is quoted as saying the Center underestimated Emily's strength. Mr Case went on to describe Emily as a small, compact, tightly-knit hurricane. Her cloud canopy was 200 miles (320 km) across – relatively small compared to the 600-mile (960-km) spread of other hurricanes that have raged through the Gulf of Mexico. The Center felt the storm had only a 28 percent chance of striking the island. But Bermuda was hit by Emily's "strongest possible punch" with "downbursts" forcing its most violent conditions to ground level.

The valuable National Trust properties Verdmont and Winterhaven suffered badly, as did the historic walls around the town of St George's. About $100,000 worth of damage occurred to the Southampton Princess Hotel, when the hurricane shattered windows in 80 rooms.

"I've never seen such chaos before in my life and I've lived here for 58 years," observed one local. By 8pm that Friday night, less than 12 hours after Emily made her presence felt, the fire service had already responded to 275 calls. There were several reports of bravery and no incidents of looting after Hurricane Emily, which reflects well on the island and its behaviour in a crisis. ❏

LEFT: gale-force winds can pack a punch.

Map
on page
198

wings form the shape of a cross. The **Edmund Gibbons Nature Reserve** is situated in Devonshire along the South Road near the junction with Collector's Hill. Rare birds and exotic flora inhabit the marshy land, and visitors are advised to stick to the designated paths and observe from a distance.

Toward Devonshire Bay, on the South Road, is a lovely traditional Bermudian home called **Palm Grove** ❼ (open Mon–Thurs 9am–4.30pm). The house is privately owned, but during the week the grounds are open to the public. There's a moongate and a small aviary with noisy, colourful tropical birds, but be sure not to miss the pond that lies just behind the house; in the middle of the pool is a miniature replica of the Bermuda islands.

Southeast of Hamilton

A short drive from the capital, in the parish of Paget on Point Finger Road, lie the **Botanical Gardens** ❽ (open daily from dawn to dusk; tel: 236 5291). This 36-acre (15-hectare) site features 15 permanent attractions, including an "Exotic House" of orchids and waterfalls, which are housed under a partially shaded roof.

Only one type of fruit, the prickly pear, is native to Bermuda, but avocados, loquats and bananas all thrive in the subtropical fruit gardens. The Botanical's "Garden for the Blind" is unique among its displays. Created in 1960, this enclosed, rectangular area is planted with blossoms recognised immediately by their taste and smell. There are lemon mint, lavender cotton, dandelion (including instructions as to how to cook it), plus spearmint and spices galore. Free tours of the gardens (which tend to begin in the car park or the garden's visitors' centre) are held throughout the year.

It's easy to be side-tracked on the way to **Camden** ❾ (open Tues and Fri noon–2pm; sometimes closed for an official engagement), the official residence of Bermuda's Premier, located deep in the boughs of the Botanical Gardens. The eye

BELOW: don't miss the pond at Palm Grove.

is constantly diverted by different plants, not least by a particular type of tree with a trunk so gnarled and coarsened it looks like a dozen trees all entangled. The roots of this dazzling specimen, called a banyan tree, spread out toward the pathway and threaten to overtake with long, spider-like legs. Alice in Wonderland would feel at home walking through these grounds.

The lawns surrounding Camden itself are less ethereal, more genteel, in keeping with a residence which is used primarily for official entertaining. Built in the 1700s and looking rather like a colonial mansion in the American south, Camden contains elegant watercolours and items created by local craftsmen. The cedar panelling in the dining room and entrance hall, plus the furniture in the dining room, were the work of a local cabinet maker named Jackson, who lived in the mid-1880s. They took nearly 30 years to complete. Be sure to note, in the ornate dining room, not only the cedar moulding on the ceiling but also the cedar serving plates.

The view from Camden's verandahs, which were probably added in the 19th century, sweeps over the Botanical Gardens and all the way out to sea. It is a tranquil spot, enlivened by the occasional cry of a peacock from the nearby aviary.

South of the Botanical Gardens lies **Hungry Bay**, a popular spot for visitors and fishermen. In 1988 there were 301 registered fishermen, more than two-thirds of whom had their own boats. By 1998 that number had dwindled to 288. The life of a commercial fisherman is not an easy one, as local waters are in danger of being over-fished.

The late Alfred Birdsey was one of the island's best-known contemporary artists. His watercolours concentrate on landscapes and birds, with an overall effect, as described in the essay on art in this book *(see page 116)*, "as if a butterfly on the wing had brushed the paper, and a spider had tracked it after wading through an inkwell". Birdsey's Stowe Hill studio, in the grounds of his Paget home, Rosecote,

BELOW: the Botanical Gardens have a large expanse of trees and flowers.

Map on page 198

is known as the **Birdsey Studio** (open Mon–Fri 10.30am–1pm, or by appointment; tel: 236 6658). Birdsey's daughter Jo Birdsey Linberg, also a well-known artist, runs the studio today.

South of Hamilton

The scenic and attractive **Harbour Road** borders Hamilton Harbour for several miles before coming to an end opposite Darrell's Island, the green islet which was the site of Bermuda's first airport. Bermuda International airport opened in 1947. Today the island is a popular campground. Ferries ply the route regularly from the capital to this southern peninsula, landing at an attractive spot called, appropriately, **Lower Ferry ⓾**. Some visitors consider the Lower Ferry area the ideal spot to stay on Bermuda, not only for the views of the capital across the sparkling waters, but also for sheer convenience.

The sea is just a hike away if heading south; Hamilton with its shops and parks

an approximately equal distance to the north. An evening spent in one of the capital's many entertaining restaurants can be enhanced by a boat ride back to home base.

East of Lower Ferry is **Waterville ⓫** (tel: 236 6483), an 18th-century private residence which is also the headquarters of the Bermuda National Trust. As well as owning some of the most distinguished historic properties on the island, the National Trust also organises spring tours of private homes and gardens not normally open to the public. It's worth enquiring at the Visitor Information Centre in Hamilton *(see page 177)* as to when and where these are taking place.

Clermont, another handsome house in the area is a private residence, which was built in 1800. Chief Justice Sir Brownlow Gray, a later owner, became such a keen fan of tennis, then a purely British sport, that he ordered the construction of the island's first courts on an isolated piece of his property. One

BELOW: the much-missed artist Alfred Birdsey: his studio can be visited.

year later an enamoured guest named Mary Outerbridge, clutching a racquet and a rule book, sailed to the US, where she introduced tennis to the Staten Island Cricket Club in 1874. This marked the first time the sport had been played in America. Sir Brownlow Gray's grass court can still be seen.

Inland from Harbour Road, off Lover's Lane, is important **Paget Marsh** ⑫, one of the island's most interesting nature reserves. Its open areas are of ecological interest owing to the number of endangered plants and trees contained within its 18 acres (7 hectares). The fragile status of the land previously required visitors to arrange an appointment to walk around the marsh. However, philanthropist and former president of the Bermuda National Trust, Dennis Sherwin, donated millions of dollars to build a boardwalk through the marsh, allowing access without damaging the land. The marsh is arguably the best venue for close-up views of the red mangroves. The boardwalk is well signposted

for a self-guided tour, although guided tours are sometimes available. Contact the National Trust for details; alternatively, any visitor information centre can help arrange a guided tour of the marsh and the footpaths in the surrounding area *(see Travel Tips, page 300)*. The original marsh has been enlarged by additional land presented to the Trust by the Society for the Prevention of Cruelty to Animals.

The South Shore

Bermuda's glorious coastline is most richly observed along the South Shore. No fewer than 23 beaches or coves comprise this coast, and the turquoise sea is rarely out of sight. Some beaches are attached to hotels, for this is also an area of lavish "cottage colonies", which are fully serviced bungalows offering the seclusion of a private home with the facilities of a luxury hotel.

Bermudians are permitted to use the beaches attached to certain hotels, such as Elbow Beach, in exchange for the payment of a small fee, but most local people

BELOW: the South Shore contains 23 beaches and coves.

Map on page 198

don't bother. Their reluctance to do so is twofold. First is a genuine desire not to impose upon holidaying visitors. The second reason soon becomes evident: Bermuda's public beaches are, quite simply, spectacularly beautiful.

The short stretch from **Warwick Long Bay** ⑬ to **Horseshoe Bay** ⑭ backs onto South Shore park to stunning effect: rippling blue water to the front, trees, greenery and nature trails behind. During the summer, Bermudians observe their right to camp on this stretch of land (a privilege denied to tourists), for the warm summer months are the only time locals will dip into the sea. A joke is told that any time before Queen Victoria's birthday, on 24 May, the season is still officially "winter". Before this date the beaches are always dotted with sunbathing foreigners, but Bermudians stay well away and keep bundled up.

The South Shore is meticulously maintained. Litter seemingly evaporates, and "beach sweepers" have been known to occasionally collide with early morning joggers. **Elbow Beach** ⑮, along the eastern edge, is said to be the longest strand on the island. No one seems to know, however, the origin of its distinctive name. Elbow Beach Hotel occupies land fronting a beautiful beach, with fine sand. Facilities include changing rooms and a beachfront snack bar.

The area west from Elbow Beach to pretty **Coral Beach** was once known as the Sand Banks, due to the hills created by centuries of shifting sands. Information obtained by taking samples from the sand mounds has long fascinated geologists, and the Sand Banks have provided them with important data on the island's early formation.

Beaches serve different functions for different people. Hotel guests frequent the beaches on the eastern part of South Shore while Bermudians and many non-resident guests favour the beaches to the west, in Warwick and Southampton. The more isolated **Church Bay** in Southampton, once

BELOW: a Bermuda beach babe. **RIGHT:** a novel sunshade.

a popular spot for snorkellers, was badly damaged during Hurricane Fabian, in 2003. Beware the red sponge and Portuguese man-of-war, which can sting. Otherwise, bathers have little to fear when swimming off the South Shore coast.

It is said that sailors can see the bright beam of **Gibbs Hill lighthouse** ⑯ (Lighthouse Road; open 9am–4.30pm; entrance fee; tel: 238 0524), from up to 40 miles (65 km) away, an important beacon for those negotiating Bermuda's reefs. The lighthouse is a commanding structure, made in Great Britain of cast iron and shipped to the island in pieces around the mid-19th century. Visitors can climb to the top via a series of steep steps, for the lighthouse is open to the public every day of the year.

The view from the top is one of the most impressive in Bermuda, as the lighthouse's beam shines from a height of 362 ft (110 metres) above sea level. A small walkway around the top offers an all-encompassing view, from Ireland Island at its western tip to St David's Head at its eastern. Don't despair, however, if the prospect of climbing 185 steps appears daunting – the panorama from Gibbs Hill, at the base of the lighthouse, is only marginally less spectacular. The former lighthouse-keeper's cottage at the base is now the Lighthouse Tearoom (open from springtime), which serves tasty breakfasts, lunches and afternoon teas.

Map on page 198

West Whale Bay, a public park that can be reached by turning west off Middle Road in the parish of Southampton, is a lovely spot to watch the sun set. The meandering **Railway Trail** criss-crosses Middle Road several times in this area, so the parish is a popular one with walkers. Whale Bay Park slopes down to a beach that tends to be less crowded than its glamorous South Shore neighbours. In fact, much of Southampton is bypassed by visitors, a bonus to those in search of a tranquil holiday.

Whale Bay Battery ⑰ (open daily; free) lies in the park itself, the ruins of a small defensive fortress completed in 1876. Its function was to control access to the delightfully named Hog Fish Cut, a small channel that leads to the massive defences mounted at the Royal Naval Dockyard on Ireland Island (now called the West End). A portion of an even earlier, semi-circular fort, can be seen in front of the battery, as can the ammunition magazine and barracks, hidden behind an earthen rampart.

The northern end of Southampton is best known for the **Port Royal** ⑱ 18-hole golf course, and for the former US Naval Air Station Annexe, which was located on a peninsula to the east. The strip of land that contained the military base, which closed in 1995, was originally called Tucker's Island.

These acreages were the "overplus" from Norwood's Survey of 1616, which Daniel Tucker intended to have as his own. This is commemorated in the area by a street called "Overplus Lane". The story of the greedy governor of Bermuda and his quest for personal property is recounted in the history section of this book (*see page 47*).

LEFT: the view from the Gibbs Hill lighthouse is impressive. **RIGHT:** ❑ scooter city.

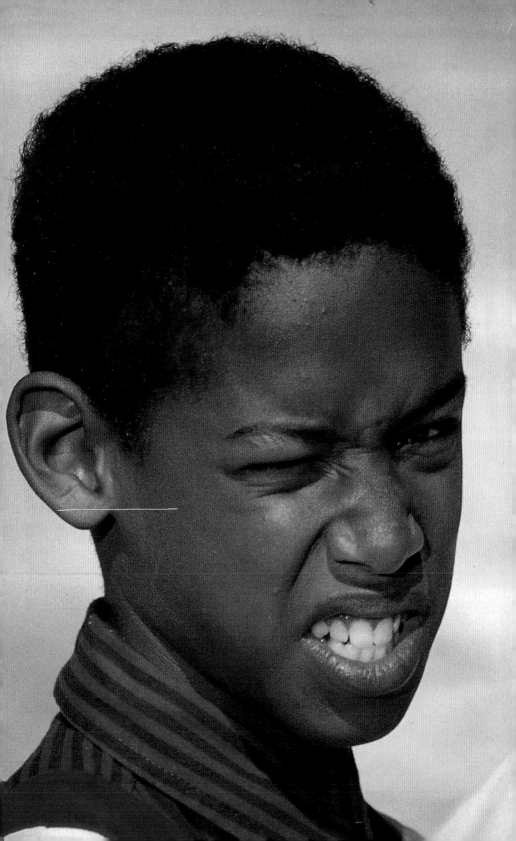

Map on page 168

provided by a pirate. The cedar population suffered again during the 1940s, when a scale insect blight destroyed almost all of the native cedar trees.

The implications, justifiable or not, of the pole on **Gibbet Island** at the entrance to **Flatts Inlet** are discussed in the *Small Islands* chapter of this book *(see page 279)*. Trail walkers might anyhow like to imagine (or not, as the case may be) poles along this stretch of shoreline adorned with the quartered bits of Indian John, incompetent burglar and failed murderer. Witches, too, met their violent end on this small island.

The attractions of **Flatts Village** are gentler. The tide, racing through the narrow passage to **Harrington Sound**, has boats bobbing at their moorings. The **Bermuda Aquarium** in the same village contains nearly 100 species of fish in several tanks, the largest being a 140,000-gallon (636,500-litre) reef tank. The grounds around the aquarium house birds and animals – flamingoes, macaws, giant

tortoises, etc – and there are special facilities for children *(see page 244)*.

The trail continues through **Shelly Bay Park and Nature Reserve** and along a fine stretch of wild coastline, which may work up a thirst, quenchable, on reaching **Baileys Bay**, in the stylishly tatty **Swizzle Inn**, which also provides nourishing snacks and tasty pub meals at fairly reasonable prices. The crossing from **Coney Island** to **Ferry Point** is the boundary between Hamilton Parish and historic St George's, the change heralded by two **ancient forts**, or their remains. The shoreline is different, too, suddenly bleak and in winter lashed by gales. The bodies of soldiers who died from yellow fever were brought to this place and buried in the **old cemetery**.

Astor's Halt is the nostalgic terminus of the Bermuda railway proper. It was here that a private line took over for the descent into St George's. Trail walkers could do worse than absorb the view from **Sugarloaf Hill** before making the descent. ❑

BELOW: parts of the Railway Trail can be travelled by moped.
RIGHT: this banyan tree, spotted on the trail, originally came from tropical India.

Map on page 168

THE RAILWAY TRAIL

*The trains and the track of Bermuda's only railroad have long gone,
but the paths that have been left behind provide a great opportunity
to explore on foot, on horseback, or on a moped*

The railway sagas which tend to grip popular imagination are journeys chugging across Siberia, the American prairie or some such immense tract. Failing that, the mind's eye has passengers groping along corridors in dressing gowns because of some untoward incident at an international border at dead of night. Bermuda, a group of pocket-sized islands which collectively could not pack in more than 21 miles (34 km) of track, would not seem cut out for a railway, much less a railway saga, yet somehow it has contrived to end up with a healthy railway saga but no railway.

As visitors are the main beneficiaries of Bermuda's trainless railway system, they may wish to consider the evidence of the matter before passing judgement on this curious state of affairs.

Before World War II, it ought to be recalled, Bermuda was without motor vehicles; any journey beyond walking distance was, of necessity, by carriage or boat, often the latter because in the absence of cars there was no pressing need to do much about roads. The idea of a railway was brought up in 1899 and acted upon in 1922, by which time the local money had concluded it was a crackpot idea and the funding had to be sought from abroad. The first train rolled on 31 October 1931, and the first-class passengers travelled in wicker chairs, the *hoi polloi* on benches.

After the war, Bermudians were captivated by the novelty of the automobile and not inclined to stump up the £1 million required to make good "Old Rattle and Shake", which was thereupon sold off to British Guyana for further duties. Closer acquaintance with the problems associated with automobiles led to remorse, and with every passing restriction on the use of cars – some visitors would not be stretching their legs on this railway trail but for the ban on self-drive hire cars – Bermudians ask themselves whether they did the right thing. The soul-searching continues to this day.

The wrangling over the route of the proposed railway has turned out well for present purposes. Property owners wanted it nowhere near them, so the engineers were obliged to pick their way as far as possible along the shore. Ten percent of the track was elevated on 33 bridges, and as half of these cross water the line provides walkers with many splendid vistas. There are some tunnels and conventional railway cuttings, but on the whole the meandering **Railway Trail** is as good a way to take in Bermuda as any. Lazy walkers may wish to remind themselves that trains avoid steep hills too.

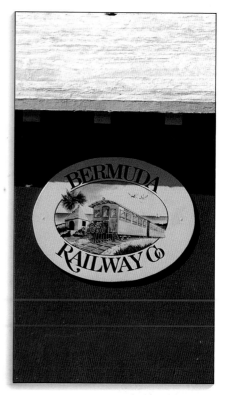

PRECEDING PAGES: island art in Somerset; the Devonshire coast. **LEFT:** facing the world head on. **RIGHT:** the Bermuda railway looms large in local memory.

On the trail

The Bermuda Department of Tourism publishes a free guide to the Railway Trail. It is not now continuous because certain sections, especially round **Hamilton**, were taken up by new roads. The department's map indicates points of access for walkers arriving by bus and helpfully recommends stretches that, having been negotiated at a dawdling pace for anywhere between 1½ and 3 hours, will deposit them at a point where they can easily catch a bus back to their hotels. Parts of the trail are open to self-propelled visitors on motor scooters and are safe spots for novices to familiarise themselves with the controls.

Guests staying in the lovely hotels along the south coast are within walking distance of the section of the trail that forms the spine of the **Paget-Warwick-Southampton isthmus** between the South Road roundabout on the outskirts of Hamilton and Somerset village. Moving in that direction, the trail connects soon after a 450-ft (135-metre) tunnel with

roads leading to spectacular **Elbow Beach** in Paget *(see page 205)*. Remember to take along your swimsuit.

There follows a fine opportunity to reflect on the architectural features of old Bermuda houses which prompted Ralph Adams Cram, the American architect, to observe: "I wonder if Bermudians realise how unique, charming and distinguished are these dwellings, great and small, of the 17th and 18th centuries. They are absolutely indigenous, built almost automatically by men of instinctive good taste."

The points to look out for are the distinctive white wedding-cake roofs made from limestone, which drain precious rain water into a domed tank designed to keep it cool, and store it in the basement of most buildings. The small, square outbuildings with pyramid roofs are butteries, a slight misnomer because they were used to store all perishables before the invention of refrigeration.

A group of allspice trees beyond the **Belmont Hills Golf Course** conceals the

BELOW: a train on opening day, 31 October 1931.

Map on page 168

small Warwick Pond bird sanctuary. West of the pond the so-called **Khyber Pass** is a bit of harmless hyperbole, less Rudyard Kipling than chain gang, because this is where a large amount of Bermuda's building stone was and is quarried. There is a clear distinction between the lower sections, which were worked by hand, and the bigger swathes cut above by modern machinery.

Tribe Road 7 runs down through the **South Shore Beach Parklands**. This is a possible diversion from the trail which must be weighed up, if time is short, against another farther along, which leads to **Gibbs Hill lighthouse**. Beyond the lighthouse the trail hugs the inside of the arc forming **Little Sound** against a backdrop of dunes and rock formations.

Readers of the history section of the book may now like to put themselves into the shoes of the 17th-century surveyor, Richard Norwood, under instructions from the autocratic governor, Daniel Tucker, to keep an eye open for desirable agricultural land which Tucker felt ought to belong to him, by hook or by crook *(see pages 47–8)*.

Norwood, a blameless party to all this, began to recognise when he reached this section what he thought Tucker had in mind. Norwood's judgement was vindicated by the fact that, while agriculture in Bermuda generally was made unviable by prohibitive American tariffs, most of the 600 acres (245 hectares) that are still worth farming are in this region.

The scandal created by Tucker's machinations was Bermuda's 17th-century Watergate. It was known as "overplus" and survives as the name of the lane that bears sharp left to take trail-walkers on to **Middle Road** and thence to **Somerset Bridge**, "the smallest drawbridge in the world". It was probably built in the year (1619) that Tucker was grudgingly awarded a small share of his "overplus" claim. The centre section of the bridge, 22 inches (55 cm) wide, is opened by hand in order to let a sailboat mast pass through.

BELOW: train crossing trestle bridge at Baileys Bay.

Visitors staying in or near the capital should be aware of the chance to take a ferry from Hamilton to Somerset Bridge, either to backtrack on the sections described above or to advance along the remainder of the trail to picturesque **Somerset Village**, a short walk of less than 2 miles (3 km).

This stretch, however, could easily occupy a morning or afternoon because there is much of interest: historic **Scaur Hill Fort**, clear views of **Ely's Harbour**, **Spanish Point** and (in the distance) **St George's**, as well as the 43-acre (17-hectare) **Heydon Trust** estate and its 17th century chapel, not to mention **Springfield** and the **Gilbert Nature Reserve**. The Somerset bus terminal at the end of the trail is the original railway station.

The Railway Trail running from outside the City of Hamilton, through Hamilton parish, to St George's and beyond begins at **Palmetto Park**. Shortly after, it passes near **Palmetto House**, a lovely 300-year-old home. Sitting on the North Shore

facing the sea, Palmetto House is built with its wings in the shape of a cross, a common architectural feature of its time. When the British army was stationed nearby, the house was used as a golf course clubhouse. Walkers on the Railway Trail are welcome to visit Palmetto House, but special arrangements must be made in advance. The National Trust headquarters at Waterville can advise.

The hillside that runs along beside **North Shore Road** down to Flatts Village has many examples of the Bermudian cedar which was so vital to the colony's early development. The tree is different from more common types of cedar, the most important from a shipbuilding point of view being the exceedingly fine grain that is watertight without the need for seasoning. Many cedars were deliberately sacrificed by burning in the interest of exterminating a plague of rats which in the 17th century threatened to devour practically everything. The rats were an unsuspected part of a consignment of grain

BELOW: Somerset Bridge is a landmark.

Map
on page
224

THE WEST END

*You can see picturesque western Bermuda by road or, better still, by ferry.
Whatever your choice, all routes lead to Dockyard, an historical
maritime landmark that is brimming with things to do and see*

Bermuda consists of an East End and a West End, names which owe much to the island's British heritage, for these terms also define specific areas in London. Bermuda's West End has little to do with Parliament, art galleries and theatreland, however, and much to do with maritime activities.

The parish of Sandys, plus the islands of Somerset, Watford, Boaz and Ireland, have long been dominated by the great base at **Royal Naval Dockyard ❶**, and even today, with warships replaced by ferryboats and the barracks by bijou attractions, the tug toward Dockyard is strong. There is only one road (with various names) and it, too, ends at this historic site – specifically, in front of Bermuda's Maritime Museum, with its important collection of exhibits.

The scenic route

Along the way to Dockyard, though, are lovely churches, shops and pastel-painted Victorian mansions echoing the past. The Railway Trail, the nature track which follows Bermuda's now-abandoned attempt at railway transport, is especially scenic through Somerset and the western parish of Sandys.

But perhaps most fun of all is the ferry ride from Hamilton. There are three ferry stops along this part of the island, handily located near sites of interest. It is an apt reminder of Bermuda's early history that most visitors choose to arrive at the West End by boat.

The ferry from Hamilton to Somerset Bridge, the first stop, squeezes through a channel called Timlin's Narrows before threading a picturesque path past islets and rocky outcrops. More than 30 of these islets are scattered around the **Great Sound ❷**, which is the basin formed by the left "hook" of Bermuda. Most are residential or barren, but a few are used by locals for recreational purposes, such as camping trips or nature hikes. Curiously, for Bermuda has few indigenous animals, this northeast section houses a virtual menagerie – islets with names like Goat Island, Bird Island, Goose, Partridge and Cat Islands.

The ferry from Hamilton docks at a tiny white shelter, empty save for a (working) telephone and palm trees on the horizon. But this part of the island is set for major changes, such as the development of the **Morgan's Point** resort on the site of a former US Naval Annex in the Great Sound. Facilities planned include an 18-hole golf course, a marina, a cottage colony and housing. On the other side of the island, **Tudor Hill** – adjacent to the

Port Royal Golf Club – is also slated for housing and tourism development.

A short walk down a tree-lined lane leads to **Somerset Bridge** ❸, which connects Somerset Island to the mainland of Bermuda and is believed to be the smallest drawbridge in the world. Its 22-inch (55 cm) draw is opened by hand to allow just enough space for the mast of a boat to pass through it. The bridge is a much-loved and photographed landmark, and even appears, sailboat at the ready, on the Bermudian $20 bill. There is a ferry landing at the bridge.

Sandys is an attractive parish, with marinas or boatyards at most strategic inlets, and stone staircases which lead off the main road. The people of the West End are fiercely independent. During the American Civil War, when the rest of Bermuda supported the South, the defiant residents of Somerset threw their hats in with the "damned Yankees" of the North. Both were united, however, in defence of Queen and Country.

Scaur Hill Fort ❹ (open daily May–Oct 9am–4pm; Nov–Mar 10am–4.30pm; free; tel: 234 0908), on Somerset Road, was built on the highest point of Somerset Island in the 1870s. Its position is strategic; it has a view that stretches in all directions and far out over **Ely's Harbour**. Enemy armies advancing towards the royal naval base at Dockyard could be spotted well in advance of attack.

This vista from Scaur's high ramparts can still be admired through the telescope provided. Also on display are the remains of an innovative gun carriage known as a Moncrieff Disappearing Carriage. The British were usurped as caretakers during World War II, when American troops used the fort as a US Marine outpost and nicknamed it "Cockroach Gulley". The fort is a fine spot for a picnic (no cockroaches in sight) and tables are scattered across its grounds. If you go for a walk on the north side of the slope facing the Sound, look for an isolated marker which wistfully states: "London 3,076 miles".

LEFT:
Scaur Hill Fort.

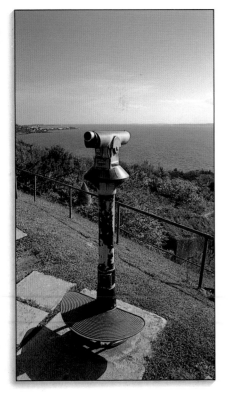

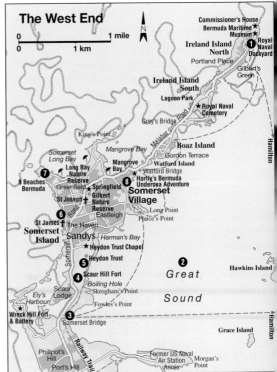

Map on page 224

Peace and tranquillity

Sandys parish is bisected by pleasant **Somerset Road** – which is not designed for pedestrians. Skirting the high walls of Scaur Hill Fort while negotiating the curves of the narrow lane, a hapless foot-soldier might end up impaled on one of the (albeit historic) stone walls. A winding uphill lane off Somerset Road leads to the **Heydon Trust** ➎, one of Bermuda's few private parks. The park's owner, a Christian charitable trust, allows the public to wander through its 43 acres (18 hectares) between sunrise and sunset every day.

Even on a Saturday afternoon, the grounds are blissfully quiet: cardinal birds and butterflies flit through groves of banana trees and benches are provided to allow visitors to pause and savour the views. But the vegetation is too lush to allow for more than fleeting glimpses of the sea and lingering is best enjoyed farther up the hill where the path levels off.

Tiny **Heydon chapel** is a squat, white building in traditional island style, with an interior almost monastic in its simplicity: whitewashed walls, three pews and a modest altar of cedar. Built in the early 19th century as a farm cottage, it was consecrated in 1970 and is still used as a denominational chapel.

A stone tablet outside reads in part: "Lift up a song to Him/Who rides upon the clouds." A wooden cross stands on the crest of the hill with sea views in every direction; sails flutter on the ocean below.

From Somerset Road, on the left, **St James's church** ➏ appears perfectly proportioned. Whitewashed tombs flank a long driveway; beyond is the slate, grey-and-white facade of the church and behind it, the sea. Although an earlier wooden structure probably existed on this site, much of the present church dates from 1789. Inside, although attention is drawn to the handsome organ and handsome polished cedar doors, the rear of the church is also of interest. A long wooden balcony with connecting stairs on either side takes up the rear wall. This modest construction

was presumably for black members of the churchgoing community. Unusually, there is only one stained-glass window, perhaps due to the lightning that struck the church in 1937, toppling the grand spire into the nave. Whatever the reason, cheerful sunlight floods into the room from colonial, arched windows.

Springfield is a perfect example of colonial architecture. Formerly the private home of the Gilbert family, its grounds have been turned into the **Gilbert Nature Reserve** (open until sunset), which includes 5 acres (2 hectares) of unspoiled land. A walk around the back of this National Trust house reveals the original entrance to Springfield, plus a series of fascinating outbuildings: a kitchen, slave quarters and a buttery. All now have other functions, either as a nursery school or private apartments or, in the case of Springfield House itself, a government community centre.

For many years Springfield House served as the Somerset Library, but this closed and the National Trust devoted years to restoration of the valuable mid-18th century structure. While the community centre is open to the public, there is little to see inside it now. The verandah, however – thought to have been a later addition to the house – looks out over the lawns, acres of banana plants and the nature reserve.

At Somerset Long Bay, on the northwestern peninsula near Daniel's Island, **9 Beaches Bermuda ❼** caters to the visitor seeking beach and water sports fun, and relaxation. The resort comprises around 80 cabin tents, all with views of the water.

The road toward **Long Bay Beach** and **Nature Reserve** leads past the tiny little cottage, buried in bougainvillea, that housed the original Irish Linen Shop. Called **Torwood**, this was the 18th-century home of the family that founded the linen shop. It was in the cellars of this cottage that the idea of importing fabric from Ireland, then selling it embellished

LEFT: street signs. **BELOW:** father and son go fishing.

Map on page 224

with embroidery, was conceived. At the time, in 1949, finances were simple. The linens were sold at whatever the owners felt was a fair price. Nothing went to waste: the wooden packing cases, in which the linen was transported from Ireland, were offered to local farmers for chicken coops.

In keeping with tradition tea was served in the drawing room at four o'clock for customers and staff. Now, the busy shop at the corner of Front and Queen streets in Hamilton handles the business, but Torwood offers a nostalgic glimpse of bygone days.

Long Bay is a popular spot for family picnics. The water is shallow and almost always calm, while a grassy area beyond the beach is ideal for cricket. A nature reserve edged with bamboo to the west of the beach is much loved by birdwatchers who in the autumn can spot migratory birds from the US and South America. Occasionally, birds such as the Siberian flycatcher, drop in from Russia.

Beaches and hamlets

Mangrove Bay is a curving sweep of idyllic beach from which, in the summer, it is possible to hire sailboats, rowing sculls, motorboats, kayaks, snorkelling equipment, even rafts and fishing tackle. Mangrove trees *(Rhizophora mangle)* were once so plentiful they gave their name to this tranquil little lagoon but, although the species still exists on other parts of the island, it can not now be found near the bay itself.

Hugging the northern shore of Mangrove Bay is **Somerset Village** ❽, a tidy hamlet dominated by Sandys Boat Club and a restaurant-cum-tavern called the Country Squire. Visitors with money to spare can find much to choose from in the small selection of boutiques and local craft centres.

Somerset Pharmacy has tea, coffee, sodas and pastries for people in need of a snack on the way to Dockyard. A welcome throwback to the 1950s, when American kids went to sox hops and

BELOW: high fliers.

drank malteds at the local drugstore. In the rear of this shop is a glorious soda-fountain with gleaming chrome stools, a Coca-Cola dispenser and quick snacks ranging from hot dogs (now microwaved) to chilli and curried chicken.

Somerset Village also marks one end of Bermuda's **Railway Trail** *(see page 213)*. If you plan to walk any of the trail, this is the ideal place to begin.

Just before Watford Bridge, a detour down East Shore Road leads to the **Gladys Morrell Nature Reserve**, a 2-acre (1 hectare) patch of unspoiled land presented to the National Trust in 1973.

The three islands, **Watford**, **Boaz** and **Ireland Island South**, which link up to Somerset like a slightly accusing finger, point the way to a place considered to be the most important site in the West End: the Royal Naval Dockyard. Bermudian street names like Honeysuckle Lane give way to stout English names (Victoria Row), emphasising the importance of the massive British naval base at Dockyard.

Until the **Watford Bridge** was built around the end of the 19th century, workers at the massive Dockyard had no idea whether they would be able to arrive at work, or even return home again, so erratic was the ferry service.

The erecting of this unassuming bridge contributed in no small measure to the defence of the country. Crossing from Boaz (Gates Island in Bermuda's history books) into Ireland Island South, the road divides and then encircles beautiful **Lagoon Park**, an open space with nature trails and a central watery refuge for wild birds. Visitors may see yellow-crowned night herons, which are particularly visible as they roost on the mangroves.

The road to the south is the scenic route, travelling along a narrow band between the lagoon and the sheltered sea before arriving at a beach cove and picnic site known as **Parson's Bay**. The main, northern road passes near two evocative burial grounds, the 19th-century **naval cemetery** and the equally historic **old convict**

BELOW: fish and ships at the Royal Naval Dockyard.

Maps on pages 224/229

cemetery, where the labourers who built Dockyard were laid to rest.

The Royal Naval Dockyard

At the beginning of the 19th century, when Britannia ruled the waves, the Royal Navy needed a safe haven in the Atlantic. The Crown wanted to keep an eye not only on French privateers in the waters but also on the Americans who, after their successful revolution in 1776, closed all ports to the British.

Bermuda was the obvious site and, in 1809, the Royal Naval Dockyard, the most ambitious building scheme upon which the island ever engaged, was commenced. This was none too soon.

The fleet that attacked Washington DC in 1814 set sail from here, and there has not been a major war since in which Dockyard has not played a role. Over 9,000 slave labourers and English convicts toiled for 39 years under intolerable conditions to construct the wharfs, workshops and outbuildings that were to

BELOW: the Clocktower Centre.

become the bastion of British power in the Western Atlantic. The stone walls of the fortress are 3 ft (1 metre) thick. After the British pulled out of Bermuda in 1951, the Georgian buildings were abandoned, and it wasn't until the early 1990s that the commercial potential of Dockyard was fully exploited.

The site on Ireland Island North has now been turned into a vast, upscale recreational complex, consisting of shops, fine restaurants, a well-appointed marina, a number of workshops and craft centres and a sightseeing train.

A tour of Dockyard is fascinating and visitors should allow themselves a day to explore the museums and historical sights here. It begins in the large building opposite the Keep, where barrels of drink were once housed. This building is the premises of the **Craft Market A** (open daily 9.30am–5pm; tel: 234 3208) and it is the pungent smell of cedar, rather than ale, that fills the air, emanating from a small wood-turners' shop in the corner. The

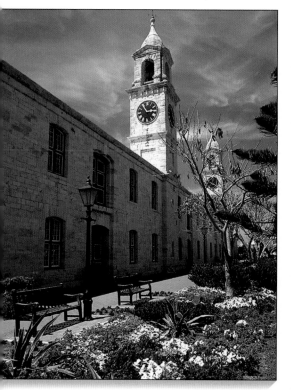

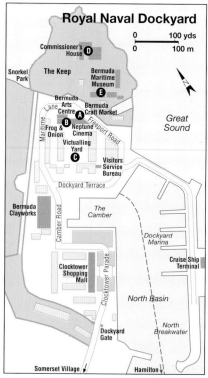

The Salvaging of the *Sea Venture*

A chance to go helmet diving at the age of 14 was to prove a turning point in the life of Allan "Smokey" Wingood (1915–2006). Years later, having survived World War II as a bomber pilot, and having retired from his successful diving/ underwater construction business, Smokey would prove that the remains of a shipwreck off the southeastern tip of Bermuda were those of the historic *Sea Venture*, which sunk in 1609.

Smokey was so enamoured of his first underwater experience that he resolved to get his own diving helmet. Since a manufactured one was beyond his reach, the schoolboy had to build his own. Working in their spare time, he and a friend crafted the helmet from a paint tin, affixed a lead collar to it and, after many failures, managed to insert a watertight glass face panel. There was no fancy air supply, and hence no air hose. Small wonder, then, that

Smokey's father was under the impression he was trying to kill himself.

With the outbreak of World War II, Smokey joined the RAF and was later presented with the Distinguished Flying Cross "for bravery and devotion to duty" by King George VI at Buckingham Palace. Back in Bermuda, the time had come for Smokey to realise his dream: to form a marine construction company. Eventually, he wound up diving for the Bermuda Maritime Museum, which triggered a lasting interest in marine archaeology.

In 1958 an American diver, Edmund Downing, discovered what he claimed was the wreck of the *Sea Venture* off the coast of St George's. With the island's 350th anniversary looming the following year, his find seemed too convenient to be believed. Two decades would pass before Smokey pressed for an investigation of Downing's find.

"The *Sea Venture* was never really lost, as the flat on which the ship sits is called Sea Venture Flat," Smokey explained. "The wreck is located three-quarters of a mile (1.2 km) from the shore off the most southeasterly point of Bermuda – and those are the things given in a contemporary account of the shipwreck."

Smokey formed the Sea Venture Trust and obtained permission to be the sole diver on the wreck. The Maritime Museum would take possession of any artefacts brought up.

The project soon became an all-consuming passion. Shards of pottery from the wreck were trekked around the museums of England until finally one in Plymouth confirmed that they matched similar shards found in the Plymouth and Bristol areas, and which conformed to the period when the *Sea Venture* foundered.

Further confirmation came from Ivor Noel Hume, chief archaeologist in Williamsburg, Virginia, who reported that the Wingood shards matched pottery he was excavating in Martin's Hundred, near Jamestown, Virginia – where, incidentally, the *Sea Venture* had been sailing before foundering on the reefs of Bermuda.

"So now it has been accepted that the wreck is the *Sea Venture*, and Downing was right," Smokey said proudly at the time. "How many other countries can say they have found the wreck of the ship that founded the colony?"

Queen Elizabeth II recognised Smokey's work by awarding him the Queen's Certificate and Badge of Honour in 1989.

LEFT: a man of honour.

Map
on page
229

fullest collection of island crafts in Bermuda can be found here, from stained glass examples of indigenous birds, to cunning Gombey dolls in a variety of shapes and forms. Across the breezeway was the **Smithy**, with its huge fireplace made of hard local stone.

Another fireplace is located in the lobby of the **Cooperage Theatre**, home of the **Neptune Cinema**, which shows Hollywood movies. Just across the way, the **Frog & Onion** ❸ pub is popular, with indoor and patio dining and a selection of shellfish and fish. The pub is always busy on Sundays with sightseers and "Onions", as Bermudians refer to themselves.

The grassy expanse in the middle of the complex was the **Victualling (Vittling) Yard** ❸, where all supplies for the base were stored. It's a stately spot, surrounded by imposing two-storey Georgian buildings with arched windows. If you walk to the middle of the manicured lawn and look toward the Cooperage, it's possible to see a large house on the right. This was the

Commissioner's House ❹, where all materials, like the Welsh slate roof and marble fireplaces, mahogany woodwork and even domestic fittings, were shipped 3,000 miles (5,000 km) from the United Kingdom. It also contains a detailed mural depicting Bermuda's history, painted by well-known local artist Graham Foster.

Construction of the impressive stone building began in 1823 and it is believed to be one of the first in the world with a cast-iron frame. The house, which affords good views over the island, underwent a lengthy, multi-million dollar restoration and is part of the Maritime Museum *(see page 234)*. It is also used for special events and exhibitions, such as a **coin collection** previously held at the Bank of Bermuda in Hamilton. The collection traces Bermudian currency from the 16th century to the present day. Doll-like replicas of each monarch denote which coins were used under which sovereign, and many of them bear further scrutiny, especially the bank's reserves of historic Hog

BELOW: the Victualling Yard: over 9,000 convicts laboured to build Dockyard.

Money, consisting of seven one shilling pieces, seven sixpences and the rare three-pences, of which only six others are known to exist. Note, too, the very British coins, which were standard currency until 1969, and the very American-style coins that were adopted in 1970.

The convicts who were forced to work in Dockyard were paid three pennies a day for their back-breaking labours: one penny went towards food, one penny towards housing and the sole remaining penny went into their pockets.

Overlooking the massive dockyard area is Casemates, previously used as a bar-racks and then a prison until West Gate, a modern maximum-security prison facility opened nearby. It is interesting to specu-late what the inmates must have pondered when gazing down on the well-heeled visitors below wandering around the flourishing tourist complex.

As a reminder of past glories, on occa-sion there is still a small naval presence berthed in the **South Basin**. On the far side of the harbour are blue-and-white terminals for the large cruise ships which stop here. Nearer the dock are modern "tenders", which transport passengers from the cruise ships into Hamilton.

Two towers

One of the later buildings to be con-structed at Dockyard was the handsome **Great Eastern Storehouse**, a building with twin clocktowers. Its facade is smoother than earlier buildings, presuma-bly because, over the years, the convicts learned their trade. In front of the store-house are the **King's Steps**, with the intriguing engraving "William IV Rex". No one is quite sure why the markings are retained, as he never came to Bermuda.

The clocks appear to tell slightly dif-ferent times, but this can be explained because one tells the time of day while the other is said to indicate high tide. Below the towers the former storehouse is now a smart shopping mall with chic boutiques, galleries and souvenir shops ideal for

BELOW: pottering around in Dockyard.

Map on page 229

cruise ship passengers in a hurry, and not unreasonably priced.

If you are hungry after a morning of sightseeing or shopping in the small mall a good place to stop before heading farther into Dockyard is the **Freeport Seafood Restaurant and Bar** near the complex entrance gates. Open during the summer season, the eatery is patronised by locals and visitors who enjoy the tasty, fresh seafood concoctions on the menu.

On the weekend Dockyard is at its busiest, with many visitors arriving by car, bus or ferry, simply to stroll or rest in one of the shaded benches dotted around.

Because local stone is too porous to construct an ample dry dock, three ships towed the **floating dock** from England in 1869. Once a familiar sight at Dockyard, today it stands idle at Spanish Point Park in Pembroke.

Behind the Eastern Storehouse is a building with an intriguing history. The **Sail Loft** was built in 1860. Its handsome floor was made of teak to prevent splinters from getting into the sails. But by the time the building was completed, steam power had virtually replaced sails, and the loft saw little action in its intended function. The loft later had a brief but rowdy period as a dance-hall.

The **ramparts** offer wonderful views out to sea; directly below them is reclaimed land. Huge warehouses are now the premises of the **Island Pottery**, the **Bermuda Clayworks** and other workshops, where it is possible to watch potters at their craft. The **Bermuda Arts Centre** (open daily 10am–5pm; free) was opened by Princess Margaret in 1984. A non-profit organisation mostly run by volunteers, the arts centre holds exhibitions which change almost every month.

The work of five resident artists, along with other notables, is on display and on sale. Visitors can browse through the stalls which display original sculptures, paintings, jewellery and textile designs.

The most important building at Dockyard was undoubtedly **the Keep**, with its

BELOW: a wife shops while a husband flops.

moat, drawbridge, watergate and inner lagoon, where small boats were loaded with munitions and supplies for larger ships at anchor. The Keep was the last line of defence in the protection of Dockyard, should an enemy successfully pass the other massive fortresses protecting its approaches by land and sea.

The Maritime Museum

This handsome building (actually, a series of eight buildings) is now the **Bermuda Maritime Museum E** (open daily Apr–Oct 9.30am–5pm; Nov–Mar 10am–5pm; entrance fee; tel: 234 1418; www.bmm. bm). Fascinating displays include the Tucker Treasure, part of which is a replica of the Tucker Cross, a gold and emerald piece salvaged from the *San Pedro*, which disappeared in 1975 while on its way to the museum *(see page 123)*. There are exhibits on diving, navigation, shipping, whaling, plus an interesting walk around **the Keep's ramparts**, which measure a towering 30 ft (9 metres) high.

Map on page 229

The Maritime Museum with its six exhibition halls, vividly illustrates Bermuda's intimate connections with the sea. According to *Life at Sea*, published in 1750, at any one time one-third of the adult male population was manning the island's sailing vessels. Strict regulations governed the number of free men aboard these ships, to ensure that enough manpower remained at home to prevent uprisings by enslaved men and women. But enslaved men went to sea, too, usually as crew, but occasionally rising to positions of power. And while at sea, these sailors were also allowed to vote.

Privateer sloops carried the largest crews, often manned by ex-pirates, but the risk on board was so great, either from each other or from enemy privateers, that every man, regardless of status, voted on whether to do battle. This was almost 200 years before black people played a significant role in political decisions on land, and is a striking example of the irregularities of life at sea.

The enclosed waterway, known as the Keep Pond, was a secure channel that allowed safe ship repairs. Today the Pond is home to the island's dolphinarium.

To many people, the most fascinating room in the museum is the **Treasury**. The exhibition of shipwreck archaeology features Bermuda's treasures, retrieved by Teddy Tucker and many others from the island's reefs. Most of the booty is Spanish, such as the gold bar weighing 35 oz (984 g), as the Spanish were "easy victims". They sailed to the Old World laden with treasures from Spain's New World, South America.

Bermudians, who were notorious for their wrecking and salvaging, happened to be on hand. Archaeologists are particularly excited when "pieces of eight" are discovered. Over 2,000 of these silver coins have come to light, which provide important clues to the wreck being salvaged.

The position of caretaker has been held by, among others, the late Douglas Little. With his sailor's hat and peg leg, this man was the epitome of a seafaring Bermudian. The fact that Mr Little was a confirmed landlubber should cast no doubt on the veracity of the museum. ❏

LEFT: Dockyard took 39 years to complete. **RIGHT:** the late Douglas Little, former caretaker at the Maritime Museum.

Map
on page
242

HARRINGTON SOUND

*Around the great saltwater lake known as the Sound
lie Bermuda's zoo and aquarium and beautiful architecture.
Here, too, spectacular caves and tunnels wind their way underground*

Harrington Sound is a salt-water lake almost 6 miles (10 km) long. It is ringed by nature reserves and natural caves, many of which form Bermuda's premier tourist attractions. The surrounding area is lush and extensive. Much of Harrington Sound lies in Hamilton parish, which bears no relation to the capital, but Verdmont, the most interesting of Bermuda's historic houses, lies in neighbouring Smith's.

Historic home

On the corner of Collectors Hill and Sayle Road is **Verdmont House Museum ①** (open Tues–Sat 10am–4pm; entrance fee; tel: 236 7369; www.bnt.bm), built around 1710 in the style of a small English manor house. This peach-coloured home was in continuous residence until the early 1950s, when it was sold to the National Trust. The last owner, a Miss Lillian Joell, never bothered to modernise the property, preferring instead to illuminate it with oil lamps and to cook by kerosene. Inside, the floorboards are bare and a little bit scuffed, the walls are peeling in places, as if a hand too busy with other matters attempted to slap on a coat of paint.

This adds to, rather than detracts from Verdmont's charm, for its cosy atmosphere is in direct contrast to the French-polished formality of many historic homes around the world. Rumours – which have circulated for years – that the National Trust plans to "smarten up" Verdmont's interior, which would be a great pity.

Verdmont is approached by a flag-stoned path, wonderfully fragrant with wild flowers. To truly appreciate its proportions, go around to the south side, as the house was constructed to look out over the sea. Verdmont's four great chimneys, two at either end, allowed for a fireplace in each room; the cedar balcony replaces a Victorian portico and was added by restorers.

The gardens are delightful, skimming down towards the sea in graceful undulations. Although the volunteer guide may claim that the shrubberies date from the 18th century, which means they would have weathered many a gale, this is a romantic view; they were in fact planted by the National Trust from several varieties which grew on the island at the time.

Inside, much of the furniture, assembled from other island properties, is of Bermuda cedar and made by local craftsmen. The wooden armchair in the dining room, called a "Cromwellian", is probably the oldest piece, and pre-dates Verdmont by 50 years.

Although there is much to see in the sunny drawing room and the library with its fine roll-top desk, the real charm lies upstairs in the **nursery**. Strewn around a miniature canopied bed is an eccentric collection of Victorian toys including a rocking horse with no ears and a horse-headed tricycle, operating in quite the opposite manner to modern bicycles, for it was propelled by the arms while steering with the legs.

A Dresden doll lies in a baby cradle – rare for its day and even more valuable now – for the doll has brown eyes rather than the regulatory blue pair.

Note for modern parents: a slim volume discovered in the nursery's bookcase, *Etiquette for Little Folks*, which was published in Boston in 1856, reads in part: "Modesty is a polite accomplishment, and generally attendant upon merit. It is engaging, in the highest degree, and wins the hearts of all with whom we are acquainted. None are more disgusting in company than the impudent…"

Nature's havens

East of Verdmont on South Road lies **Spittal Pond** ❷ (open daily from dawn to dusk), the island's largest wildlife sanctuary. Unlike some other reserves, which can be visited only by appointment, Spittal Pond's 60 acres (25 hectares) offers good public access, although visitors are requested to keep to the pathways.

About 25 species of waterfowl choose to winter in Bermuda, and most of them opt for this open space with its large waterway. Visiting birds in the winter include great, cattle and snowy egrets, and also little blue, tricoloured and green herons. In fact, yellow-crowned night herons are Bermuda residents, having been introduced to the island in the 1970s to combat the land crab invasion of the golf courses. In winter they often roost on the low lying branches of Mexican pepper bushes that shelter part of the pond. Spring and summer longtails, or white-tailed tropic birds, swoop in and out of the south shore cliffs. In summer thousands

LEFT: explore the pretty lane by moped.

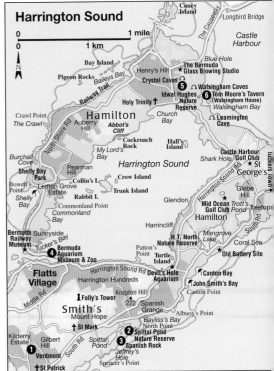

Map
on page
242

of other pelagic birds migrating north can be seen (through binoculars or telescope) from the South Shore. The most common are shearwaters, the Greater, Manx, Cory's and Sooty, but sometimes Jaegers can be spotted as well. During the fall the sanctuary is a favourite rest stop for varieties of warblers, thrushes, sandpipers and plover and grebes.

Off the pathway at the western end is an interesting geological formation aptly named the Chequerboard. A flat floor of rock is scored into squares and is surrounded by crags and boulders overlooking the ocean. A little beyond and situated high on a hill between Spittal Pond and the meandering south shore is **Spanish Rock ❸**, which holds an intriguing little tale. When the early colonists arrived in Bermuda they found, carved into this rock, the date 1543 and some initials, which remain unclear, but are thought to be an "R" and a cross.

Some argue that they are the monogram of "R.P." which, with the cross, could rep-

resent the Portuguese Order of Christ, *Rex Portugalie*. The engraving was probably left by shipwrecked Portuguese sailors, so arguably this spot should really be called "Portuguese Rock". A cast of the inscription can be seen in the Bermuda Library, and since the original initials on the rock have been eroded, a bronze plaque taken from this cast now marks the spot.

Another nature reserve lies nearby: the **H.T. North Nature Reserve** at the western end of Mangrove Lake on the border of Hamilton parish. Bermuda's reserves are not just of interest to ornithologists, however, for in addition to exotic birds there are many examples of rare flowers, which thrive on the protected land.

Knapton Hill Road leads directly to **Devil's Hole** and its **Aquarium** (open daily 9.30am–4.30pm; tel: 293 2072), the island's first tourist attraction, established in 1834. The "hole" is actually a natural pool where, for the price of an admission fee, it's possible to fish with hookless lines for sharks, Moray eels, fish, and with

EFT: island ceramic.
RIGHT: scooting around Flatts village.

luck one may see protected loggerhead turtles. Entrance is, eccentrically, through the Angel Wings café (avoid fish on the menu), but the best possible description of Devil's Hole has been written by its owner and is posted out front. It reads as follows: "The beauties of nature abound around a pool of 32 foot depth of clear blue water alive with the silent movement of beautiful and ferocious fish invites relaxation and rest or arouses the spirit for sport fishing." Enough said. The nearby rock in Harrington Sound is called, appropriately, **Turtle Island**.

Around the Sound

Devil's Hole marks the beginning of a circular route around the Sound, which can be undertaken on foot, by motorbike or, for the privileged, by car. Heading north up Harrington Sound Road, the first junction reached is the village of **Flatts**. Rumour has it that Flatts was once a smugglers' cove, and its position, on a spindly neck of land which leads to the

open sea, would lend credence to this theory. It is now a popular stopping-off point for yachts, whose tall masts make ghostly silhouettes on the Sound at sunset. All in all, Flatts is a very pretty spot, with a tasteful blend of new and old buildings painted in a variety of ice-cream colours. The new buildings, although attractive, replace an elegant hotel whose loss is mourned by Bermudians, an example of the island's increasing capitulation to commerce.

Fish and other friends

The **Bermuda Aquarium, Natural History Museum and Zoo** ❹ (open daily 9am–5pm, last admission at 4pm; guided tours; entrance fee; tel: 293 2727), all located within the same sprawling grounds, has its own landing dock for the loading and unloading of animals. The cool, shady verandah of the Bermuda Aquarium is a perfect place to observe the comings and goings of Flatts.

The interior of this sea-green building is

BELOW: old-fashioned exterior but with modern facilities.

Map
on page
242

ultra modern, belying its opening date of 1928. Tanks are filled with unfiltered salt water and coral prised from the seabed. A lot of thought has gone into making life agreeable for the fish, all of which are native to Bermuda: a reef tank with a "tide" was installed for species that depend on the ebb and flow of the sea.

Visitors can observe the exotic specimens such as the peacock flounder who lies down so that he can see: both eyes are on the same side of his body. Seahorses trot merrily through smaller tanks, but the darker side of marine life is not over-looked.

In the coral reef North Rock Exhibit, in a tank, which covers an entire wall, swim barracuda, a dusky shark that can grow up to 12 ft (4 metres) in length, a huge hawksbill turtle and assorted other fish. The shark's dinner is these "other fish", who form excited little schools to protect themselves. It is quite disturbing to have a front-row seat at mealtime, for the smaller fish, trapped in a glass corner, are close

enough to reveal their terror seconds before being gobbled up. Children love this spectacle, however, and egg on the shark with glee. They also enjoy watching scuba divers who periodically swim with the fish to clean the tanks.

Other animals seem happy enough. The aquarium's resident family of harbour seals, which has been breeding successfully, can be seen waddling in a pool just outside the Aquarium. In the Bermuda Zoo, a reptile walkway provides views of tortoises, lizards, terrapins and alligators in "natural" settings. The skink enclosure reveals the island's indigenous lizard. The Galapagos tortoises, an endangered species, were first bred outside their native island in the Bermuda Zoo.

Inside the terrestrial room of the Natural History Museum, it is possible to watch a movie (through a porthole) detailing an attempt to duplicate the success of the Beebe Project. This was an experiment conducted in 1934 by Dr William Beebe to descend deep into the ocean off the

BELOW:
in the swim:
Holacanthus
tricolor, or
Rock Beauty.

coast of Bermuda to document fish and marine life never seen before. Dr Beebe, director of Tropical Research for the New York Zoological Society, descended over half a mile (800 metres).

The local attempt (as documented in the movie) was less successful, but a replica of the original bathysphere, the "underwater laboratory" which Dr William Beebe used for his feat, can be viewed outside the museum.

A scenic route

Leaving Flatts, Harrington Sound Road temporarily becomes the continuation of **North Shore Road**, the long, unswerving and fairly traffic-free boulevard which starts at Spanish Point in the parish of Pembroke and extends all the way to the fertile greenery of **Coney Island**. It is a beautiful route which parallels the well-trodden Railway Trail, and this stretch offers some of the finest scenery in the parish of Hamilton.

Both **Shelly Bay**, with its beach, nature reserve and park, and Shelly's eastern neighbour, **Baileys Bay**, are named after early Bermudian settlers. **Crawl Hill**, just before Baileys, is the highest point in Hamilton parish and worth a short stop for the view. Within the Baileys Bay area are a popular ice-cream parlour and the well-known **Swizzle Inn**, a hostelry serving up copious quantities of the island speciality – rum swizzles – along with good pub grub.

Blue Hole Park, just before the Causeway on the way to the airport, is small but magical. Once the home of the Blue Grotto Dolphin Show, it has trails leading to small caves, a lagoon, and a mangrove and cherry-tree jungle that connects with Walsingham Park.

Church Bay in Harrington Sound is so named because of handsome, historic **Holy Trinity Church**, one of the oldest on the island. It dates back at least to the 1660s when it consisted of one room and a palmetto thatched roof. Nineteenth and 20th-century additions have transformed

BELOW: lush Coney Island.

Map on page 242

the church into a cruciform shape, complete with chancel, sanctuary and spire. It is well worth a visit, if only to view its stained-glass windows, five of which were designed by the 19th-century artist, Sir Edward Burne-Jones.

The region around Church Bay is riddled with caves. For centuries cave exploration was a popular activity in Bermuda, since it was commonly believed that gold and precious diamonds had been hidden by extinct tribes.

Beauty underground

Pot-holers should note that some caves can be reached only on hands and knees; others are underwater. It is claimed that a team of local divers discovered one cave full of blind shrimps. Other caverns are accessible, like the two caves attached to the Grotto Bay Beach hotel grounds.

The most breathtaking caverns of the lot are undoubtedly the **Crystal Caves ❺** (open daily 9.30am–4.30pm [final tour]; entrance fee; tel: 293 0640), located,

appropriately, on Crystal Caves Road, a tranquil cul-de-sac that winds through a small plantation of palms and open fields. These caves were discovered in 1907 by two small boys pursuing a lost ball that had rolled down a hole in the ground. Further exploration revealed an enormous cavern surrounding an underground lake of clear water. Although the 120-ft (37-metre) descent was originally made by ladder, today the lake can be reached by a gently sloping path and a few steps.

The interior is truly astonishing; an underground cathedral of crystal and water. As Cahow Lake is salt water, with two tides a day, there is constant movement. This movement creates ripples that, together with underwater spotlights, cause the water to shimmer in a myriad of shades from turquoise to midnight black. Two of the stalagmites are over a million years old, while other rock formations are reflected in the water in fascinating shapes – the Manhattan skyline, for instance, or a very watery Buddha.

BELOW: schoolboys discovered Cahow Lake in the Crystal Caves.

The climate underground feels cool in the summer and warm in the winter, for the temperature remains constant at 68° F (20° C). The Crystal Caves might well be Bermuda's premier visitors' attraction and should not be missed. And in case you were wondering, no, the boys never did get their ball back. At the same location is **Fantasea Cave**, which is also open to the public. Its stalactites and stalagmites are markedly different from the neighbouring caves – they are believed to resemble orange spaghetti.

Near to the Crystal Caves lies **Walsingham Bay**, which is closely linked to the 19th-century Irish poet Tom Moore, who arrived in Bermuda to take up a government post and wreak havoc with the hearts of young ladies. Moore had achieved considerable fame in Britain, and at one point was even mooted as Poet Laureate of Ireland. According to William Zuill, in his booklet *Tom Moore's Bermuda Poems*, the Bermuda position was merely a fee-paying job and, after four months (and several scandals), Moore returned to Ireland and literary achievement.

Moore spent some time at **Walsingham House**, which had in its grounds a calabash tree. From this memory Moore composed the lines: *'Twas thus, by the shade of a calabash-tree, With a few, who could feel and remember like me, The charm, that to sweeten my goblet I threw, Was a sigh to the past and a blessing on you!*

Moore spent many more hours in the town of St George's than he did at Walsingham House *(see The East End, page 255),* so it remains a mystery as to why this particular spot should claim his name. Nevertheless, Walsingham House, hidden from the road by vegetation, is now an elegant restaurant called **Tom Moore's Tavern ❻**, and a very pretty spot it is, too.

The east coast of Harrington Sound was well known in Bermuda's history. The area around **Castle Harbour** was designated by governor Daniel Tucker to replace St George's as the island's new capital. He modestly proposed to call it Tucker's Town. Whether the plan actually got off the ground or remained a figment of the governor's imagination remains unknown. In either case, the present-day **Tucker's Town** is an exclusive residential area where properties change hands for millions of dollars.

Tucker's Town is surrounded by several golf courses. Two of the most popular members-only clubs are **Tucker's Point Golf course**, which lies to the northwest, and **Mid Ocean Club**, situated toward the remains of the once spectacular rock formations, the **Natural Arches**, which were devastated by powerful Hurricane Fabian in 2003.

The Mid Ocean is Bermuda's most famous golf course, designed by an American champion in 1921. The famous or merely wealthy flock to suffer the challenges of its fairways, which overlook the sea and undulate toward two separate bodies of water, **Trott's Pond** and **Mangrove Lake**. Eisenhower met Churchill at the Mid Ocean Club, but it remains unrecorded as to which world leader had the greater handicap.

Map on page 242

LEFT: ❏ Tom Moore.

Survival Notes for Nervous Drivers

Bermudians have cars. Visitors have motorbikes. This idea – clear, direct, and wonderfully discriminating – has kept many a holidaymaker off Bermuda's roads entirely. A shame, really, for some of the island's best-kept secrets are hidden down tiny lanes or half-way up hillsides where buses never venture.

However, just because Bermuda is small and the speed limit is 20 mph (35 kph) doesn't mean that accidents don't happen here. They do. Visitors used to driving on the right side of the road sometimes forget at crucial moments that right on Bermuda's roads is wrong. Also drivers can be unpredictable – some think nothing of stopping suddenly to have a chat with another car driver or of honking their horns just to say hello.

By all means hire a motor scooter if you have nerves of steel, but take some sensible precautions. Avoid hitting the road during rush hour traffic (7.45–9.15am and 4.45–6.15pm), and don't be tempted to go faster if there is a sudden torrent of rain. Wet roads can cause skids. Try not to cling to the sides of narrow roads; it's safer to drive in the middle of the lane. And above all else, make sure you get proper instruction.

Rental centres include an introductory lesson, but instructors tend to be rev-happy teenagers unconversant with a beginner's fears. Be firm and ask to be shown again. Check the brakes. Helmets must be worn at all times, and it's wise to take a sweater in the summer or a leather jacket in the winter; you'd be wise to carry a rain-proof jacket at any time. In Bermuda you must drive on the *left-hand side* of the road.

The route a nervous driver selects for that all-important first run can make or break the decision to ride again. There are many choices around the island, from the peace of the Railway Trail to the clockwise charm of Harrington Sound.

One tried-and-tested route is to drive the distance from Hamilton to St George's – at least half the distance of the entire island – without stopping. This circuit is nicknamed the "Go For It Route" as it caters for people determined to conquer their fear of the roads.

This route can be travelled in 40 minutes. It involves a couple of right-hand turnings to get out of Hamilton, a few dodgy moments while checking out roadsigns, and then levels off at the North Shore Road – every nervous driver's dream. It runs in a straight line to your precise destination. It is relatively free of traffic, with scenery pleasant enough to be appealing but not so awe-inspiring as to divert from the mission at hand: getting to St George's.

The tedious business of stopping, starting, and winding through traffic over, exhilaration sets in, along with the realisation that anything difficult has already been accomplished. The long smooth road ahead – every sign pointing to St George's – is intoxicating.

Once in St George's, park the scooter by the harbour. Then lock it: insurance against theft is not included in the rental. Enter the nearest café, and indulge in a well-earned treat. For the faint-hearted, buses lead straight back to Hamilton but proud victors will never use public transport again. ❑

RIGHT: getting around Bermuda is easy on two wheels.

Map on page 256

THE EAST END

The cobbled streets and narrow alleys of St George's hold colourful secrets, while neighbouring St David's bears the scars of a past military presence

Progress in Bermuda – in terms of a bridge here, a causeway there, nothing too radical – has blurred but not quite obliterated the distinctive characteristics of individual islands. **St David's** which together with **St George's** (the island, as opposed to merely the town) makes up the bulk of the eastern wing of Bermuda, retained an extraordinary degree of cultural insularity until, and even after, the 1930s, when a bridge finally replaced the old ferry link with the other islands.

A St David's man, probably with features revealing Native American blood, may still claim a closer identification with that island than Bermuda as a whole, although such a remark ought not to be taken too literally. The issue is parochial pride rather than festering secessionist tendencies. E.A. McCallan's highly enjoyable memoirs, *Life on Old St David's*, published by the Bermuda Historical Society and found in local bookstores, rattles on as if the rest of Bermuda scarcely existed.

Bridging the gap

The bridge that joins St David's and St George's – the two names are respectively those of the patron saints of Wales and England – was pointedly named after the Severn Bridge which links the two British neighbours over the River Severn. The constant flow of traffic on an uninterrupted road right across Bermuda now makes such claims sound less quaintly defiant than gratuitously silly.

Nevertheless, while time and communications have eroded the barriers, Bermudian loyalties are divided between Hamilton and St George's, with even smaller pockets of allegiance to hamlets like Somerset and Flatts. The instincts which, for example, steered sympathies into one or other camp during the Ameri-

can Revolution and subsequently in the Civil War, as well as in domestic disputes, are not quite ready to be buried.

"The harbour of St George is one of the most beautiful and secure harbours in the world," a Dr Theodore L. Godet noted in 1860. In his medical opinion, Bermuda was ideal for "natives of cold countries who, from general delicacy of constitution, are unable to undergo active continuous labour with exposure", but St George's was an exception. Dr Godet, it should be noted, was a West Ender. "The streets are extremely narrow", he sniffed, "which is a great disadvantage, as the accumulation of much confined air is occasioned thereby, which consequently renders the town unhealthy".

PRECEDING PAGES: St George's; a reflective portrait of children.
LEFT: Bermuda's town criers, past and present, have won awards.
RIGHT: a hoax occurred in the Town Hall.

The old town of St George

What was true of **St George ❶** then is not much changed now, and it is difficult to understand what the good doctor was going on about. No building was higher than two storeys, the population was measured in hundreds, and refreshing breezes swept in from thousands of square miles of open ocean.

The narrow "streets" that worried Dr Godet are, for modern visitors, aesthetic assets with appealing names like **One Gun Alley**, **Shinbone Alley** and **Featherbed Alley**. **Old Maid's Lane**, for example, was once Cumberland Lane; the nickname was inspired by the number of spinsters who coincidentally happened to live there. Their strenuous efforts to resist the creeping use of the new name included the erection of a sign upon which "Cumberland Lane" was written emphatically large.

Although their rearguard campaign proved futile, they may have derived some posthumous consolation from the lane's later role as a kind of Juliet's balcony in Bermuda's most celebrated romance. The story, denied as fantasy by some, involved Nea, wife of one of the indomitable Tucker clan, and the visiting Irish poet Thomas Moore who, until eclipsed by the man himself, had a precocious, Byronic reputation in English society. He first caught sight of young Nea walking down the lane and that set him off:

> *And thou, when at dawn, thou shalt happen to roam*
> *Through the lime-covered alley that leads to thy home*

With Moore bringing round little notes with lines like "Sweet Nea! let us roam no more" the House of Tucker put its foot down. He was banished from the house, although presumably not even the Tuckers could deny him the right to gaze up Old Maid's Lane with a throbbing heart. His infatuation later received official blessing, or at least recognition, with the naming of an adjacent lane after Nea.

A **bust of Tom Moore Ⓐ** is to be found in a small, walled garden near **Bridge**

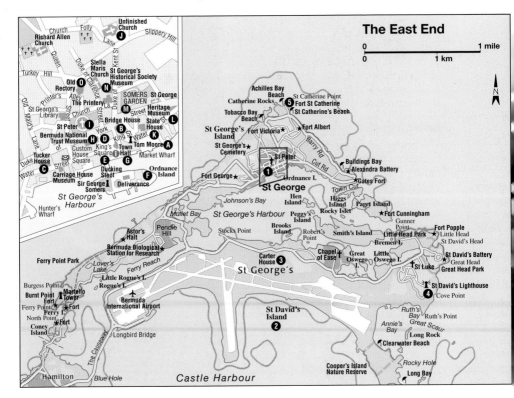

Map on page 256

House **B**, home to several governors and to Bridger Goodrich, hero to some and pirate to others, not least Thomas Jefferson.

The Tuckers had another, grander house at the corner of Water Street and Barber's Alley, the latter a reference to a freed American slave named Joseph Rainey who escaped to Bermuda at the outset of the Civil War. He and his French wife lived and worked in the kitchen of **Tucker House C** (open Mon–Sat 10am–4pm; entrance fee; tel: 297 0545), he as a barber and she as a dressmaker. He planned to return after the war and pursue a career in the church, but went into politics instead and, unprecedented for a black man, was elected to the House of Representatives in 1870. The Tucker House is now a National Trust property housing a museum containing handsome Bermudian cedar wood furnishings, antique silver and other valuable artefacts. The building itself has many important architectural features (see *Island Architecture*, page 88, for a guide to Bermudian style).

St George's rich anecdotal history, set down in William Zuill's 1946 *Bermuda Journey* and works by the tireless Mrs Terry Tucker, from Britain's Isle of Wight who married into the family, greatly enhances what most visitors would wish to do in the town, which is simply to stroll about at a leisurely pace.

From the beginning of the 19th century, most of Bermuda's development was concentrated around Hamilton, which replaced St George's as capital in 1815, a bitter pill for St Georgians. The differences lay in the harbours. Reefs made the approaches to St George's treacherously narrow, and as ships grew larger they could not cope. The channels were widened but it was always too little too late. At the approach of the 21st century, the corporation of St George's embarked upon an ambitious programme to develop the 17th-century town. However, assurances have been given that this will not result in a Disneyland-style replica. Such is the town's historical importance that it

BELOW: the Tucker House has important architectural features.

has been designated a World Heritage Site, and restoration plans include burying unsightly modern cables underground, providing street lighting reminiscent of days past and development of the waterfront area. It remains a wonderful place to explore.

Visitors – and, one suspects, most St Georgians – now relish the commercial neglect that left the town virtually unchanged. The alleys have not expanded beyond the width needed to roll a barrel. Concessions made to the car were minimal. St George's is practically as old as Jamestown, the first European settlement in America, and it feels as unaffectedly pristine as any town in the New World.

Gravity draws the winding alleys in the old part of the town down to old **King's Square** , also known as Market Square, which resembles a film set in the absence of jarring anachronisms. It is the invariable fate of a photographer's travelling companion to pose contritely in the preserved pillory and stocks.

Although the **ducking stool** was used even-handedly for petty offenders of either gender, it is best remembered (or resented) as a summary lesson for wives who nagged or were otherwise tiresome. A certain Goodwife Prosser, evidently an appalling creature, was forever being shown her errors – on one occasion her foul-mouthed behaviour warranted no fewer than six successive dips.

The stool is still wheeled over to the water's edge for practical demonstrations, although the wet seat once occupied by petulant wretches like Goodwife Prosser now tends to be filled by a volunteer, possibly an attractive member of the crew of a visiting yacht or a selflessly dedicated employee of the Department of Tourism.

Added to all this, David Frith, the congenial Town Crier, garbed in period attire, shows visitors around and is not averse to an invitation to pull up a stool in, say, the venerable White Horse Tavern, across the square from the Town Hall.

LEFT AND BELOW: before… and after.

Map on page 256

A walking tour

A great deal of Bermuda's turbulent early history evolved in and around King's Square. Chronologically, a walking tour ought to begin with the replica of *Deliverance* (open daily Apr–Nov; 9am–5pm; entrance fee) sited on ancient **Ordnance Island** F, a former British army arsenal. A certain amount of educated guesswork went into the reconstruction of the ship because the original was improvised out of the salvage from *Sea Venture*, the ship which struck a reef while carrying some of the first settlers to Virginia.

Deliverance (and a second vessel, *Patience*) took over a year to build, during which time some of the settlers began to wonder whether Bermuda, without any hostile native Indians, might be a better bet than Jamestown, Virginia, their original destination.

The interior of the ship is tiny, with little headroom and even less space for sleeping. Conditions during the 14-day journey to Virginia must have been intolerable.

Those who stayed behind set up camp on Smith's Island.

The choice of St George's as the main settlement was made by the governor in charge of Bermuda's first intentional settlers who, attracted by contrary reports reaching England about these supposedly dreadful dots in the mid-Atlantic, arrived in 1612 – just as the "three kings", as those who held the fort came to be known, were planning to leave. The islands of Bermuda were then thickly wooded with cedar and palmetto trees which were an easy source of building materials.

Disappearing act

The **Town Hall** G (open Mon–Sat 10am–4pm, closed public holidays; free), focal point of King's Square, was built of stone some 200 years later and was used for all sorts of non-municipal purposes, including entertainment. At the entrance are stone tiles brought back by the town crier from a visit to St George's twin town, Lyme Regis, in Dorset in the United Kingdom.

BELOW: café viewing on the waterfront.

Furnished with beautiful Bermuda cedar, the small building is still used for council meetings today.

In his book, *Bermuda Journey*, Zuill recounts a splendid hoax. The hall was packed to capacity in anticipation of *Ali Baba and the Forty Thieves*, a production staged by a certain Professor Trott. The audience, growing restless with a delay well beyond the advertised starting time, cheered with relief when the professor's head at last poked through the curtains to say: "Now you see me and now you don't", or words to that effect. Still nothing happened; in due course the head reemerged with the same comforting, though somewhat enigmatic, message. This baffling routine was repeated a third time, but yet again without result.

The mood of the audience degenerated from impatience to anger. The professor's head failed to reappear. Ticket holders eventually barged through the curtains to find a bare stage: no Professor Trott, no sign of any preparations for *Ali Baba* and absolutely no chance of a refund. The evening ended in chaos and no explanation was forthcoming until, two days later, "Professor Trott" put in another appearance – on this occasion, in the police court, where he was charged with the theft of a safe while his theatre-loving victims were, of course, otherwise occupied.

The disgruntled audience very likely filed across the square to the historic **White Horse Tavern** for a drink. The pub was no stranger to bizarre practices. It was once the home of John Davenport, a paranoid entrepreneur who kept his money in arrowroot kegs in a basement fortress to ward off a world which, he felt, was out to rob him.

Which of the kegs contained the money was a secret entrusted only to his manservant, who was required to accompany Davenport down to the basement each day and hold up a candle while he bored a gimlet into the relevant keg. The hardness of metal beneath a layer of arrowroot pro-

BELOW: the White Horse Tavern.

Map
on page
256

vided sure confirmation to both men that all was well.

This ritual was followed until Davenport's death, when his executors had to sort out the kegs. They were removed one by one over several days, emptied and, in the case of those riddled with gimlet holes, the contents counted. The final tally was an astonishing £75,000 in gold and silver. Today, the White Horse is the place for a refreshing glass of beer, but don't forget it is illegal to take drinks outside onto the square itself.

The studio of well-known water colour artist Carole Holding is nearby. For many years, Holding worked out of the St George's Historical Society; the artist also has studios on Front Street and at Dockyard.

Another building of interest on the edge of the square is the **Bermuda National Trust Museum** ⊕ (open Mon–Sat 10am–4pm; entrance fee; tel: 297 1423), formerly the Globe Hotel and, for the duration of the American Civil War,

the headquarters of the Confederate agent, Major Norman Walker. The Union was represented in St George's by a consul, Charles Maxwell Allen, whose fairly frequent abuse at the hands of locals who favoured the Confederacy did not dissuade him from finally settling in Bermuda after the war.

Local support for the southern states did not necessarily reflect high moral principles. There were fortunes to be made out of blockade-running trade with the south, a prospect that turned St George's into a rip-roaring magnet for adventurers, some in the "gentleman" class, others not. "Dr Blackburn" was definitely in the latter category. Ostensibly a philanthropic physician, he was actually a Confederate agent who collected the infected clothing of the victims of a yellow fever epidemic then sweeping Bermuda, with a view to making poisonous presents of it to the civilian population in the North.

The museum's exhibit entitled "Rogues and Runners: Bermuda and the American

LEFT: inside the Bermuda National Trust Museum.
RIGHT: mind your head in Featherbed Alley.

Civil War" examines the period when the island made a small fortune from the blockade-running trade. Also featured is a video, "Bermuda: Centre of the Atlantic," which uses rarely seen paintings and documents to tell the story of the island and the forces that shaped its history. Another display is a model of the *Sea Venture*, the ship that brought the first accidental settlers to Bermuda.

St Peter's on the hill

The beautifully preserved **St Peter's** ❶ above King's Square, on York Street, was no ordinary parish church during Bermuda's early days; more often than not, it was centre stage for bruising battles that might have nothing to do with God and religion. The conflict between the established Church and the Puritans in England did surface in ferocious local microcosm, but there were also purely secular vendettas that often exploded in the middle of a service, leading to brawls. The church was later used as a courthouse for a while, the scaffold being conveniently situated down the hill on Ordnance Island.

The first church on the site, a thatched hut, was replaced by a more substantial structure in 1619. The basis of the existing building goes back to 1713. One way or another, St Peter's is said to be "the oldest Anglican church in continuous use in the western hemisphere".

The altar is of local cedar, much darkened since it was made in 1624, the year before the parish was presented with its silver chalice by the Bermuda Company in London. The triple-decker pulpit is 17th century, as is a massive set of communion silver, the gift of King William III and engraved with his initials. The walls are lined with commemorative tablets whose inscriptions provided a colourful, though necessarily selective, commentary on the passing show. A burial ground for enslaved Bermudians can be found in the church yard.

St Peter's was very nearly lost to future generations. Its condition in the 19th cen-

BELOW: the Unfinished Church, like a spiritual *Marie Celeste*.

Map
on page
256

tury led to a campaign for something rather better, and in 1874 work commenced on what was to be a fine neo-Gothic cathedral. As the roof went on and the tower rose, so did the cost. The restoration of St Peter's began to look more and more sensible and the new project was summarily abandoned.

The ghostly hulk of the serene and soaring **Unfinished Church** ❶, a spiritual *Marie Celeste* now sprouting undergrowth between blocks of masonry just as the workmen left them, has assumed the nobility of an ancient monument and is photographed by visitors more assiduously than would have been the case had it ever been finished.

Bermuda's gunpowder plot

The **State House** ❻ (open Wed 10am–4pm), east of King's Square, was constructed in 1620, the first stone building in Bermuda. To the discomfort of Assembly members, it served a secondary role as a gunpowder magazine. The governor was prevailed upon to place this potential bomb elsewhere and, with a fine disregard for his own safety, had it installed in the grounds of his residence on Retreat Hill.

The danger came from a wholly different quarter – from the Tuckers, who, in concert with others, stole the powder in order to sell it to a grateful General Washington in the American Revolution. The enraged governor promptly restored what little powder was left to its former place in the State House, pointedly above the heads of some of those whom he suspected of complicity.

St George's lost its State House when the capital was moved to Hamilton, and the building was given over to the Masonic Lodge at a peppercorn rent, a ceremony that is re-enacted annually with much pomp and circumstance. The present **post office** also has connections with the American Revolution: it was a hell-hole of a prison for captured rebels.

Near to the State House at the junction of Water and York streets the **Heritage**

BELOW: red, white and blue: St George's had connections with the American Revolution.

Museum ❶ (open Tues–Sat 10am–3pm; entrance fee; tel: 297 4126), housed in the Samaritans Lodge, traces the history of black people in Bermuda. The Independent Order of Good Samaritans and the Daughters of Samaria, founded in the 19th century, were among the island's various benevolent organisations. This small community museum includes replica artefacts such as a freedom cottage used by emancipated slaves, art and historical displays.

Garden memorial

Not far from the State House is the **Somers Garden ⓜ** (open daily 8am–4pm), a favourite spot for local artists. The garden is named after Sir George Somers, the admiral who was among the Jamestown settlers wrecked on Bermuda in 1609. It is his statue, arms aloft on sighting Bermuda after the fearful passage in *Sea Venture*, that stands near the replica of *Deliverance*.

Although Sir George was paid the tribute of having the Somers Islands named after him (before they became "Bermuda"), the disposal of his remains after his death in St George's in 1610 was not as ceremonial as might have been expected. His heart was removed for local burial; the rest of him had to be shipped back to England disguised as general cargo in deference to seafaring superstition about transporting bodies. Some years later, Governor Butler discovered an overgrown patch where the heart had been buried. He put matters right with a stone tomb and an epitaph of his own composition.

A second Somers memorial in the park was added in 1876 by one of Butler's successors, Governor Lefroy. A rather macabre exhumation of the Somers tomb in 1819 produced a broken bottle, a pebble and a few bones.

A little cottage – the **Gwynn House** – stands well back from the road in the western part of the town as a monument to less glorious memories. In 1826 Joseph Gwynn, a hot-tempered tailor, armed himself with a pistol to settle a score with the

BELOW: the State House is believed to be the first stone building in Bermuda.

Map on page 256

local magistrate, who had just sent his son to prison. Unable to find the magistrate, Gwynn shot dead his blameless brother-in-law. Gwynn was seen leaving the scene of the crime and it was never doubted that he was guilty.

He seemed to vanish, however, and the elderly Mrs Gwynn purported to be as nonplussed as anyone else. She took her loss badly, refusing to leave a rocking chair for days on end while she nursed her grief. A soldier on guard at Fort George happened to train his telescope on the distraught woman and witness a furtive ritual whereby she checked that the coast was clear and pushed the rocking chair aside to reveal a trap door. A pair of hands reaching for a plate of food gave the game away.

The police hurried round but Mrs Gwynn, back in her customary position, refused to budge. She was lifted in her chair and the hapless Gwynn fished out. The *Bermuda Gazette* described how he was "launched into Eternity" at the con-

clusion of a trial, the execution being staged, as was often the case, at the scene of the crime, near the entrance to the Somers Garden.

The **Printery** in Featherbed Alley is a historical landmark in its own right – the ancient press is kept in working order – but there is additional interest in the small shuttered window in the side of the building, which was once used as a jail. Next door is the **Featherbed Art Studio** run by artists Charles Zuill and Emma Ingham Denouk (tel: 297-2468 for an appointment).

A short distance from the Printery are the **St George's Historical Society Museum** Ⓝ (3 Featherbed Alley; open Apr–Oct Mon–Sat 10am–4pm; Nov and Jan–Mar 11am–3pm; entrance fee; tel: 293-0423), with its fine cedar furniture and interesting relics, and the **Old Rectory** Ⓞ (open Nov–Mar: Wed noon–5pm) on Broad Alley, built in 1705 by a repentant pirate and later, but only temporarily, used as a rectory. The Rectory's churchyard contains many old

BELOW: tall palms provide shade in Somers Garden.

Spirit of Bermuda

As any Bermudian will tell you, Bermuda takes its daily greetings very seriously. In restaurants, in offices, in shops and in banks, work cannot begin until "Good Mornings" are said. Emergencies make no difference – no greeting given, no offer of help. Just an expectant stare. However, even Bermudians were surprised to see a beaming figure at the Crow Lane roundabout waving frantically and yelling out to passers by and motorists coming into Hamilton, early one morning. Many people called him crazy or foolish. That was in 1983 and octogenarian retired bus driver, Johnny Barnes, has been greeting people on their way to work ever since. Each weekday, at 5am exactly, he arrives at the roundabout, and remains there until 10am when he picks up his umbrella and takes the bus back home to Paget where he lives with his wife of more than 60 years, Belbina.

He's always smartly dressed, sports an immaculately pressed shirt, trousers and a

wide brimmed straw hat, which shades his friendly face and curly white beard. And he always gives individual greetings to the myriad faces caught in the snarl of traffic. "I love you darling", he calls, blowing kisses to a woman negotiating the roundabout. "God bless you, God loves you", he adds. Sometimes schoolchildren give him hibiscus flowers from the back window of their cars. Occasionally, people noticing wear and tear on his jacket or his hat supply him with new ones. And sometimes volunteers stand with him holding placards publicising their favourite charities.

Far from thinking he's crazy, these days people have come to rely on him. He's a fixture, a part of the island's early-morning rhythm, no matter the weather. If it's wet, he dons his raincoat and pulls up his hood. Johnny has become a symbol of cheerful perseverance – more than that, a national institution. He's Bermuda's official but unpaid greeter.

Some years ago he failed to show up at the roundabout. A frisson rippled through the community. Was Johnny all right? Was he sick? How could the day go right without his ebullient welcome? As it happened, he had spent the day in hospital undergoing a minor operation. Soon afterwards he was back on the job. But that day without Johnny precipitated the Spirit of Bermuda charity, which commissioned local sculptor Desmond Fountain to cast a full-sized bronze statue of Johnny. Originally, the idea was to create the statue after his death. But, as he explains, "I told them, 'You want to do something for me? Do it for me while I'm alive and can enjoy it.'" Some spoilsports took exception to this – why spend some $70,000 honouring a man who's still alive? Sir George Somers, who accidentally got the Bermuda settlement started in 1609, had to wait 375 years before his statue was unveiled in St. George's. But Johnny's has been erected on the side of East Broadway. And a great likeness of him it is too.

But whatever possessed him all those years ago to suddenly stop and say hi to commuters, there's no chance he'll retire from this calling any time soon. He says, "it was the Good Lord who put me here and it's the Good Lord who'll decide when it's enough." ❏

LEFT: Johnny Barnes and the *Spirit of Bermuda*.

Map on page 256

headstones; look for the slaves' graves to the west, behind the wall. Though the Rectory is a National Trust property it is also a private residence.

St David's

The geography of eastern Bermuda was turned topsy-turvy by the landfill operation that created the World War II military base and **Bermuda airport**. Many of the islands around St David's were swallowed whole; the shape of St David's changed forever.

The US Naval Air Station, as it was called, opened in 1941 with a 99-year lease, but closed in 1995, and the 700-acre (283-hectare) site is under development by the Bermuda Land Development Company (BLDC). The developers have dubbed the site "Southside", and hope to lure tenants for the various buildings of the former base – the 24,000-sq. ft (2,230-sq. metre) Channel House, the similarly sized Lilyfield Place and the much smaller Corregidor House. The BLDC points out

that rentals are as much at 50 percent below those in Hamilton, and, as a further inducement, advertise the nearby parklands, walking trails, tennis courts and lovely beaches, as well as the proximity to the airport and St George's.

The closure of the US base noticeably affected employment in the surrounding area. Local people had for years worked on the base which had its own school, hospital, theatre and other facilities. This was the only place in Bermuda to have a MacDonald's restaurant, so when the Americans left the burgers went too.

St David's Island ❷ is the site of Bermuda's oldest residence. Called the **Carter House** ❸ (call St George's Visitor Information Centre, tel: 297 8000 for opening times), it was the home of the descendants of one of the "three kings" *(see Beginnings, page 39)* and a perfect example of the distinctive indigenous architecture. No one knows exactly when the house was constructed, but historians speculate that it was built *circa* 1670.

BELOW: watery view of St David's Island.

Map
on page
256

As the house was on the grounds of the US Naval Air Station, access to it was limited to Wednesday afternoon, and special arrangements had to be made in advance. The air base maintained the 17th-century house, and when the base closed, the future of the house was in doubt. In 1998, the St David's Historical Society was formed for the purpose of obtaining the house and opening it as a museum. The Society pays the government an annual rental of one lily bulb – following an ancient tradition that has the tenants of the State House in St George's presenting an annual rental of one peppercorn and the Maritime Museum making an annual payment of one cannonball. Historical Society officials and local people raised more than $130,000, used to restore Carter House, now a museum. It is estimated that another $600,000 will be required to run it. To the house's collection of period furnishings, the Society has added portraits of some old St David's Islanders – portraits borrowed from the Masterworks Collection. One particularly appealing exhibit is the late Claude Pitcher's passport. It has just one stamp in it – Philadelphia – but he used the blank pages for his shopping lists, which included every day items such as: "dettol", "m. magnesia" and "Geritol tablets".

Touring the East End

Using St George's as a base to explore the east end of Bermuda on a scooter is a sound proposition. The excursions possible from the town are either a circular drive which begins clockwise around St George's Harbour, then turns back on itself past **Gates Fort** (Cut Road; open dawn to dusk; free). Next is **Buildings Bay** (where *Deliverance* was built) and finally to Fort St Catherine. Or, take the road that follows the southern shore of the harbour across to **St David's lighthouse** ❹ (Lighthouse Hill; opening times vary; tel: 236 5902), without encroaching on the former naval base land. The striking red-and-white beacon not only guides ships, it is also a popular lookout spot during the Newport-Bermuda boat race.

The reward at the end of the latter journey ought to be a meal at the splendidly eccentric **Dennis's Hideaway** (Cashew City Road; tel: 297-0044), where Sea Egg, son of the original proprietor, the late Dennis Lamb, serves up a selection of specialities, notably shark hash, conch fritters and mussel stew.

Bermuda was fortified for over 400 years with the finest defences available; as the islands were never attacked in earnest, many of them survive in exceptional condition and, as an example of 19th-century military architecture, stately **Fort St Catherine** ❺ (15 Coot Pond Road; open daily 10am–4.30pm; entrance fee; tel: 297 1920) cannot be bettered. The 11-inch (28-cm) guns, capable of firing 400 lb (180 kg) projectiles, are in excellent order, as are the mechanical magazines which fed them. A video, shown at frequent intervals, provides a fascinating insight into the development of this "Gibraltar of the West". ❑

LEFT: a smile from Elliot Darrell. **RIGHT:** St David's Lighthouse.

Map on page 168

Island in Harrington Sound as a hermit's retreat as rather wasteful. One half of **Ordnance Island** in St George's, where the *Deliverance* replica stands, was once known as "Gallows Island", handy for those sentenced to death in St Peter's Church, when that was used as a courthouse, or afterwards in the State House.

The island was originally two, and these formed the basis of Bermuda's second example of sharp real estate practice, the first being Governor Daniel Tucker's devious dealings in the so-called "overplus" scandal. An American entrepreneur bought the islands, which were individually not much use for anything bar a scaffold, filled in the channel separating them and sold his creation at a vast profit. The British Army later took it over as an ammunition dump.

A second Gallows Island, which was renamed **Gibbet**, is to be found at the entrance to Flatts Inlet. In 1681, a slave called Indian John, who had been taken prisoner in New England, was responsible for one of Bermuda's rather less compe-

tent capital crimes. He broke into the Orange Grove mansion, stole a gun and hat, started a fire and crept outside again with the intention of shooting the occupants as they fled. Instead, the family woke up and put out the flames without difficulty.

A look in the shrubbery revealed Indian John wearing his new hat. He made a full confession, leaving Governor Florentius Seymour to do the necessary. Indian John was to be "executed at or by the Gibbet at the Flatts mouth and there to have his head cut off and be quartered and the head and quarters put upon poles at such remarkable places as the sheriff shall think fit".

A pole that is visible from the road running past the island is said to be the very one on which Indian John's head was displayed. To suggest otherwise – it looks like an ordinary pole holding up a navigation light – may be construed as the sort of scepticism which reduces the number of Bermuda's islands to less than the magical 365. On an even fishier note, Gibbet is a rewarding site for snorkelling. ❏

BELOW: view of the islands.

Map on page 168

THE SMALL ISLANDS

The collection of islands that makes up Bermuda have a colourful past, used as sites for early fortifications, a prison and execution spots. Today many remain unspoilt and uninhabited, protected as nature reserves

When Spanish sailors in Christopher Columbus's time came up with the name "Isle of Devils", their use of the singular noun when referring to what were manifestly many islands set a precedent whereby the early names – e.g. Bermudas or Bermuda, Somers Island or Summers Islands – were casually either singular or plural. Consistency was introduced with general recognition of "Bermuda", and that was taken to mean the main islands lying in close formation in the shape of a fish hook and all the smaller ones.

Every-day islands

The exact number of smaller islands was a folkloric toss-up, rather like the number of churches on a Greek island. In such cases the claim is often "365" – fortuitously, of course, one for each day of the year. Sure enough, Bermuda was said to have 365 islands.

It is not in the spirit of such claims to go out and coldly count the things, although in Bermuda the writer Terry Tucker, never one to leave a stone unturned, almost did. She arrived at 120 islands, some masquerading under more than one name. A government survey using different criteria later settled on 181 islands, Cockroach Rock being just large enough to escape the ignominy of being classed as a rock.

A typical complication in getting everyone to agree on the number is **Cooper's Island**, which features in Bermuda's history as a suspected treasure trove and favourite nesting place of the amazing cahow, but ceased to exist as an independent entity when St David's was expanded to accommodate the naval base and airport. Nearby **Longbird Island** suffered a similar fate. Prewar air traffic consisted of flying boats which used **Darrell Island** as a base.

As Mrs Tucker demonstrated in her survey *(Islands)*, a copy of which may be consulted in the Historical Society Museum in Hamilton, the small islands collectively have a large and varied story to tell. There are no organised island tours as such. The ferries that ply the Great Sound between Hamilton and the western parishes pass close to some islands, while visits to others may be possible during a scuba-diving or sailing trip.

The first settlements were based at the eastern end of Bermuda (the "three kings" preferred **Smith's Island** but were nevertheless overruled in favour of St George's), and the islands straddling the entrances to St George's and Castle Harbours had to be fortified quickly because a Spanish invasion was thought to be imminent. The first fort to taste

PRECEDING PAGES: sea and sand; sailing through the small islands. **LEFT:** isolated shores are one of Bermuda's attractions. **RIGHT:** Oriental mystery on Ordnance Island.

action, when two Spanish merchantmen poked their noses in, was the one that then became known as King's Castle on **Castle Island**.

The result for the home team could easily have gone the other way: only one cannon was in working order, the ammunition stock amounted to three cannon balls, and the floor was perilously covered in spilled gunpowder which, amid the bangs and flashes and noise, miraculously did not explode.

Things were apt to go wrong on Castle Island. A rally to drum up support for the hopeless cause of Captain Miles Kendall, a drunkard seconded to the post of governor in 1615, was to be kicked off by the ceremonial firing of a cannon. Kendall's campaign manager, as it were, a Lieutenant Wood, sailed over to the island to confirm the arrangements. He checked the readiness of the cannon by poking a metal-tipped pike down the barrel. His scraping caused a spark which ignited the charge. The efficient Wood,

who could not have been in a worse position, was blasted bodily into the channel.

He was pulled out of the water in a sorry state and died the next day "to the extreme passionate grief of the Governor and the dismay of his confederates". On a later occasion, a night-firing exercise at King's Castle sent shells whistling around a startled Bolivian warship that was innocently in the vicinity.

Fort Cunningham was constructed on **Paget Island** as a precaution against the newly independent, belligerent United States. It was designed as "the strongest colonial structure of its kind in the British domain". The cost of importing millions of bricks, iron and stone from England because the local limestone was considered too fragile caused members of the House of Commons to ask whether Fort Cunningham was being made of gold. The forts on Castle and Paget Islands are not readily accessible, but a telephone call to the curator at Fort St Catherine will advise on the possibility of special arrangements.

BELOW: Denslow's designs from around 1900.

Map on page 168

Off to see the Wizard of Oz

Visitors canny enough to select a renegade captain on one of the glass-bottomed boat trips might find themselves recipients of a journey through unexpected waters.

Locations pointed out on this trip can be fascinating, like the rock called Fern Island, but more commonly known as **Sin Island**, because of its popularity as a venue for yachting parties, and the privately owned **Denslow's Island**. Though it is today owned by the Bluck family, Denslow's Island is named for William Wallace Denslow, who lived in Bermuda around the turn of the 20th century. Denslow was the underrated artist who created – perhaps in the large house with its handsome tower which he built – the characters depicted in *The Wizard of Oz*.

The Wonderful Wizard of Oz, as the book was first known, was written in 1900 by talented journalist-cum-children's-writer L. Frank Baum. The success of this book was due in no small measure to the distinctive characters drawn by Denslow,

BELOW: W.W. Denslow's remarkably enduring characters.

the first person to visualise Dorothy, the Cowardly Lion, the Scarecrow and the Tin Woodman. Denslow's highly individual drawings have been remarkably enduring, establishing forever the way these characters are envisioned.

The popularity of *Oz* produced 13 sequels by Baum, many additions to the series by another author after Baum's death, several stage productions and, of course, the 1939 movie starring Judy Garland. In every one of these cases, excepting a grown-up Dorothy to allow for Garland's singing talent, Denslow's influence on the characters can clearly be seen.

Visitors under their own steam in self-drive or skippered hire boats ought to make enquiries before landing on any of the small islands. Barging through a nature reserve could upset years of painstaking work; **Nonsuch Island** is a case in point: before the docking facilities were damaged during Hurricane Fabian in 2003, access to the 14-acre (6-hectare) island was possible, but only on a guided tour run every

Thursday by the Bermuda Biological Station. Unfortunately Nonsuch Island is currently closed to visitors. **Castle Island** and its neighbouring islets in the East End are part of a nature reserve set up to protect the area's rare sea birds. The approved campgrounds are on **Port's**, **White's**, **Darrell** and **Coney islands**.

Island interns

Passengers on the Hamilton to Somerset Bridge ferry pass, on the port side, **Burt** and **Darrell islands**. The former was once used as an isolation station for passengers arriving from smallpox areas and at the turn of the 19th century, together with Darrell and others in the group, as a camp for Boer prisoners of war. Most of them seemed to pass their time happily carving souvenirs, which found a ready market among tourists.

One of them, however, decided to swim for freedom. It is hard to say what he had in mind, particularly when he had gone as far as he could on Bermuda and, poised on the beach for the last leg, realised there was still some way to go before reaching Pretoria.

The end of the war created the problem of Boers who refused to take the oath of allegiance, which would have seen them on a ship home, wouldn't take jobs locally, and declined offers of free passage to the port of their choice. They were dubbed the "Irreconcilables" and remained a lugubrious presence in their wide-brimmed hats and long beards until forcibly removed in 1903.

The Boer prisoners left behind on Burt Island the grave of a man named Skeeter. He had murdered his wife and thrown her body into the sea weighted with an 80-lb (36-kg) boulder. A hurricane freakishly washed the body ashore, the boulder still attached. The judge stipulated that Burt's should be the place of execution and burial and added the provision that the boulder in question should serve as the condemned man's headstone.

Governors and judges made full use of the islands in this way and would probably have regarded the use of **Trunk**

LEFT: footsteps to nowhere.
BELOW: shading from the sun.

INSIGHT GUIDES
TRAVEL TIPS

CONTENTS

Getting Acquainted

The Place 282
Climate 282
Geography 282
Government 282
Culture & Customs 282

Planning the Trip

Getting There 283
Visas 283
Entry Regulations 283
Extensions of Stay 284
Accommodation 284
Tax..............................284
Animals 284
Drugs..........................284
Offensive Weapons......285
Health 285
Money 285
What to Bring 285
Public Holidays............285
What to Wear 286
Tourist Offices 286

Practical Tips

Useful Addresses 286
Disabled Visitors..........286
Business Hours 286
Banks..........................286
Religious Services 286
The Media 286
Postal Services............287

Phone, Fax & Internet ..287
Dialling Codes 287
Emergencies 287
Medical Services 287
Consulates 287

Getting Around

Orientation 288
Airport/City..................288
Public Transport 288
Private Transport 289
Travel with Children 289
Guided Tours 289

Where to Stay

Accommodation 289
Hotel Categories..........290
Resort Hotels 290
Small Hotels................291
Cottage Colonies 291
Guesthouses 293
Apartments 293

Where to Eat

Asian 294
Bermudian 294
Continental..................295
Island Cuisine..............295
Italian..........................295
Mexican 295
Pubs............................296
Afternoon Tea 296
Coffee Shops 296

Sites

Museums & Historic
  Buildings....................296
Forts 297
Other Attractions 298
Tourism Website............298

Sport & Leisure

Festivals......................298
Spectator Sports 299
Walks..........................300
Nature Reserves..........300
Beaches......................300
Watersports 300

Nightlife

Clubs, Bars & Hotels....300

Shopping

What to Buy 301
Where to Buy 301
Export Procedures 301

Further Reading

General 302
Other Insight Guides....302

Art/Photo Credits 303
Index 304

Getting Acquainted

Area 21 sq. miles (54 sq. km)
Population 66,000 (2007 estimate). Around 55 percent are black, 34 percent are white, 6 percent mixed heritage and three percent are Asian or other ethnicity.
Capital Hamilton
Language English
Religion 23 percent Anglican, 15 percent Roman Catholic, 11 percent African Methodist Episcopal, seven percent Seventh Day Adventists.
Time Zone GMT -4 hours. Daylight Saving Time is in effect from the second Sunday in April until the first Sunday in November.
Currency Bermuda dollar (Bd$). US dollars also accepted.
Weights and Measures Although the metric system is usually used in shops, the imperial system is employed in everyday conversation.
Electricity 110 volts, 60 cycles (as in US and Canada).
International Dialling Code +441

Climate

Bermuda is a sub-tropical island, and the Gulf Stream, flowing between Bermuda and North America, keeps the climate temperate. The island has two seasons and two "changes of season". The heat rarely rises above 85°F (29.5°C) and there is often a cool breeze at night.

Bermuda's spring-like weather lasts from mid-December to late March, with an average temperature of around 70°F (21°C). In December and January it is often still warm enough to go swimming, though Bermudians don't tend to take to the sea until after 24 May. Summer temperatures prevail from May to mid-November; the warmest weather is from July to September. Rain showers are a possibility any time of the year.

Geography

Bermuda is 600 miles (965 km) east of Cape Hatteras (North Carolina) on the east coast of the US. It consists of seven main islands linked by bridges, and is 22 miles (35 km) long and 21 sq. miles (54 sq. km) in area. The widest point is 2 miles (3 km) across.

Government

Bermuda's government is based on the British Parliamentary system. Queen Elizabeth II is the head of state, represented by a governor appointed in London. The governor selects the premier, nominating the leader of the party elected with the majority of votes. Considerable power rests with the premier, who, in turn, appoints a cabinet.

Culture & Customs

Bermuda feels very British, in some ways even more so than Britain itself. People on the island drive on the left and call soccer "football", many policemen wear hard-topped "bobby" helmets, and the British monarch's birthday is celebrated as an official holiday.

However, Bermuda is also very American in character. Most of its consumables are shipped from the US East Coast. The currency is pegged to the US dollar, and many Bermudians head to the States for weekend getaways.

Bermudians acknowledge anyone they meet, from close friends to total strangers, with a "Good Morning" or "Good Evening". They expect the greeting to be returned in the same friendly spirit. For visitors, especially those from large cities, responding can feel uncomfortable, until they discover that this simple courteous gesture reaps dividends, including ensuring better service.

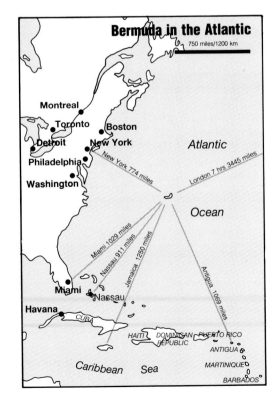

Bermuda in the Atlantic
750 miles/1200 km

Montreal
Toronto
Boston
Detroit
New York
Philadelphia
Washington
New York 774 miles
Atlantic
London 7 hrs 3445 miles
Ocean
Miami 1029 miles
Nassau 911 miles
Jamaica 1250 miles
Antigua 1069 miles
Miami
Nassau
Havana
CUBA
HAITI
DOMINICAN REPUBLIC
PUERTO RICO
ANTIGUA
MARTINIQUE
BARBADOS
Caribbean Sea

Planning the Trip

By Air

Bermuda can be reached in less than two hours from the East Coast of North America and in less than seven hours from the UK. There is a baggage allowance of two checked-in pieces of luggage and one carry-on bag of specified sizes and weights. Airline schedules are subject to change.

From the US:
All flights are non-stop.
American Airlines – from New York, JFK (daily) and Miami (Wednesday–Sunday).
Continental – from Newark (daily).
Delta – from Boston (daily) and Atlanta (daily).
Jet Blue – from New York (daily).
US Airways – from New York, La Guardia (daily), Boston (daily) and Philadelphia (daily), Washington (Sunday and Thursday).
USA 3000 – from Baltimore (Tuesday and Friday), Newark (Tuesday and Friday) and Philadelphia (Wednesday and Saturday).

From Canada:
Air Canada – daily non-stop from Toronto and weekly non-stop from Halifax (during the summer) with connecting services throughout Canada, the US and Europe.

From the UK:
British Airways – non-stop from London, Gatwick (daily).
Zoom – from London Gatwick (Monday and Friday).

By Sea

It is advisable to contact a travel agent for current information. Bermuda is a popular cruise ship destination. It is rare to be able to book a one-way passage on a ship, but ask your agent about cruise-and-stay options.

Cruise season is May–October. All the major cruise lines sail to Bermuda – including Royal Caribbean, Norwegian Cruise Lines, Carnival, Costa Cruises and Fred Olsen. Most cruises calling in Bermuda depart from US ports. Ships from other cruise lines call in Bermuda on fall and spring "repositioning" trips from ports along the US eastern seaboard.

A **return** or **onward ticket** or other document of onward travel to a country which, at that time, the passenger has right of entry, is required by all visitors. Most bona-fide visitors with a confirmed return ticket and a place of accommodation will have no difficulties with Bermuda Immigration Control. There is a special Secondary Immigration Control section at the airport to deal with any unusual circumstances posed by arriving visitors.
Bermuda immigration authorities may restrict the length of stay, generally three weeks. For example, in the case of passengers arriving with an open return ticket, a time limit will be imposed.

A valid passport is the required entry document for all visitors. **Passports** are required by all visitors from countries that, in turn, need a passport for re-entry purposes or for entry through another country to which the passenger has right of entry.

Visitors from the US are required to produce a current **US Passport** when entering Bermuda. All persons travelling by air between the US, Canada and Bermuda are required to present a valid passport, non-citizens of the US must also carry a US Green Card and a US re-entry permit to enter or re-enter the United States. Check the State Department website: www.travel.state.gov/travel for detailed information.

Visitors from Canada are required to have in their possession a **valid Canadian passport**. Or, for people born outside Canada, a **Canadian Certificate of Citizenship** or **Canadian Permanent Resident Card**.

Visitors from the European Union (including the UK) are required to produce a **valid passport**.

Persons wishing to enter Bermuda for the purpose of residence and/or **employment** or for indefinite periods will not be permitted to land, unless they have prior authorisation from the immigration authorities to do so. It is illegal for visitors to seek work while in Bermuda; those who do so risk deportation.

Married women whose identification documents are published in their maiden name but who are travelling under their married name should carry a marriage certificate or certified copy as proof of identity.

Children travelling alone or with their parents must present a valid passport. Adults travelling with children who are not their own must

Visas are not required by nationals of Australia, New Zealand, EU countries, Canada and the US.

For permanent residents of the US or Canada, who were not born in either country, but hold a valid US Alien Registration Card or valid proof of Canadian Landed Immigrant Status or resident status plus a valid passport, a visa to enter Bermuda is not required. However, persons requiring visas to enter other countries on departure from Bermuda must be in possession of the respective visas before arriving in Bermuda.

For other nationalities, visas to enter Bermuda may be obtained from the Visa Section of any British Embassy or other British Foreign Service representation abroad, for example, a consulate.

have the child(ren)'s travel documents as noted above and a letter from the child(ren)'s parent(s) authorising that the child(ren) are allowed to be accompanied by the respective adult for the visit to Bermuda.

Visit www.bermudatourism.com for up-to-date visa and passport information.

Extensions of Stay

Applications to extend a length of stay must be made in person at the Immigration Headquarters at 30 Parliament Street, Hamilton, tel: (441) 295-5151. A fee may be charged for processing an application.

Tax

On Arrival

Visitors entering Bermuda may claim up to a Bd$30 duty-free allowance for gifts, and import 50 cigars, 200 cigarettes, 0.5kg tobacco, 1 litre of wine and 1 litre of spirits.

Incoming visitors may bring duty-free, all clothes and articles for their personal use, including sports equipment, cameras, golf bags, etc. Visitors are also permitted to bring in duty-free unlimited quantities of cooked, dried or otherwise preserved meat and approximately 50 lbs (22 kg) of fresh meat,

Accommodation

Anyone arriving in Bermuda without **accommodation booked prior to departure** runs the risk of being turned away by immigration officials at Bermuda International Airport, who regularly enquire as to where you will be staying.

Always arrange your holiday through a reputable travel agent or, if booking independently, be sure to secure proof of accommodation before leaving home. Keep the address to hand, especially if you are staying with friends who live on the island.

although it and other foodstuffs may be dutiable up to 22.25 percent of their value.

The importation of all fresh fruits, plants and vegetables is strictly regulated and these may be held for inspection. You can download a copy of the official Customs Regulations brochure from www.bermudatourism.com.

On Departure

All visitors not in direct transit are taxable under the Passenger Tax Act of 1972. The departure tax for air passengers is Bd$25 and Bd$80 for ship passengers; the tax is included in the airfare and ship passage, respectively. Children under the age of two are exempt.

US Customs pre-clearance is available in Bermuda for all scheduled flights. All passengers departing to the US must fill out written declaration forms before clearing US Customs in Bermuda. These forms are available at all hotels, travel agencies and airlines on the island. Be sure to arrive at the airport at least two hours before departure, as clearing US Customs is a very time-consuming business.

Bermuda Duty Free Ltd operates two airport shops, both offering wines, spirits, perfumes, cosmetics, jewellery and clothing plus gourmet products and cigarettes.

The stores are situated on the US departures concourse and inside the international departure lounge. Executive lounges are also available for first and business class passengers travelling on US carriers and British Airways.

Visitors are permitted to buy merchandise, duty-free, up to the following amounts:

US citizens: purchases worth up to $800 after 48 hours on the island and every subsequent 30 days. Duty-free allowances vary from state to state, but US citizens may import 100 cigars and 200 cigarettes and, if over 21, 1 litre (33.8 oz) of liquor every 30 days. Cuban cigars, available in Bermuda, may not be taken to the US.

Canadian citizens: purchases

worth up to $300 after 48 hours and any number of trips per year, or $750 after seven days each calendar year.

UK citizens: purchases worth up to £145. Plus, 200 cigarettes or 100 cigarillos or 50 cigars or 250 gms of tobacco, as well as 1 litre of spirits or 2 litres of fortified wine and 2 litres of table wine. Plant materials for propagating in the UK cannot be imported without prior permission from British authorities.

Animals

Animals arriving without proper documentation will be refused entry and returned to the port of origin. There is no quarantine facility. For information consult Bermuda's Customs Regulations brochure *(see above)* or contact:
Department of Environmental Protection, PO Box HM 834, Hamilton HM CX, Bermuda.
Tel: 236-4201
Fax: 236-7582
www.animals.gov.bm

Drugs

Importation of, possession of, or dealing with unlawful drugs (including marijuana) is an offence. Anyone contravening the Misuse of Drugs Act is liable to fines of up to Bd$1 million or 10 years to life imprisonment or both. Conviction on indictment carries a maximum penalty of a fine or imprisonment for life, or both. Sniffer dogs are used at both the airport and cruise ship terminals.

Customs officers may, at their discretion, conduct body searches for drugs and other smuggled goods. Bermuda considers itself serious about controlling the importation of drugs. Visitors in possession of even small amounts for personal use may be prosecuted for importation.

Bermuda will not accept medical use as a defence in an importation charge.

Visitors may bring with them sufficient prescription drugs for the duration of their stay. All medication should be in the original containers – do not bring unlabelled pills or herbal remedies into the country.

Offensive Weapons

The importation of any firearm, part of a firearm or ammunition into Bermuda is forbidden except under the authority of a licence granted by the Commissioner of Police. Even toy guns and replicas may not be carried onto the island.

Spear-guns and a variety of dangerous weapons including Verey pistols or signal guns are treated as firearms, but antique weapons manufactured 100 years or more ago can be imported if the importer can show they are genuine antiques. It is a serious criminal offence to import firearms or ammunition into Bermuda without a licence, and anyone seeking to do so may be imprisoned or heavily fined. Other forbidden weapons include throwing knives, spiked wristbands, swords, crossbows and concealed knives.

Health

No vaccinations are required. Visitors on a short-term holiday have little to fear when it comes to health matters. The island is very clean and all beaches, hotels and restaurants meticulously maintained. Despite the island's "garden" appearance, the climate is quite kind even to hay fever sufferers; pollens of most noxious weeds tend to be blown out to sea.

Snakes are non-existent, owing to Bermuda's isolated position in the middle of the Atlantic. However, don't be startled by the shy, harmless lizards you will see.

The chirping noise you hear on warm nights is the whistling of tree frogs, also harmless, as are the extremely unattractive toads and large brown cockroaches that thrive in the dampness.

Swimmers should beware of two sea creatures that can cause particularly nasty stings: the red sponge and the Portuguese man-of-war. Seek immediate medical attention if you are stung. The sea egg (urchin) leaves a series of pinprick-sized holes in the feet if stepped on, so be sure to tread with care or to wear plastic shoes in the sea.

The island's most serious long-term health problem is Aids. Intravenous drug users and homosexuals have been the main victims; but, as elsewhere in the world, contraction of the virus through heterosexual activity is increasing. Avoid unprotected sex.

Money

Legal tender is the Bermuda dollar (Bd$), which is divided into 100 cents. The Bermuda dollar is pegged, through gold, to the US dollar: Bd$1 = US$1. US currency is interchangeable with Bermudian and is accepted in shops, restaurants and hotels, with many cashiers returning change to visitors in US dollars – a helpful gesture which negates the need to change money again at the airport if heading to the US. Bermuda currency is not sold and cannot be purchased at banks or exchange bureaux outside Bermuda. Automated teller machines (ATM) dispense Bermuda dollars.

Exchange rates for all other currencies are liable to the usual fluctuation; current rates can be obtained from any bank and many hotels. Credit card transactions or any other banking matters involving foreign currencies are subject to these exchange rates. Major credit cards such as American Express, MasterCard, Visa and Diners Club are accepted at most places, and can be used to obtain cash at all local bank branches.

Traveller's cheques in US dollars are accepted everywhere, and with much more grace than in most cities in the US. Proof of identity is rarely required, but carry your passport just in case.

Public Holidays

Bermuda observes **New Year's Day**, **Good Friday**, **Labour Day** (first Monday in September), **Remembrance Day** (11 November), **Christmas Day** and **Boxing Day** (26 December) as holidays.

Public holidays falling on a Saturday or Sunday are normally observed the following Monday. Please note that on these holidays all shops and businesses, and many restaurants, close.

Three public holidays are particularly special to Bermuda. The specific days may alter slightly from year to year, but tend to be celebrated around the time of the dates shown:

- 24 May: **Bermuda Day**
- 18 June: **Queen's Birthday**
- 2 and 3 August: **Cup Match** (see page 105); on the first day of the event **Emancipation Day** is celebrated, while the second is **Somers Day**.

What to Bring

During certain seasons, Bermuda imitates its mother country, Britain, in having a variable climate. Islands have notoriously unpredictable weather patterns, and mid-November until late December and late March to late April, Bermuda can experience anything from hot sunshine to chilly winter gales. Poor weather blows away quickly, however, so it is sensible to bring a combination of clothes, preferably in coordinating colours, so that you can add or subtract layers according to the temperature.

During the warmer months (May to mid-November) women should bring summer-weight sports clothes, cotton dresses, swimsuits, a light, dressy wrap for the evening, plus cocktail-type outfits to wear when dining out. Men should bring light sports clothes, swimming gear, plus a lightweight suit or sports jacket and tie for evenings. In all seasons, everyone should bring a raincoat or waterproof windcheater, especially important when riding on chilly motor scooters. Scarves are also a good idea.

In the cooler months (December to late March) bring light woollen clothes, a warmer jacket, a raincoat and a windcheater, plus a swimsuit for the occasional really warm days (or the heated hotel pool).

What to Wear

In general, Bermudians prefer formal and modest attire, for both daytime and evening. Casual "resort wear" is acceptable on the beach and by the pool, but outside these areas revealing clothing is considered inappropriate. A few restaurants and clubs ask men to wear a jacket and tie after 6pm, and women should don informal but fairly dressy evening attire. Some cottage colonies have "casual nights", but this may just mean that no tie is required.

Bermuda shorts are perfectly OK for men, accepted but less OK for women. However, short shorts (and bare feet) are out of the question in public areas. It is an offence to ride cycles or appear in public without a shirt. Nude or topless sunbathing is not permitted.

Tourist Offices

In Bermuda: Global House, 43 Church Street, Hamilton MH 12. Tel: (441) 292-0023.
In the UK: Tel: 020 7096 4246; cjoell-deshields@bermuda tourism.com. Calls are answered by a representative Monday–Friday mornings only.
In the US: Tel: 1-800 237 6832 Georgia: Suite 803, 245 Peachtree Center Ave. NE, Atlanta, Georgia 30303. Tel: (404) 524 1541. New York: 675 Third Ave., New York, NY 10017. Tel: 800 223 6106. For general tourist information visit: www.bermudatourism.com www.bermuda-online.org

Practical Tips

Useful Addresses

Local **Visitor Information Centres** can help with all kinds of queries, including those about tours, opening hours and accommodation.
Hamilton: Walker Christopher, Emporium, 69 Front Street, tel: 536-4636.
Royal Naval Dockyard: on Clocktower Parade, tel: 799-4842
St George's: off Water Street Plaza, tel: 297-8000.
L.F. Wade International Airport: tel: 299-4857.

National Trust

The **Bermuda National Trust** provides details of historic buildings, selected nature reserves and private gardens which are open to the public on certain days in spring. The Trust's headquarters are at Waterville, Paget, tel: 236-6483; www.bnt.bm. Members of the National Trust in other countries enjoy reciprocal privileges.

Disabled Visitors

Bermuda is not an ideal destination for disabled visitors. Although a national policy on disability has been agreed in principle, it has not yet been implemented and there is no legislation requiring organisations or businesses to make their facilities accessible to the disabled.

Getting around is not easy: roads and pavements are generally busy and crowded. Hamilton has pavements with ramps, but this is not always the case elsewhere. In addition, visitors, disabled or otherwise, are not permitted to hire

cars or electric mobility vehicles. Buses are not suitable for wheelchair users. On the plus side, the ferries are a great way to see the islands. The following organisations can provide information on disabled access:
National Office for Seniors and Physically Challenged (NOSPC; a government department), Stonehall, 60 Victoria Street, Hamilton.
Access Bermuda, www.access.bm, is run by a wheelchair user and can provide information and organise tours.
Bermuda Physically Handicapped Association (BPHA), PO Box HM8, Hamilton HM AX, tel: 295 5035; www.bermuda-online.org/bpha. A few hotels have specially adapted rooms; this is noted in the Accommodation section (see pages 289–93). Visit www.bermuda tourism.com for a list of attractions with wheelchair access.

Business Hours

Most shops open Mon–Sat 9am–5.30pm. Some, however, open at 9.15am and close at 5pm, so it's wise to enquire first. During the summer months, some Hamilton shops are open late, particularly on Wednesday, when Front Street becomes a street festival: Harbour Nights.

On Sundays, only a few grocery stores and the shops at Dockyard's Clocktower Mall are open.

Banks

• All **Bank of Bermuda** branches in Hamilton open Mon–Fri 9am–4.30pm.
• **Bank of Butterfield** Mon–Thurs 9am–3.30pm, Fri 9am–4.30pm.
• **Bermuda Commercial Bank** Mon–Thurs 9.30–3pm, Fri 9.30am–4.30pm.
All banks close on Saturday, Sunday and public holidays.

Religious Services

Bermuda has a surprisingly large number of houses of worship of all denominations: Anglican, Roman

Catholic, AME, Seventh Day Adventists, Presbyterian, Jehovah's Witness, Pentecostal, and Muslim to name a few. Consult the *Yellow Pages* of the Bermuda telephone directory for addresses.

Media

Print

Bermuda's only daily paper is *The Royal Gazette*, published Monday to Saturday. *The Bermuda Sun* (published Wednesday and Friday) is a bi-weekly tabloid; the *Mid-Ocean News* (published Friday) is a broadsheet with colour magazine and is the *Gazette*'s sister paper.

British newspapers can arrive as early as 5pm on the day of publication (otherwise the following day), while North American newspapers arrive around 3pm on the day of publication.

Bermudian Business is a glossy monthly magazine aimed at the business and financial sector, while the long-established *The Bermudian* tends to feature articles on history, culture and the arts.

Two free magazines geared towards tourists are: *This Week in Bermuda* and *Preview*. They provide calendars of events and activities and are available at hotels and at Visitor Information Centres.

Radio

Radio station VSB-1160 (AM) offers the BBC World Service 24 hours a day and coverage of local events. Other AM radio stations include: ZBM-1340 (Talk Radio); ZFB-1230 (Community Relations); VSB-1450 ("The Music You Know" from the 1950s–1980s); VSB-1280 (Bible Broadcast Network).

There are three radio stations on the FM frequency: ZFB-FM-95 (Urban contemporary); VSB-FM-106 (Contemporary music and news); ZBM-FM-89 (Hits and favourites); Hott-FM-107.5 (Contemporary music and talk show). Good for hurricane news is the Government Emergency Channel on FM 100.

Television

Three Bermuda television stations

are linked to American national networks. Channel 9, ZBM, shows programmes from CBS; Channel 7, ZFB, shows programmes from ABC. Channel 11, VSB, is the NBC affiliate. Many hotels also have cable television.

Postal Services

Stamps can be bought, and postcards, letters and parcels mailed from picturesque Perot's Post Office on Queen Street in Hamilton. The main post office for Bermuda is on the corner of Church Street and Parliament Street in Hamilton. There are also post office branches across the island.

Dialling Codes

● **US and Canada**: dial 1, then the regional area code, then the seven-digit telephone number
● **All other countries**: dial 011, then the country code, then the regional area code minus the initial zero, then the number.

Phone, Fax & Internet

Most hotels and guesthouses add service charges on calls made from hotel rooms. Calls are charged according to when they are made:
US: Full rate is in effect 10am–7pm; discount 7–11pm and 7–10am; the economy rate applies 11pm–7am.
Canada: Full rate 7am–9pm; discount rate 9pm–7am. No economy rate.
UK: Full rate 7am–6pm; discount rate 6pm–7am. No economy rate.

Telephone cards can be bought at a variety of places around the island including hotels, pharmacies and post offices. Local mobile telephone providers have roaming agreements with overseas services. Mobile and GSM coverage is good.
International access codes:
AT&T: 1-800 872 2881.
MCI: 1-800 623 0484 (C&W); or 1-800 888 8888 (TBI/Worldphone).
Sprint: 1-800 623 0877.
Most hotels and guest houses have

fax facilities and direct **Internet** access may be available too. Bermuda also has a growing number of Internet cafés and shops where you can check e-mail, the Twice Told Tales book shop (Parliament Street, Hamilton), ArtCetera art supplies store (Burnaby Hill, Hamilton) and Café Latte (bus station, St. George's).

Consulates in Bermuda

UK: Government House 11 Langton Hill, Pembroke HM13 Tel: 292-2587
US: Crown Hill, 16 Middle Road Devonshire DV 03
Tel: 295-1342
Fax: 295-1592
Canada: Canadian Consul, Reid House, 31 Church Street, HM 12. Tel: 294-3611
Many other countries have honourary consuls in Bermuda. See the white pages of the Bermuda Telephone Directory.

Emergencies

Security & Crime

On the whole, Bermudians are honest people and you need do no more than take the same precautions you would elsewhere: lock up accommodation and motor scooters, tie valuable bags to the basket of your bike or scooter so they can't be snatched, and avoid walking alone in isolated areas. If you visit clubs and bars, exercise the same caution you would at home. In the unlikely event of a crime, dial **295-0011** or **911**.

Medical Services

In emergencies, dial **911**. King Edward Memorial Hospital is on Point Finger Road, Paget. Tel: **239-2009** for emergencies. Tel: **236-2345** for general enquiries.
See the *Yellow Pages* of the Bermuda directory for dentists and doctors, or ask at your hotel.

Getting Around

Orientation

Once a group of seven islands connected only by boat, Bermuda is now fully linked from east to west by a series of bridges. When the term "The Bermudas" is employed, this includes all the smaller islands located along the shores of its major islands. These small islands are used as camp-sites and recreation grounds. Some are privately owned, while others are mere lumps of rock.

Bermuda roughly forms the shape of a fish hook. It is divided into nine parishes (districts), seven of which are named after the principal investors in the Bermuda Company: Robert Rich, Earl of Warwick; William Herbert, Earl of Pembroke; Sir Thomas Smith; Sir Edwyn Sandys; James, Marquis of Hamilton; William Cavendish, Earl of Devonshire; and Henry Wriothesley, Earl of Southampton. The two other parishes are Paget, on the South Coast, and St George's, with the same name as its principal town.

The capital, Hamilton, is not located in the parish of Hamilton, but in the parish of Pembroke. The area commonly referred to as "The East End" is St George's parish, while "The West End" is Sandys parish, centred around the village of Somerset and the Royal Naval Dockyard.

Airport/City

Bermuda's airport lies on reclaimed land in the parish of St George's. Ironically, the view upon landing is probably the most unsightly the island offers. Visitors should not be disappointed, however, for within

minutes of leaving the airport things improve immeasurably. Except for anyone staying in St George's, the first real view of Bermuda is seen when crossing The Causeway, a narrow bridge linking St George's with Hamilton parish. Surrounded by turquoise sea on all sides and, on the horizon, pastel houses shimmering in bright sunlight, only the most jaded of travellers could fail to be excited.

Taxis are usually plentiful just outside the airport. It's 30 minutes from the airport to Hamilton and the fare is around Bd$30. Drivers are typically honest and shouldn't rip off unsuspecting tourists, and the islands contain so few roads that it's virtually impossible to take "the scenic route" to bump up the fare.

A passenger coach serves hotels and guest houses, making several stops along the way. It can be pre-arranged by calling Bee Line Transportation, tel: 293-0303. *(See page 289).*

Public Transport

By Road: Bermudians drive on the **left-hand side** of the road. The stated speed limit is 20 miles (35 km) per hour, but the usual pace is faster. Few people honk their horn, except in greeting. There is no private car hire. Visitors may rent 50-cc motorbikes (also known as "scooters"), which carry one or two people.

By Bus: Buses are frequent and very good, with comprehensive timetables (they almost always run on time) but a complicated fare system. The island is divided into 14 different zones of about 2 miles (3 km) each, with different fares charged according to how many zones are crossed.

You must have the exact fare (in coins only) to board a bus. It's advisable to buy pre-paid tickets or a pass. Not only does this save fumbling for coins, but it is better value. Books of tickets are available from the bus terminal on Church Street, Hamilton, next to City Hall, or from any post office.

Passes on sale at Hamilton's bus terminal or Visitor Information Centres cover all zones and therefore are a good choice. Available for one, three or seven days; for extended visits there are passes for one or three months. The pass allows unlimited travel, the flexibility of jumping on and off the buses, and will also cover ferry journeys. Timetables that include a list of where to catch buses to popular tourist sites are available either from the bus terminal, Visitor Information Centres, or from your hotel.

On the Buses

Bermuda's public buses are a joy to use; they are clean, reliable and the drivers are usually very helpful. If you want to explore the island independently, pick up a bus and ferry timetable at the bus station or Visitor Information Centres, which includes a timed do-it-yourself tour. Then just ask the driver to put you off at the relevant stop – be sure to sit near the front of the bus.

By Ferry: Ferries are fun and reliable. They run to schedule but, contrary to popular myth, do not wait if they see a latecomer scrambling to board.

● The Hamilton/Somerset/ Dockyard route is a popular excursion, calling in at Somerset Bridge, and passing near the village of Somerset before arriving at Dockyard, the westernmost tip of Bermuda. It's a perfect way to see the small islets located in the Great Sound. Bicycles can be taken on board free of charge; motor scooters cost one extra fare. No half fares for children.

● The Hamilton/Paget/Warwick ferry goes past White's island with its sailboats moored in the harbour, and is the only public transport available to points in Paget and Warwick parishes located on the southern side of Hamilton Harbour.

● The Hamilton/Dockyard/St. George's route, which runs

weekdays, during summer, is an ideal way to see most of Bermuda from the sea.

The main ferry terminal for the island is in Hamilton Harbour.

Private Transport

Note that it is not possible for visitors to Bermuda to hire cars. **By bike/scooter/motorcycle:** For a comprehensive briefing, see the feature *Notes for Nervous Drivers* on page 249. Motor scooters can be hired by the hour, by the day or by the week. You must be 16 years of age, but pillion (passenger) cycles can be rented for carrying small children. Scooter shops are located all around the island. Rates vary, but the daily fee tends to be from around Bd$50. All customers are required to pay a mandatory non-refundable damage waiver fee of Bd$30. Rates include third-party insurance, delivery and collection, service in case the bike breaks down, and the first tank of petrol. Rates decrease the longer the bike is hired.

Guided Tours

Taxis with qualified tour guides may be hired by the hour (minimum three hours) or the day. See By Taxi page 289 for more details about taxi tours. For information about sightseeing tours contact: **Bee-Line Transportation** (tel: 293-0303) or **Bermuda Hosts** (tel: 293-1334) or ask at a Visitor Information Centre.

By Taxi: Taxis may be hired by the hour, day, or mile (a day is considered to be six consecutive daylight hours). Rates per cab are currently the same for any number of passengers, from one person up to a maximum of six, for normal transport and general sightseeing. Rates may be higher after midnight or on Sundays and holidays. All taxis are metered and the tariff is fixed by law. If a taxi sports a blue flag, it belongs to a qualified tour

guide – a good way to see the island. Rates for taxi tours are Bd$40 per hour for 1–4 passengers, more for 5–6. **On Foot:** Walking the trails and parks in Bermuda is fascinating; walking along public roads is frustrating. Walls and hedges can be high, obscuring vision, and motor scooters whizzing around corners appear without warning. It's best, too, to refrain from hitch-hiking in Bermuda, not because it's dangerous, but because it's considered unmannerly.

Travel with Children

Despite the fact that some resort hotels have excellent children's programmes, Bermuda is more an island for grown-ups, especially when it is raining. Although Bermudians themselves are welcoming towards children, hotel dining rooms are formal, as is the way of life. The absence of cars prevents anything resembling a "traditional family holiday", as very little can be carried around on a motor scooter, even one built for two.

Some of the beaches, of course, are ideal for children, with shallow waters and a gently sloping shelf. Shelly Bay on the North Shore is ideal, with public conveniences nearby; so is Somerset Long Bay. Admiralty House Park, at the junction of North Shore and Spanish Point Roads in Pembroke has a cove with an almost land-locked beach. Children also usually love the caves, the zoo and aquarium, so if you are staying in self-catering accommodation and are willing to travel by ferry or bus, both parents and children will no doubt have an excellent time.

Where to Stay

Accommodation

The **Department of Tourism** and the **Bermuda Hotel Association** recommend using the services of a professional travel agent. It is important to have confirmed reservations before arriving *(see Entry Regulations page 283)*. The immigration authorities may ask where you'll be staying and you must indicate this on your landing card.

All room rates are subject to a 7.25 percent Government Hotel Occupancy Tax, to be paid on check-out. A two-day deposit may be required by the majority of hotels, which may be non-refundable if cancelled less than 14 to 21 days before the arrival date. Any service charge indicated is in lieu of tips and is added to the bill for room and board only. It does not cover bar charges, extra meals, etc. Most hotels accept major credit cards; smaller guesthouses may not. Always check in advance.

Hotel dining rooms tend to serve excellent food, and meal plans are commonplace. MAP (Modified American Plan) means room, breakfast and dinner. AP (American Plan) means room, breakfast, lunch and dinner. BP (Bermuda Plan) is room and full breakfast. CP (Continental Plan) is room and light breakfast. EP (European Plan) means room only. Meal plans are considerably cheaper than dining out in restaurants each night.

Almost all properties, even many small guest houses, have cable TV. Many hotels have Internet connection, voice mail and services to entice business guests. Virtually every property on the island provides guests with in-room irons.

Hotel Categories

Hotels and cottages are grouped into five categories: resort hotels, small hotels, cottage colonies, guesthouses and housekeeping cottages & apartments. The Department of Tourism's website (www.bermudatourism.com) accommodation list also includes Bed & Breakfast establishments.

Resort Hotels are full-service properties with restaurants, swimming pool(s), private beaches, nightclubs, beauty salons, motorbike rentals and a spa.

Small Hotels are private and intimate, and offer more personal attention; most have dining rooms, and/or room service, swimming pools and access to the beach.

Cottage Colonies, unique to Bermuda and considered by many to be *the* place to stay, are on the beach, with luxury private cottage rooms and suites built around a main clubhouse with pool, bar and restaurant.

Guesthouses, often in private homes, usually have neither pool nor restaurant, but offer personal attention, and breakfast.

Cottages & Apartments, many of which are located near the beach, have kitchens or kitchenettes stocked with dishes and cutlery, sometimes a pool, and can usually sleep more than two.

The front desk in each of the categories can assist with arrangements for watersports, golf, dining and other activities.

Price Guide

Prices quoted are for a standard room, during high season (mid-May until mid-November), exclusive of tax and gratuities.

$$$$ = over 400 Bd dollars
$$$ = 300–399 Bd dollars
$$ = 200–299 Bd dollars
$ = under 199 Bd dollars

Credit cards: AE = American Express; DC = Diners Club; MC = MasterCard; V = Visa.

Resort Hotels

Hamilton (Pembroke)
Fairmont Hamilton Princess
P.O. Box HM 837
Hamilton CM CX
Tel: 295 3000; 800-257-7544 (US)
Fax: 295-1914
www.fairmont.com/hamilton
This luxurious hotel was originally built in 1884, and is located on the picturesque harbour, near downtown Hamilton. The Princess has 413 rooms/suites decorated in the old-world tradition, with a sophisticated atmosphere and first-rate restaurants. Some rooms adapted for disabled guests. One of the best places for afternoon tea and Happy Hour. There are watersports and guests can complete scuba certification (PADI). Ferry access to all of the beach-resort facilities of its sister resort, the Fairmont Southampton. AE, DC, MC, V. **$$$$**

Hamilton Parish
Grotto Bay Beach Resort
11 Blue Hole Hill
Hamilton Parish CR 04
Tel: 293-8333; 800-582-3190 (US); 800-463-0851 (Canada)
Fax: 293-2306
www.grottobay.com
This oceanfront property overlooks 21 acres (8 hectares) of manicured gardens and man-made beaches. A friendly resort, with tennis, sailboarding, sailing, snorkelling and diving. There's a 500,000-year-old cave you can swim in. A poolside bar and restaurants offer a delicious Bermuda experience with live evening entertainment; children's activities. Close to the airport, with 201 suites in lodge-type accommodation on three floors. No lift (elevator). All-inclusive packages are available. AE, MC, V. **$$$**

Paget
Elbow Beach
60 South Shore Road
P.O. Box HM 455
Hamilton HM BX
Tel: 236-3535; 800-223-7434 (US and Canada)
Fax: 236-5882
www.mandarinoriental.com/bermuda
This luxurious property occupies 55 acres (22 hectares) of landscaped gardens overlooking Bermuda's south shore and one of the island's spectacular pink-sand beaches. Accommodation is in the main hotel, cottages and lanais. Facilities include children's programme, fitness centre, beauty salon, pool, tennis courts and watersports. Award-winning restaurants (formal or casual) and cocktail bars: the Deep nightclub, is open till 3am and Mickey's Beach Bar is open for lunch, dinner and evening drinks (May–October). AE, DC, MC, V. **$$$**

Southampton
Fairmont Southampton
P.O. Box HM 1379
Hamilton HM FX
Tel: 238-8000; 800-257-7544 (US and Canada); 0506 863 6310 (UK)
Fax: 238-8968
www.fairmont.com
Large (593 rooms/suites) and luxurious, this resort sits on a hill with commanding views of the south shore and the Great Sound. A popular conference hotel that's also a favourite with tourists. Facilities include tennis, water sports, a challenging par-3 golf course, a private beach, spa and fitness centre, award-winning restaurants, bars and a children's programme. Some rooms adapted for disabled guests. A ferry takes hotel guests between this property and the Fairmont Hamilton Princess. AE, DC, MC, V. **$$$$**

Small Hotels

Hamilton (Pembroke)
Rosedon
P.O. Box HM 290
Hamilton HM AX
Tel: 295-1640
Fax: 295-5904
www.rosedon.com
Traditional afternoon tea and Internet access are among the paradoxical charms of this award-winning property known for its attention to detail. This 47-room friendly hotel has no formal dining room but breakfast, lunch and light evening meals are available – they'll

even pack you a picnic lunch. Tastefully decorated, elegant rooms in the main colonial house, with spacious but less attractive, simple rooms around the gardens and swimming pool. It's within walking distance of the centre of Hamilton and round-trip transport is provided to a south shore beach and tennis club. AE, MC, V. **$$**

Royal Palms
P.O. Box HM 499
Hamilton HM CX
Tel: 292-1854; 800-678-0783 (UK, US and Canada)
Fax: 292-1946
www.royalpalms.bm
This elegant, award-winning property, with rooms and suites in two century-old manor houses and a handful of cottages (with kitchenettes), combines the intimacy of a family-run establishment with amenities usually found only in large hotels. All 32 rooms have Internet access. There is a freshwater pool surrounded by manicured gardens and one of the island's most popular restaurants, Ascots, as well as a well-stocked wine bar. It's situated on a tree-lined avenue, a short distance from downtown Hamilton. AE, MC, V. **$$–$$$**

Hamilton Parish
Clear View Suites and Villas
Sandy Lane
Crawl Hill
Hamilton CR 02
Tel: 293-0484
Perfect for visitors wanting easy access to both St George's and Hamilton. A 20-minute bus ride will take you to either town. The hotel's 40 rooms have beautiful views of the North Shore; suites are bright and cheerful and all have fully-equipped kitchenettes. There are two swimming pools and a tennis court for the use of guests only. The Landfall restaurant is open for breakfast, lunch and dinner. This place is close to the Railway Trail which leads to nearby Shelly Bay, and Flatt's Village and the Bermuda Aquarium, Museum and Zoo are just five minutes away. AE, MC, V. **$$**

Paget
Coco Reef Resort
P.O. Box HM 523
Hamilton HM CX
Tel: 236-5416; 800-648-0799
Fax: 236-9766
www.cocoreefbermuda.com
This refurbished hotel was formerly the Bermuda Hospitality Training Centre and is set on a wide beach of lovely pink sand surrounded by manicured grounds. Snorkelling and tennis (lessons available) for the active holidaymaker, and those who prefer to relax can enjoy the beach. Guests can dine on the terrace or indoors, or have a drink in the welcoming bar in the lobby. Rooms have terraces or balconies with ocean views; cottages also available. AE, DC, MC, V. **$$$$**

The Wharf Executive Suites Hotel
P.O. Box PG 176
1 Harbour Road
Paget PG 01
Tel: 232-4008
Fax: 232-4008
www.wharfexecutivesuites.com
Bermuda's first hotel built specifically for business executives who want more of a home setting than an anonymous hotel. Rooms have balconies with great views of Hamilton Harbour and its 15 units can accommodate up to 40 guests and include equipped kitchens or kitchen areas as well as desks and chairs. Computer equipment and complimentary wireless Internet make working from The Wharf easy. Guests can take the nearby ferry for a seven-minute ride into Hamilton. Rates include continental breakfast served in the guest lounge. AE, MC, V. **$$**

Southampton
The Reefs
56 South Road
Southampton SN 02
Tel: 238-0222; 800-742-2008
Fax: 238-8372
www.thereefs.com
In a spectacular setting, on the cliffs above one of the south shore's great beaches, this is a small luxury hotel that's won numerous awards for its hospitality, its service, its food and its architecture. It offers elegant suites and beautifully decorated smaller rooms, as well as eight 1- to 4-bedroom cottages. Three good restaurants (one outdoors) have varied cuisine and its Sunday brunch is well-known. Internet access, pool, spa, a fitness centre, tennis, snorkelling and kayaking as well as a beautiful private beach. AE, MC, V. **$$$$**

Warwick
Surf Side Beach Club
90 South Road
Warwick WK 08
Tel: 236-7100; 800-553-9990
www.surfsidebermuda.com
The rooms, apartments and suites with Island decor and furnishings have vista views overlooking the South Shore. Cliff paths in the surrounding palmetto gardens lead down to the beach, and there is also an outdoor swimming pool. Some of the suites have fully equipped kitchens. The Palms restaurant is much loved by local people and known for its excellent French cuisine, and bar. A mini spa offers beauty treatments. The hotel is on a bus route and within easy reach of Hamilton for shopping and business. AE, MC, V. **$$$**

Cottage Colonies

Hamilton Parish
Pink Beach Club and Cottage Colony
116 South Road
Tucker's Town HS 02
Tel: 293-1666; 800-355-6161
Fax: 293-8935
www.pinkbeach.com
Refurbished, all-suite accommodation in this upscale part of Bermuda with private balconies overlooking 13 acres (5 hectares) of ocean front with views of the South Shore reef. The cottages, all with Italian marble bathrooms, are surrounded by gardens, with the Mid Ocean Golf Course nearby. A swimming pool overlooks the ocean and there are two tennis courts. Some rates include breakfast (brought to your room every morning by your personal

Price Guide

Prices quoted are for a standard room, during high season (mid-May until mid-November), exclusive of tax and gratuities.

$$$$ = over 400 Bd dollars
$$$ = 300–399 Bd dollars
$$ = 200–299 Bd dollars
$ = under 199 Bd dollars

Credit cards: AE American Express; DC Diners Club; MC MasterCard; V = Visa.

housekeeper), afternoon tea and a five-course gourmet dinner. Well known for its stretch of pink, soft sand, this hotel is an ideal venue for romantic occasions. It also has a resident masseur and offers other luxurious in-room body treatments. AE, MC, V. **$$$$**

Paget
Fourways Inn
P.O. Box PG 294
Paget PG BX
Tel: 236-6517; 800-962-7654 (US)
Fax: 236-5528
www.fourwaysinn.com
Home to one of the island's finest restaurants. Its 11 cottages are scattered over a grandly luxurious property on Middle Road, roughly midway between the ferries of the harbour and the sands of south shore. Peaceful, and the atmosphere is old-world Bermuda, but with modern amenities. Not least among its attractions are the freshly baked goodies from the on-site bakery. Each room and suite has its own kitchenette. AE, MC, V. **$$–$$$**

Sandys
9 Beaches
4 Daniels Head Lane
P.O. Box MA 238
Sandys MA BX
Tel: 239-2999; 866-841-9009 (US)
www.9beaches.com
This casual resort is a good place for visitors looking for fun and relaxation away from it all. The place comprises 84 canvas-roofed cabanas, all with delightful ocean views. Some of the accommodation is positioned on stilts above the water, with glass windows in the floor for viewing passing fish and marine life. There is also a separate 2-storey, 3-bedroomed house available for rent on the resort property. **$$$**

Cambridge Beaches
30 King's Point Road
Sandys MA 02
Tel: 234-0331; 800-468-7300 (US and Canada)
Fax: 234-3352
www.cambridgebeaches.com
Repeat visitors keep this outstanding property busy year-round. The antiques-filled cottages and guest rooms sit on a private 25-acre (10-hectare) beach-fringed peninsula. Offers both relaxation and recreation. Facilities include a range of watersports, a marina, tennis and a spa and health club. Its meals are known for their variety and good quality. AE, MC, V. **$$$$**

Willowbank
P.O. Box MA 296
Sandys MA BX
Tel: 234-1616; 800-752-8493 (US); 800-463-8444 (Canada)
Fax: 234-3373
www.willowbank.bm
A former country house, Willowbank is a non-denominational, non-profit Christian hotel set in landscaped gardens with views overlooking Ely's Harbour and the south shore. Accommodation is in small, simply furnished cottages which have no telephone or TV. The philosophy of this peaceful, friendly place is to provide good food in a beautiful setting where people can relax free from the pressures of modern, day-to-day life. There is a summer programme for children aged 4–12 years old. MC, V. **$$$**

Southampton
Pompano Beach Club
36 Pompano Beach Road
Southampton SB 03
Tel: 234-0222; 800-343-4155 (US/Canada)
Fax: 234-1694
www.pompanobeachclub.com
A friendly, family-run hotel in a breathtaking ocean setting. The best seat in the house for spectacular sunsets is in the excellent dining room of this popular cottage colony. The property is known for its beautiful beach, which has a wide sandbar, extensive watersports facilities and for its elegantly casual atmosphere. You can wade out 400 yards (365 metres) in warm, knee-to-chest-deep water; very young guests have their own wading pool. There's also tennis, fishing, a fitness centre and a spa – the pool and jacuzzi are open 24 hours. The place is also a golfer's paradise, since it's located adjacent to the Port Royal Golf Course, a par-71 championship course. Tee times can be booked when you reserve your room. The cottage colony offers lovely rooms and suites as well as personal attention and great food. Guests on the Modified American Plan can also participate in a dining exchange with nearby hotels including: The Reefs, Cambridge Beaches and Coco Reef. The Sunset Lounge is ideal for a quiet drink in the early evening, but is transformed when the music starts. AE, MC, V. **$$$$**

St George's
St George's Club
P.O. Box GE 92
St George's GE BX
Tel: 297-1200
Fax: 297-1022
On a hill overlooking the historic town of St. George's, this is a time-share property, with one- or two-bedroom apartments and fully equipped kitchens. It has an adjacent golf course, three pools (one heated), private beach club, floodlit tennis courts and a good restaurant. A convenience store is situated on the premises, and staff at the activities desk are on hand to assist you with watersports and entertainment arrangements. AE, DC, MC, V. **$$$$**

Guesthouses

Hamilton (Pembroke)

Oxford House
Woodbourne Avenue
P.O. Box HM 374
Hamilton HM BX
Tel: 295-0503/800-548-7758
(US)/800-272-2306 (Canada)
Fax: 295-0250
www.oxfordhouse.bm
A charming, award-winning 12-room bed and breakfast within a two-minute walk of downtown Hamilton. Large, light-filled guest rooms recreate the atmosphere of an elegant private residence, with traditional decor and furnishings. Air-conditioned rooms have private bathrooms and include singles, doubles, triples and quads. Homely atmosphere and plenty of personal attention. AE, MC, V. **$$**

Robin's Nest
10 Vale Close
Pembroke HM 04
Tel/Fax: 292-4347
www.robinsnest.com
An apartment complex in a residential area of the island. For the budget conscious. All 11 apartments have clear views of the north shore and also include fully equipped kitchens. The patio areas outside are ideal for al-fresco dining. Unusually, rates include service charges and government tax. An ideal venue for both business travellers and for families. No credit cards. **$**

Paget

Greenbank Guesthouse and Cottages
Salt Kettle Road
P.O. Box PG 201
Paget PG BX
Tel: 236-3615
Fax: 236-2427
www.greenbankbermuda.com
Situated on the Salt Kettle peninsular, Greenbank is a short ferry ride away from Hamilton and a 10-minute taxi or scooter ride from the South Shore beaches. Rooms and apartments have fully equipped kitchenettes and some can accommodate up to four people so this is a good choice for families.

Patio areas so that guests can enjoy the lush subtropical setting and views of the Great Sound. AE, MC, V. **$**

Little Pomander Guest House
P.O. Box HM 374
Hamilton HM BX
Tel: 236-7635
Fax: 236-8332
www.littlepomander.com
Facing Hamilton Harbour, just five minutes from the city, Little Pomander is an oasis of calm. This bed and breakfast has five guest rooms, each with cable TV, a refrigerator and microwave; there is also a barbecue grill provided for use by guests. AE, MC, V. **$**

Salt Kettle House
10 Salt Kettle Road
Paget PG 01
Tel: 236-0407
Fax: 236-8639
A full, very hearty breakfast sets guests up for the day in this popular and happy guest house, which is just off Harbour Road and a few steps from the ferry landing. Guests return year after year for its comfortable rooms, homely atmosphere, and friendly, knowledgeable proprietor. Some rooms adapted for disabled guests. No credit cards. **$**

Pembroke

Edgehill Manor Guest House
36 Rosemont Avenue
Pembroke HM 06
Tel: 295-7124
Fax: 295-3850
More colonial mansion than hotel, this place has rooms that are light, airy, chintzy but cheery. Staff are welcoming, friendly and helpful. Edgehill is ideal for the business traveller who will appreciate its location, a short walking distance from Hamilton, but tourists love it too. It has a swimming pool surrounded by vibrant flowers and shrubbery. Continental breakfast, served in the breakfast room included in the rate. AE, MC, V. **$$**

St George's

Aunt Nea's Inn at Hillcrest
P.O. Box GE 96
St George's GE BX
Tel: 297-1630; 888-392-7829 (US);
020 7084 6282 (UK)
Fax: 297-1908
www.auntneas.com
Just a short stroll from King's Square, Aunt Nea's is a bed and breakfast tucked away in one of St George's picturesque alleys. Air-conditioned rooms have canopy or sleigh beds, cedar chests and private baths – some also with whirlpools. A handful of suites have kitchenettes, and a cottage is available to rent. A good place from which to explore the historic town. AE, MC, V. **$$**

Apartments

Paget

Paraquet Guest Apartments
P.O. Box PG 173
Paget PG BX
Tel: 236-5842
Fax: 236-1665
www.paraquetapartments.com
Informal place in a residential area close to Elbow Beach. Popular choice for visitors on a budget. Rooms are clean and basic, and some have kitchenettes. There is a diner-style restaurant on the property that's popular with locals as well as guests, and a pool nearby. MC, V. **$$**

Where to Eat

Restaurants

For so small an island, Bermuda offers an extraordinary variety of dining experiences, ranging from casual Bermudian eateries to elegant Continental restaurants and excellent hotel dining rooms. Many dining spots publish sample menus in the Menu Pages of the Bermuda Telephone Directory. The diversity of the cuisine has led to a fusion of styles that makes categorisation a challenge.

ASIAN

Chopsticks
88 Reid Street, Hamilton
Tel: 292-0791
An attractive decor and fast, friendly service provide a backdrop for Hunan, Cantonese, Szechuan, Peking and Thai fare. AE, MC, V. **$**

House of India
57 North Street, Hamilton
Tel: 295-6450
A favourite with locals, this cosy spot serves authentic Indian cuisine. Samosas, pakoras, balti and curry (cooked to order) are among the mouth-watering dishes. Open for dinner, take out, and buffet lunch. MC, V. **$$**

L'Oriental
32 Bermudiana Road, Upstairs, Hamilton
Tel: 296-4477
Sushi, Teppanyaki and fusion dishes are on the creative menu. Light wood decor complements the friendly atmosphere of this sophisticated restaurant. Open Monday–Friday for lunch, Monday–Sunday for dinner. MC, V. **$$$**

Upper Crust
10 Bermudiana Road, Hamilton
Tel: 295-7789
A small place that serves mostly Chinese food, but in a bizarre twist pizza is also on the daily menu. Popular with local people, mostly for the take out. No liquor licence. MC, V. **$**

BERMUDIAN & CARIBBEAN

Black Horse Tavern Bar & Restaurant
St David's
Tel: 297-1991
There's nothing pretentious about this popular east-end spot. Here you will find traditional Bermudian fare, including fish chowder, conch fritters, and authentic shark hash. The fish is fresh and caught locally and while locals like theirs fried, the chef will cook yours any way you like it. Closed Monday. AE, MC, V. **$$**

Price Guide

The ranges given in this section are for a three-course meal for one, not including a beverage or the standard 15 percent gratuity.

$$$$ = over 60 Bd dollars
$$$ = 40–60 Bd dollars
$$ = 26–40 Bd dollars
$ = under 25 Bd dollars

Credit cards: AE American Express; DC Diners Club; MC MasterCard; V = Visa.

Bouchee
75 Pitts Bay Road, Pembroke Parish
Tel: 295-5759
Best known for its fresh fish entrées and excellent soups, Bouchee has more fusion cuisine than French, though its name suggests otherwise. Seafood is also a specialty. This restaurant is a great choice for a good meal in town. Located just outside the City of Hamilton, opposite the Fairmont Hamilton Princess Hotel. **$$$**

Freeport Seafood Restaurant
Royal Naval Dockyard
Tel: 234-1692
Seafood served with a Bermudian twist in a casual atmosphere. Popular with visitors and locals. **$$**

Green Lantern
9 Serpentine Road, Pembroke Parish
Tel: 295-6995
Fish chowder, fish and chips, and burgers are served in this very casual local restaurant that is open 9am–9pm. Traditional codfish and potato breakfast on Saturday. MC, V. No liquor licence. **$**

Jamaican Grill
32 Court Street, Hamilton
Tel: 296-6577
On the outskirts of Hamilton, this spot is popular with locals for lunch and dinner (take away or eat in). Generous servings of authentic West Indian food such as jerk pork and chicken with rice and peas. Other locations: 40 Parsons Road, Pembroke and 33 Ord Road, Paget. MC, V. **$$**

Landfall Restaurant
Clear View Suites and Villas, Sandy Lane, Crawl Hill, Hamilton
Tel: 293-0484
Good Bermudian cuisine. Try Bermuda rockfish in orange sauce, Bermuda lobster and at Christmas time traditional Bermudian cassava pie. There is also international food and diners enjoy the best views of the North Shore and St David's coastline. AE, MC, V. **$$$**

The Pickled Onion
53 Front Street, Hamilton
Tel: 295-2263
International cuisine and Bermudian favourites, such as generous portions of spicy fish chowder. Eat inside or on the pretty balcony overlooking Hamilton Harbour. Live entertainment most nights. The restaurant is popular with tourists. AE, MC, V. **$$$**

Port O'Call Restaurant
87 Front Street, Hamilton
Tel: 295-5373
The restaurant which is designed to resemble an old sailing ship, is a favourite with local people. Excellent food, attentive but unhurried service and a serious wine list make dining here a special

event. The menu is contemporary, with a good selection of fresh seafood dishes. AE, MC, V. **$$$**

Seahorse Grill
Elbow Beach Hotel,
South Shore Road, Paget
Tel: 236-3535
Beautiful award winning restaurant with an imaginative menu; the best of local produce and seafood as well as grilled beef dishes. Try the Yellow Fin Tartare with seared hamachi (yellow tail) and fennel and citrus salad. Alfresco dining on the terrace with expansive views of the South Shore. Definitely worth trying. AE, MC, V. **$$$$**

Speciality Inn
4 South Road, Smiths Parish
Tel: 236-3133
Pizza, spaghetti, sandwiches, even sushi, are served up in this very casual restaurant. Near Verdmont and Spittal Pond. AE, MC, V. **$**

The Spot
6 Burnaby Street, Hamilton
Tel: 292-6293
This casual coffee shop is always jammed at lunchtime with business people, shoppers and shopkeepers, enjoying the plate lunches, burgers and famous turkey sandwiches. Open Monday–Saturday 6.30am–10pm. No credit cards. No liquor licence. Family friendly. **$**

CONTINENTAL

Ascots
24 Rosemont Avenue,
Pembroke Parish
Tel: 295-9644
At the award-winning restaurant of the Royal Palms Hotel, dining is in an antique-filled room or poolside, surrounded by an English-style garden. A beautiful setting for expertly prepared and presented Continental fare. AE, MC, V. **$$$$**

Barracuda Grill
5 Burnaby Hill, Hamilton
Tel: 292-1609
A beautiful restaurant, which is a local favourite due to its interesting mainly fish-based menu. Great food here. The decor and atmosphere are stylish and elegant. AE, MC, V. **$$$**

Bolero Brasserie
Bermuda House Lane,
95 Front Street, Hamilton
Tel: 292-4507
A restaurant specialising in contemporary European cuisine at reasonable prices. Diners can eat on the outdoor porch overlooking Hamilton Harbour or inside the restaurant whose decor features local artwork. Good wine list. AE, MC, V. **$$–$$$**

Fourways Inn
1 Middle Road, Paget Parish
Tel: 236-6517
The kitchen turns out such fineries as foie gras and rack of lamb, accompanied by top-quality wines. AE, MC, V. **$$$$**

Greg's Steakhouse
39 Church Street, Hamilton
Tel: 297-2333
Located near the court and government buildings, this is Bermuda's only steakhouse. However, in addition to excellent steaks, fish, pork and lamb are on the menu, as well as seafood. Upstairs is Greg's Spot, a champagne and dessert bar. AE, MC, V. **$$$**

The Harbourfront Restaurant
Bermuda Underwater Exploration Institute, East Broadway, Hamilton
Tel: 292-6122
Elegant food in a harbourside restaurant attracts diners again and again. AE, MC, V. **$$$$**

Palms Restaurant and Bar
Surf Side Beach Club,
90 South Road, Warwick Parish
Tel: 236-7100
This restaurant, where guests dine alfresco, sits atop a cliff overlooking the South Shore. It is much loved by locals for its panoramic ocean view, romantic ambience and excellent French cuisine. Fish is always fresh from the sea. AE, MC, V. **$$$**

Tom Moore's Tavern
Walsingham Lane, Hamilton Parish
Tel: 293-8020
Bermuda's oldest dining establishment is named after the 19th-century Irish poet, who was a guest when this was a private residence. A very elegant eatery whose specialities include seafood and steaks, presented with a Continental flair. AE, MC, V. **$$$**

ITALIAN

La Trattoria
22 Washington Lane, Hamilton
Tel: 295-1877
Pastas, pizzas and seafood dishes are the mainstays in this very informal Italian spot, tucked in among Washington Mall's many shops. AE, MC, V. **$$**

Pasta Basta
1 Elliott Street, Hamilton
Tel: 295-9785
A variety of pastas served with a choice of sauces (meat or vegetarian) is what is on the menu at this value for money restaurant. No credit cards. No liquor licence. **$**

Portofino
20 Bermudiana Road, Hamilton
Tel: 292-2375
Pasta and pizza at this local favourite that attracts a lively crowd. AE, MC, V. **$$$**

Tio Pepe Restaurant
117 South Road,
Southampton Parish
Tel: 238-0572
Pizzas and pasta in this tiny place, where you'll need to make reservations. AE, MC, V. **$$**

MEXICAN

Rosa's Cantina
121 Front Street, Hamilton
Tel: 295-1912
The island's only Tex-Mex place has burritos, fajitas, quesadillas and Texas-style steaks, as well as Mexican beers, sangria and margaritas. Family friendly. MC, V. **$$**

Pubs

Flanagan's Irish Pub & Sports Bar
69 Front Street
Tel: 295-8299
Steak, ale and stout are among the offerings in this Irish pub, along with a great atmosphere. AE, MC, V. **$$**

Frog and Onion Pub
Freeport Road, Royal Naval Dockyard
Tel: 234-2900
A former warehouse at Dockyard, which has both indoor and patio dining and a good selection of pub grub, seafood and steaks. MC, V. **$$**

Price Guide

The ranges given in this section are for a three-course meal for one, not including a beverage or the standard 15 percent gratuity.

$$$$ = over 60 Bd dollars
$$$ = 40–60 Bd dollars
$$ = 26–40 Bd dollars
$ = under 25 Bd dollars

Credit cards: AE American Express; DC Diners Club; MC MasterCard; V = Visa.

Hog Penny
5 Burnaby Hill, Hamilton
Tel: 292-2534
Great pub fare in a great pub ambience. Offerings include bangers and mash, steak-and-kidney pie and flaming desserts, and there's often entertainment at night. AE, MC, V. **$$**

North Rock Brewing Company
South Shore, Smith's Parish
Tel: 236-6633
Here Bermuda beer brews in beautiful copper tanks as you eat and drink in the restaurant or on the patio. Food is authentic British pub fare such as steak and kidney pie and roast prime rib of beef with Yorkshire pudding, or fish fried in beer batter and chips. Friendly atmosphere. AE, MC, V. **$$$**

Swizzle Inn
3 Blue Hole Hill, Bailey's Bay
Tel: 293-1854
Steak, seafood and big juicy burgers are among the fare in this wonderful old two-storey pub, named after the island's most famous drink, the rum swizzle. It's popular with locals, especially at night, when it attracts a lively singles crowd. AE, MC, V. **$$**

Afternoon Tea

Several hotels serve formal afternoon tea: Rosedon, Cambridge Beaches and the Fairmont Hamilton Princess.

Lighthouse Restaurant
68 St Anne's Road,
Southampton Parish
Tel: 238-8679
The former light keeper's cottage at the base of Gibb's Hill Lighthouse is home to this tearoom, which serves up crumpets and scones, as well as breakfast, lunch and sinfully delicious desserts. AE, MC, V. **$**

Coffee Shops

Rock Island Coffee
48 Reid Street, Hamilton
Tel: 296-5241
Casual place with faded sofas and a patio with views of the harbour. Fresh roasted coffee, pastries and sandwiches. No credit cards. **$**

Temptations Café
31 Duke of York Street, St Georges
Tel: 297-1368
Small, friendly cafe open for breakfast, lunch with and pastries. Try the coconut cream pie, but get there early. **$**

Café Paradiso
7 Reid Street, Washington Mall,
Hamilton
Tel: 295-3263
Excellent spot for breakfast or to watch the world go by at lunch or tea time on one of Hamilton's busy shopping streets. **$**

Lemon Tree Café
7 Queen Street, Hamilton
Tel: 292-0235
Delicious lunchtime offerings of meat pies, wraps, daily specials and pastries. Take out or eat on the patio overlooking Par-La-Ville Park. A great happy hour on Fridays. MC, V. **$**

Sites

Museums & Historic Buildings

Bermudian Heritage Museum
Water and York streets, St George's
Tel: 297-4126.
Open: Tuesday–Saturday 10am–3pm; admission charge. Through exhibits, costumes, photographs and memorabilia, this museum examines the history and contribution of black people in Bermuda.

Bermuda National Trust Museum
Kings Square, St George's
Tel: 297-1423
www.bnt.bm
Open: 10am–4pm April–October Monday–Saturday, November–March Wednesday–Saturday; admission charge.
The former Globe Hotel (1698) was the headquarters of the principal Southern agent in Bermuda during the American Civil War. The museum tells the story of the Bermudian blockade runners. Good gift shop.

Bermuda Railway Museum
37 North Shore Road
Tel: 293-1774
Open: (usually) Monday–Friday, 10am–4pm; free admission. Housed in the old Aquarium station of the defunct narrow-gauge railway, this curiosity shop-cum-railway-museum has a delightful collection of memorabilia, including some of the first-class wicker chairs, plus signs and photographs.

Bermuda Underwater Exploration Institute
East Broadway, Hamilton
Tel: 292-7219
www.buei.bm
Open: Monday–Friday 9am–5pm, Saturday–Sunday 10am–5pm; admission charge.

This excellent facility explores Bermuda's oceanic origins through interactive exhibits, including a simulated dive 12,000 feet (3,660 metres) to the seabed, a Shipwreck Gallery and a large shell collection. The Harbourfront Restaurant (see page 295), on the institute site, has a sushi and tempura bar.

Carter House
St David's
Tel: 297-8000
Open: enquire at the local Visitor Information Centre; admission charge.
Built by the descendants of Christopher Carter, one of the island's earliest settlers, the renovated house is a small museum.

Deliverance
St George's
Open: daily 10am–4pm; admission charge.
This replica of one of Bermuda's founding ships is expertly built and brings to life the difficult conditions that early settlers faced when crossing the Atlantic. All proceeds are donated to local charitable organisations.

St George's Historical Society Museum
Featherbed Alley & Duke of Kent Street, St George's
Tel: 297-0423
Open: Monday–Friday 10am–4pm; admission charge.
The museum houses artefacts relating to Bermuda's past, including some excellent Bermuda cedar furniture and an old printing press.

Maritime Museum
Royal Naval Dockyard,
Ireland Island
Tel: 234 1418
www.bmm.bm
Open: daily 9.30am–4pm; admission charge.
A series of buildings and fortifications that vividly documents Bermuda's maritime activities and military history. The museum is also home to Dolphin Quest, where visitors can swim with dolphins for an additional fee, an experience that is bookable online up to one year in advance.

Bermuda National Gallery
Hamilton City Hall, Church Street
Tel: 295-9428
www.bermudanationalgallery.com
Open: Monday–Saturday 10am–4pm; donations welcome.
Permanent and changing exhibitions of Bermuda's finest paintings, dating from 1600 to the present.

Museum of the Bermuda Historical Society
Public Library Building, Queen Street
Hamilton
Tel: 295-2487
Open: Monday–Saturday 9.30am–3pm; donations welcome.
A small but fascinating museum provides visitors with a glimpse of life in early Bermuda. It's filled with household goods as well as unusual items. One interesting artefact is a copy of the letter George Washington wrote to the inhabitants of Bermuda, in 1775, asking them to send gunpowder for use in the American Revolution. (Bermudians met the request by stealing gunpowder from the British to ship to the rebellious colonies.)

The Old Rectory
Broad Alley, St George's
Tel: 297-0879
www.bnt.bm
Open: November–March Wednesday 1–5pm; donations welcome.
A Bermudian cottage built circa 1705 and lovingly maintained.

State House
King's Square, St George's
Open: most Wednesdays 10am–4pm.
The oldest building in Bermuda, the State House was built in 1620. Originally the seat of government assembly meetings, it is now a Masonic Lodge whose annual Peppercorn Ceremony, when the Masons pay their yearly rent of one peppercorn, is an occasion full of pomp and colour.

Town Hall
King's Square, St George's
Open: Monday–Saturday 9am–4pm.
The site of many historic events in Bermuda's oldest town.

Tucker House Museum
Water Street, St George's
Tel: 297-0545
www.bnt.bm

Open: 10am–4pm April–October Monday–Saturday, November–March Wednesday–Saturday; admission charge.
Former home of the Tucker family of England, Bermuda and Virginia. Fine collection of 18th-century furniture and silver.

Verdmont
Collector's Hill, Smiths Parish
Tel: 236-7369
www.bnt.bm
Open: 10am–4pm April–October Monday–Saturday, November–March Wednesday–Saturday; admission charge.
A fine late 17th-century mansion depicting life in Bermuda's early days.

The National Trust

For further information about historic buildings, contact the **Bermuda National Trust**, Waterville, Paget. Tel: 236-6483 www.bnt.bm.

Forts

Fort Hamilton
Happy Valley Road, Pembroke
Tel: 292-1234.
Open: daily 9.30am–5pm; free admission.
Fine example of the mid-Victorian polygon fort with a moat that has become a lovely garden. From November to March there is a skirling ceremony at noon, featuring Bermuda Islands Pipe Band.

Fort St Catherine
off Barry Road, St George's
Tel: 297-1920
Open: daily 10am–4pm; admission charge.
Replicas of the British Crown Jewels and a series of dioramas which clearly illustrate decisive dates in Bermuda's history. Five of its big guns, which could hurl a huge projectile over half a mile (800 metres), have been restored.

Gates Fort
Cut Road, St George's
Open: daily 10am–4.30pm; no admission charge.
Originally a small sea battery.

Scaur Hill Fort and Park
Somerset Road, Somerset
Open: daily 10am–4.30pm; free
admission.
You can picnic in the grounds of this
well-preserved historic fortification.
The views are wonderful and the
grounds are open until sunset.

Other Attractions

**Bermuda Aquarium,
Museum and Zoo**
Flatts Village, Harrington Sound
Tel: 293-2727
www.bamz.org
Open: daily 9am–5pm (last
admission 4pm); admission charge.
The 140,000-gallon (530 cubic
metre) North Rock Exhibit brings
over 200 species of reef fish and
marine invertebrates up close. The
zoo has birds and animals from
islands around the world, while the
museum gives an insight into
Bermuda's marine and geological
development.
Crystal Caves
8 Crystal Caves Road
Baileys Bay
Tel: 293-0640
Open: daily 9.30am–4.30pm;
admission charge.
This underground lake discovered
by two small boys in 1907
shimmers with reflected
stalagmites and stalactites. Guided
tours lead you 120 feet (37 metres)
below ground.
Devil's Hole
Harrington Sound Road
Smiths
Tel: 293-2072
Open: daily 10am–4.30pm;
admission charge.
At Bermuda's oldest tourist
attraction, visitors can feed the fish
and turtles.

Tourism Website

For further information on
the sites of Bermuda, visit the
website of the Bermuda Tourist
Board at:
www.bermudatourism.com

Festivals

Festivals

This is a small selection of events
that take place throughout the year.

January/February
● **Regional Bridge Tournament**
● **Bermuda Festival of the
Performing Arts**: six-week
international arts festival with world-
renowned artists. Classical music,
dance, jazz, song, poetry and drama.
● **Bermuda National Trust
Children's Nature Walk**: introduces
children to the island's plant and
animal life.

March/April
● **Bermuda National Trust Palm
Sunday Walk**: annual walk of 6–8
miles (9–12 km) through an area of
natural and/or historic significance.
● **The Bermuda International Film
Festival** (BIFF): in March it shows an
impressive array of independent
films from around the world.

April
● **Peppercorn Ceremony**: pomp and
ceremony in St George's when the
Masonic Lodge of Bermuda pays its
annual rent for its headquarters,
the Old Station House.
● **Bermuda National Exhibition**: a
three-day exhibit of Bermuda's best
fruits, flowers, vegetables and
livestock, plus equestrian events.
● **Bermuda International Film
Festival**: week-long festival. After
the movie you can talk to the
director or producer in person. See
www.bermudafilmfest.com
● **Good Friday Kite Festival**:
Usually at Horseshoe Beach. It's a
fun day with entertainment and
contests.

April–October
● **Harbour Nights**: a street festival,
with food, crafts and entertainment,
on Front Street in Hamilton, every
Wednesday evening. Many shops
stay open late.
● **St. George's Market Nights**:
similar to Harbour Nights, but on
Tuesdays, in St. George's.

*April–October
(excluding August)*
● **Beat Retreat Ceremonies**:
alternating in Hamilton, St George's
and the Royal Naval Dockyard.
Historic military re-enactment
features the Bermuda Regiment
Band, the Bermuda Isles Pipe Band
(with dancers) and members of the
Bermuda Pipe Band.

May
● **Open Houses and Gardens**:
selected Bermuda homes and
gardens are open to visitors every
Wednesday afternoon.
● **Bermuda Day Parade**: colourful
parade to celebrate Bermuda's
national holiday, 24 May.
● **Heritage Month**: many events
around the island celebrating
Bermuda's history and culture.
● **Bermuda End-to-End**: raises funds
for a different charity each year.
Participants walk, cycle, kayak or
row a boat across the island.

June
● **Queen's Birthday Parade**: public
holiday with military parade on Front
Street, Hamilton.

July
● **Association of Canadians in
Bermuda Picnic**: at Chaplin Bay, on
the Saturday closest to 1 July.
● **Alliance Française des
Bermudes**: celebrates France's
Bastille Day, 14 July.

July/August
● **Cup Match Cricket Festival**: in
St George's or Somerset in
alternate years. Two-day cricket
match between East and West also
has food and games of chance.
Last weekend in July.
● **Non-Mariners Race**: the objective
is to lose the non-race or, better,

sink the non-boat. Held at Sandy's Boat Club, Mangrove Bay.

October
● **The Bermuda Music Festival:** three nights of open-air concerts at Dockyard. Performers have included jazz, R&B and soul artists such as George Benson, Diana Krall, Diane Reeves, Kenny G, Natalie Cole, Patti Labelle and Joss Stone.
● **The Bermuda Tattoo:** international military bands join the Bermuda Regiment Band and Corps of Drums in this festival of music at the Royal Naval Dockyard.
● **Bermuda Culinary Arts Festival:** the best of food and wine.

November
● **Convening of Parliament:** the Governor opens Parliament with a military guard of honour.
● **Remembrance Day:** a parade of Bermudian, British and US military units, Bermuda Police and veterans organisations, to honour men and women who died in service.
● **World Rugby Classic:** teams of former top national players compete. There are also street parties and social events. A week-long event.

November–March
● **Bermuda Rendezvous Time:** daily activities throughout the winter season including historic events in St George's, a Market Day with local artisans, a Skirling Ceremony and walking tours. Military bands often perform in the evenings on Front Street in Hamilton.

December
● **Christmas Boat Parade:** boats are decorated with lights and seasonal themes around Hamilton Harbour.
● **Bermuda National Trust Christmas Walkabout:** the people of St George's participate in this evening of music, lights, crafts, food and fun.
● **St. George's Annual New Year's Eve Celebration:** St. George's drops a giant onion in the Town Square as entertainers ring in the new year, Bermuda style.

Sport & Leisure

Spectator Sports

Sailing
● International Race Week (April/May)
● Heritage Trophy, Fitted Dinghies (May)
● Newport–Bermuda Race (June, even years)
● Marion–Bermuda Cruising Race (June, odd years)
● King Edward VII Gold Cup Match Racing Regatta (November)

Golf
● Bermuda PGA Championship (January)
● Bermuda Amateur Matchplay (March)
● Bermuda Amateur Strokeplay (June)
● Bermuda Open Championship (October)
● Belmont Invitational Championships (November)
● Bermuda Goodwill Championships (December)

Tennis
● USTA Mother-Daughter, Father-Son Tournament (March)
● International Open (April)
● Bermuda Lawn Tennis Club Invitational (November)
● Coral Beach Club Invitational (November)

Cricket
● Central Counties Cup Final (July)
● Cup Match (Thursday and Friday before first Monday of August)
● Eastern Counties Cup Final (August)
● Western Counties Cup Final (August)

Football (Soccer)
● Diadora International Youth Cup (April)
● FA Challenge Cup Final (April)
● Martonmere Cup Final (November)
● Dudley Eve Trophy final, two legs (Christmas Day, New Year's Day)

Rugby
● Easter Classic (Easter Sunday)
● World Rugby Classic (November)

Squash
● Bermuda Open (November)

Bowling
● Annual Bermuda Invitation Rendezvous Tournament (February)

Hockey
● Bermuda Hockey Festival (September)

Powerboats
● Around the Island Race (July/August)

Cycling
● Grand Prix Aux Bermuda (April)

Triathlon
● Bermuda International Triathlon (September)
● Bermuda Triathlon (September/Oct)

Road Running
● International Race Weekend (mid-January)
● Marathon Derby (May)

Armchair Sports

For a look at the **athletics** opportunities that Bermuda can offer, read the chapter entitled Bermuda Sports *(see page 108)*. Visit the Department of Tourism's website for more general information: www.bermudatourism.com.

Walks

For walkers, there are many opportunities in the Bermudian town and countryside. The Department of Tourism pamphlet, *Explore Bermuda*, provides maps, suggests walking tours and includes a guide to the Railway Trail *(see page 213)*. The trail, which is protected as a National Park, is for walkers or scooter riders only.

GUIDED TOURS

There are a variety of historical and nature walks and tours organised by the Department of Tourism through the Visitor Information Centres. Some are seasonal, and all depend on the weather.

Nature Reserves

The most important nature reserves open to the public are: Paget Marsh (Middle Road, Paget); Spittal Pond (South Road, Smith's); Gladys Morrell (East Shore Road, Sandys) and the Gilbert Nature Reserve (Somerset Road, Somerset, Sandys). All reserves are open all year round, but you should make appointments in advance to visit them, apart from Spittal Pond, which is open daily and requires no appointment. Contact the National Trust at Waterville, (tel: 236-6483) for details. Please keep to the paths provided.

Beaches

Over half of Bermuda's coastline consists of beaches. Some are private, but many are not. The best way to find good beaches is by sampling as many as possible. Clearwater Beach in St David's has a lifeguard during the summer months, as does John Smith's Bay, on the South Shore, Smiths. Astwood Park, further along the same shore in Warwick, is a lovely picnic spot (tables provided) with a cove suitable for inshore snorkelling. At the secluded eastern end of the cove is a smaller beach.

Horseshoe Bay is a long, well-kept beach with lifeguards in summer. You can rent chairs, buy refreshments and shower at the beach entrance. The adjacent Port Royal Cove, commonly known as the "Baby Beach", is ideal for small children and the arm-band brigade. Church Bay, in Southampton, with its cosy rock-edged cove, is a splendid snorkelling area, unless the wind is blowing in from the south.

Watersports

From April to November, the number of activities in which visitors can engage while above, on top of, or actually in the water is vast. You can go para-sailing, scuba diving and snorkelling; hire motor boats and jet-skis, sailboats, windsurfers, paddle boats, rafts, rowing sculls and even yachts.

A number of cruises are offered, from glass-bottomed boat tours to observe Bermuda's extremely active marine community, to moonlight sails through the Great Sound, or dance parties on small, secluded islets. Hotel lobbies and Visitor Information Centres should have leaflets with all the details you require.

Nightlife

Most nightlife for visitors, and many locals, takes place in clubs at the larger hotels. Entertainment tends to be of the cocktail party or piano lounge variety, though increasingly, local bands perform live rock, reggae and dance music. Ask at your hotel for recommendations.

The Deep Night Club
Elbow Beach Hotel
Tel: 232-6969
This smart night spot attracts a lively mix of local people and visitors who dance till 3am.

Flanagan's Irish Pub and Restaurant
69 Front Street
Hamilton
Tel: 295-8299
Local bands perform here five nights a week, playing covers of anything from rock to reggae. TV sets are constantly tuned to sports events from both sides of the Atlantic. Casual attire. Open till 1am.

Fresco's Wine Bar and Restaurant
2 Chancery Lane, off Front Street
Hamilton
Tel: 295-5058
Popular wine bar above a continental restaurant. When the suits knock off work, many find their way here to unwind, to see and to be seen.

Swizzle Inn
3 Blue Hole Hill
Tel: 293-1854
This casual spot attracts both local people and visitors. The evenings can be quite lively, not least because the house drink is the Rum Swizzle, which looks and tastes like fruit juice, but is 90 percent rum.

Robin Hood
25 Richmond Road
Tel: 295-3314
A popular expat hang out. Its sports bar, reasonably priced ale and more

than edible food attract a noisy, mostly British crowd.

Pickled Onion
53 Front Street
Hamilton
Tel: 295-2263
Happy Hour (5–7pm) is indeed, happy at this cheerful eatery. The music's good, the food's better and the bartenders know their stuff. At 10pm live entertainment begins, which can be anything from vintage hits to country blues.

Hubie's Bar
Angle Street
Hamilton
Tel: 293-9287
Friday is the night for this unique jazz bar. It's small but full of awesome music and people of every age. The band plays from 7 till 10pm, but you'll need to arrive before 7pm to secure a seat. No credit cards.

Jasmine Lounge
Fairmont Southampton
Tel: 238-8000
This cocktail bar and restaurant has a pianist from 6pm; things liven up a bit later with a live band playing until 1am.

Splash
12 Bermudiana Road
Hamilton
Tel: 296-3328
The dance floor is downstairs and there is a lounge upstairs. DJs get the crowd going with the music. Dress smart casual, no sneakers. Open 5pm–5am daily except Sunday.

Out on the Town

Bermuda is a friendly place, but exercise the same precautions you would when dealing with strangers in bars anywhere. Watch your drink, watch your wallet and watch out for troublemakers.

Shopping

What to Buy

Products that make excellent, and authentic, Bermudian souvenirs that are worth keeping your eyes open for include: Outerbridge's sherry pepper sauce; Horton's black rum cake; Carol Holding Bacardi Rum Cakes, Bermuda spirits (Gosling's Black Seal Rum, Silver Label Light Rum, Rum Swizzle, Bermuda Gold, Banana Liqueur, Bermuda Triangle); floral perfumes by the Bermuda Perfumery and Royall Lyme; hand-made cedar candle-holders, lamps and book-ends.

Other good buys to look for on the island include: cashmeres, linens, woollens, knitwear, tartan, Liberty silk scarves, menswear and walking sticks, Wedgwood, Royal Crown Derby and other fine china and porcelain.

Where to Buy

Hamilton is the obvious place to head when shopping, from the elegant facades of Front Street to the indoor arcades behind them. Many of Hamilton's shops are family-owned businesses which date back to the 1860s. Gosling's, the liquor merchants, is even older – the shop was established in 1806.

As a break from the very busy Hamilton centre, it's refreshing to look for souvenirs in the narrow back streets of old St George's and by Mangrove Bay in the village of Somerset. At the Royal Naval Dockyard, which ranks as one of the island's top attractions, the Clocktower Mall is filled with shops. Several Front Street merchants also have branches in the mall, as do

shops that sell everything from Cuban cigars to suntan lotion.

Export Procedures

Bermuda is not the bargain-hunter's Mecca it once was. Still, unusual imported goods can still be found at reasonable prices, and some goods are sold duty free to visitors. As well as substantial savings on British goods, any gift of under $50 (US) or $20 (Canada) can be posted abroad by mail without infringing on the duty-free allowance.

So how are prices kept low? Bermuda is not a "duty-free" island, but most shops buy directly from manufacturers and avoid high distribution costs. "In bond" shopping is another way the island saves money. This "in bond" merchandise, mainly spirits and cigarettes, is priced low because, technically, the goods have not entered the country before they are sold on.

Further Reading

Bermuda has a relatively active publishing industry for a such a small place. The Bermuda Library, in Queen Street, Hamilton, has a copy of every Bermuda book. So, it seems, do the BookMart upstairs in the Phoenix Drug Store (Reid Street) and the Bermuda Book Store (Queen Street). As well as the library, out-of-print books can be found at the Craft Market at Royal Naval Dockyard.

Art & Photography

Bermuda Abstracts: Photographs by Graeme Outerbridge, Matrix Publications (1982).
Picturesque Bermuda Volume I and **Volume II** by Roland Skinner, Picturesque (1997 and 1999).
Bermuda: Gardens and Houses by Sylvia Shorto, Rizzoli (1996).

Fiction

A Matter of Time: A Faith Abbey Mystery by David Manuel, Warner Books (2003).
The Bermuda Indenture by Strudwick Marvin Rogers, Court Street Press (2001).
Spinners: The Lost Treasure of Bermuda by R.C. Farrington, Print Link (2005).
The Bermuda Virus by Bob O'Quinn, The Bermudian Publishing Company Limited (1996).
Endangered Species and Other Short Stories by Angela Barry, Peepal Tree Press Ltd (2003).

Food and Drink

A Bermuda Cook Book of Traditional and Modern Recipes, Plus the Interesting Background and Customs of Bermuda Cookery by Betsy Ross, D. Hunter (1968).
Spirit of Bermuda by Edward Bottone, The Bermudian Publishing Company Limited (1998).

For Children

Bermuda Petrel: The Bird That Would Not Die by Francine Jacobs, Olympic Marketing Corp (1981).
Fish Tales by Debbie Jones Harrisii Publishing Limited, Bermuda (1995).
The Bermuda Cedar Tree by Kevin Stevenson, The Bermudian Publishing Company Ltd. (1997).
Miracle: The True Story of the Wreck of the Sea Venture by Gail Kawoski, Darby Creek Publishing (2004).

General

Bermewjan Vurds by Peter A. Smith, Island Press (1984).
Bermuda: An Economy Which Works by Robert Stewart, The Island Press Limited (1997).
Into the Bermuda Triangle by Gian Quasar, International Marine/ Ragged Mountain Press; (2005).
Tea With Tracey by Tracey Caswell, Print Link (2003).

History

Bermuda Forts, 1612–1957 by Edward C. Harris, Bermuda Maritime Museum Press (1997).
Bermuda Shipwrecks: A Vacationing Diver's Guide to Bermuda's Shipwrecks by Daniel and Denise Berg, Aqua Explorers (1990).
Boer Prisoners of War in Bermuda by Colin H. Benbow, Bermuda College (1982).
Rogues and Runners: Bermuda and the American Civil War by Catherine Lynch Deichmann, Bermuda National Trust (2003).
The Bermuda Railway, Gone But Not Forgotten by Colin A. Pomeroy, Colin A. Pomeroy (1993).
The Story of Bermuda and Her People by W.S. Zuill, Macmillan (1973).
Bermuda Five Centuries by Rosemary Jones, Panatel VDS Ltd (2004).

Natural History

A Birdwatching Guide to Bermuda by Andrew Dobson, Arlequin Press (2002).
A Field Guide to the Birds of Bermuda by Andre Raine, Macmillan Publishers (2003).
Bermuda's Seashore Plants and Seaweeds by Wolfgang Sterrer and A. Ralph Cavaliere, Bermuda Natural History Museum (1998).
Hiking Bermuda: 20 Nature Walks and Day Hikes by Cecile Davidson, VegaNet Publications (2004).
Marine Fauna and Flora of Bermuda: A Systematic Guide to the Identification of Marine Organisms by Wolfgang Sterrer, John Wiley & Sons (1986).
The Adventurers of Bermuda, by Henry C. Wilkinson, Oxford University Press (1933).

Other Insight Guides

The companion volumes to this book are Apa Publications' trim **Insight Pocket Guide: Bermuda**, with selected itineraries plus a handy pull-out map, and **Insight Compact Guide: Bermuda**, a portable fact-packed guide. Other titles that explore the region include Insight Guides to: Miami, Bahamas and Caribbean Cruises.
    Insight FlexiMap: Bermuda combines details of the main sights. A laminated finish makes it durable and easy to fold.

ART & PHOTO CREDITS

INSIGHT GUIDE
BERMUDA

Cartographic Editor **Zoë Goodwin**
Production **Linton Donaldson**
Design Consultant
Carlotta Junger
Picture Research
Hilary Genin, Natasha Babaian

Index

Numbers in italics refer to photographs

a

accommodation 290–93
 cottage colonies 204
 Fairmont Hamilton Princess Hotel (Hamilton) 63, 171
 Rosedon Hotel (Hamilton) 172
 Southampton Princess Hotel (Southampton) 23–4, 200
 Waterloo House Hotel (Hamilton) 172, *173*
agriculture 17
Allen C.M. 60
ambergris 17, 39, 41, 43, 123
Arboretum (Pembroke) 199
architecture 85–8, 214, 257
art and crafts 113–7
 see also **museums and galleries**
 Bermuda Clayworks (Dockyard) 233
 Bermuda Society of Artists 113
 Craft Market (Dockyard) 231
 craft workshops (Baileys Bay) 245
 at Daniel's Head Village (Sandys) 226
 Island Pottery (Dockyard) 233
 Masterworks Foundation 114–5, 268
arts and entertainment
 see also **festivals and events**
 Arts Council 91
 Bermuda Arts Centre (Dockyard) 115, 233–4
 Bermuda Musical and Dramatic Society 92
 City Hall (Hamilton) *91*, 113–4, 178, 185
 Little Theatre Cinema (Hamilton) 185
 Neptune Cinema (Dockyard) 231
 Ruth Seaton James Theatre (Prospect) 91
Astor's Halt 217
Audubon Society 87

b

Baileys Bay 217, 246
 craft workshops 245
 Swizzle Inn 131, 217, 245–6
Barnes, Johnny 116, *170*, 171, 266
Beebe Project 245
Beebe, Dr William 245

Berlitz, Charles 149
 The Bermuda Triangle 149
Bermuda Aquarium 217, 244
Bermuda Archives 113
Bermuda Harbour Radio 97, 101
Bermuda Land Development Company 267
Bermuda National Trust 87, 177, 203
Bermuda Perfumery *246*, 247
 Nature Trail 246–7
Bermuda Railway 157, *213–5*
Bermuda shorts 77, *182*
Bermuda Triangle 15, 148–51
Bermuda Zoo 244
de Bermudez, Juan 31, 32
Bermudian cedar 17, *46*, 216
 burning 17, 46, 142–3, 216
 insect epidemic 17
Best, Clyde 106
Birdsey, Alfred 116, 202, *203*
Birdsey Studio 116, 203
Birdsey Linberg, Jo 116, 202
Blackburn, Joseph 113
Blackburn, Dr Luke P. 61–2
Blue Hole Park 246
Boaz Island 228
Bond, The Rev. Sampson 70
Bowen, John 125
Bruere, George James 57
Buildings Bay 36, 268
Burt Island 278
Bush, Jack
 St George's 112
Butler, Nathaniel 39, 48–50, 264–5
Butterfield, Tom 114–5

c

Caldicott, Charles 44
calypso *see* **music and dance**
Cameron, Earl 91
Cann, Vince *23*
cemeteries 199, 201
Carter, Christopher 37, 39, 41, 44, 123
 see also **"three kings"**
Castle Harbour 34, 248
Castle Island nature reserve 41, 43, *49*, 276, 277–8
Cavendish, William 47
Chard, Edward 39, 41
 see also **"three kings"**
Church Bay 205–6, 247
 Holy Trinity Church 247
churches and cathedrals
 Cathedral of the Most Holy Trinity (Hamilton) 91, *186*

Heydon chapel (Sandys) 225
Holy Trinity Church (Church Bay, Harrington Sound) 246
Kingdom Hall (Sandys) 226
Old Devonshire Church (Devonshire) 158, *197*, 199
St James' church (Sandys) *225*, 226
St Peter's church (St George's) 41, *47*, 49, *52*, 262–3
St Theresa's Cathedral (Pembroke) 195–6
Trinity church (Hamilton) *24*
Unfinished Church (St George's) 58, *262*, 263
Churchill, Winston *28*
civil rights 23–4, 72
 see also **people – slaves**
Clermont 203
climate and weather 15, 100–101, 155, 157
 Gulf Stream 15, 157
 hurricanes *200*
Coney, Richard 52
Coney Island 217, 245, 278
Cooper's Island 42, 44, 64, 123, 275
Coral Beach 205
Cram, Ralph Adams 214
crime and safety 24, 177
cruise ships 78, 174, 175, 232
Crystal Caves *247*, 247–8
customs and traditions 156, 158

d

Darrell, Jemmy 58–9
Darrell Island 203, 275, 278
Davenport, John 261
Deliverance 35–6, 37
Denslow, William Wallace 277
Denslow's Island 277
Devil's Hole and Aquarium 243
Devonshire 199, 201
 Edmund Gibbons Nature Reserve 201
 Old Devonshire Church 158, *197*, 199
 Palmetto House 201, 216
 Palmetto Park 216
 Palm Grove *201*
Dockyard 99, 197, 223, *228*, 229–34
 Bermuda Arts Centre 115, 233–4
 Bermuda Clayworks 233
 Bermuda Maritime Museum 99, 123, 223, 232, 234
 Coin Collection 233–2
 Commissioner's House 197, 232

Cooperage Theatre 231
Craft Market 229
floating dock 233
Freeport Seafood Restaurant and Bar 233
Frog & Onion 131, 231
Great Eastern Storehouse 232
Island Pottery 233
Keep 234
King's Steps 232–3
Neptune Cinema 231
ramparts 233
Sail Loft 233
Smithy 231
South Basin 232
Terrace Gallery 115
Treasury 234
Victualling (Vittling) Yard 231
Dodwell, David 78
Downing, Edmund 230
Driver, Thomas
St George's 38–9
driving 249
prewar motor car ban 99, 213
vehicle rentals 21, 249

e

East End 255–68
see also individual place names
ecology 16–17
see also wildlife
economy 17–18, 24, 79–80
Eisenhower, Dwight 28
Elbow Beach 205, 214
Elfrith, Daniel 41–2, 125
Ely's Harbour 216, 224
etiquette 20, 182

f

Fern Island see Sin Island
ferries 174, 203, 216, 223
Ferry Point 217
ancient forts 217
old cemetery 217
festivals and events 91–3, 197
Bermuda Day 108
Bermuda Exhibition 109
Bermuda Festival 91–3, 185
dinghy racing 100
national kite-flying day 158
Peppercorn Ceremony (St George's) 88, 264
skirling ceremony (Fort Hamilton) 159, 199
sporting events 105–9
fishing industry 202
Flatts Inlet 217

Flatts Village 217, 243
The Bermuda Aquarium, Natural History Museum and Zoo 217, 244–5
Fleming, Ian 63
food and drink 15, 19, 20, 129–31
Fort Hamilton 197, 199
Fort St Catherine 268
Fountain, Desmond Hale 93, 116, 177
News Flash 116–7
Spirit of Bermuda 116, 171
Frobisher, Richard 36

g

Gardiner, Jeane 51
Gates, Sir Thomas 33–6, 41
Gates Fort 41, 268
geology 15, 157
Gibbet Island 217, 279
Gibbs Hill lighthouse (Warwick) 206, 215
Gladys Morrell Nature Reserve 228
Goater, Shaun 106
Goodrich, Bridger 88
Gordon, Dr Edgar Fitzgerald 72
Gordon, The Hon. Pamela F. 72
Godet, Theodore L. 69–70, 255–6
Gray, Sir Brownlow 108, 203–4
Great Sound 223
Green, John 113
Gwynn, Joseph 265

h

H.T. North Nature Reserve 243
Hamilton 59, 98, 167, 171–87, 214
Albuoys Point 174
"Back of Town" 177
Bank of Bermuda 173–4, 188
Barr's Bay Park 173
Bermuda Book Store Ltd 180
Bermuda Library 183, 183
Bermuda Train Company 174
Bermuda Underwater Exploration Institute 180
birdcage 20, 173, 181
Bluck's 176
bus terminal 185
Cabinet Building 178–80
Cathedral of the Most Holy Trinity (Bermuda Cathedral) 91, 186
Cenotaph 64, 178–9
Chancery Lane 177
Church Street 185
City Hall 91, 113–4, 178, 185
Colonial Gallery 115

Dorothy's Coffee Shop 178
Emporium Arcade 177
Fairmont Hamilton Princess Hotel 63, 171
ferry terminal 174
Fort Hamilton 143
Front Street 166, 175, 178
Front Street West 175
Gosling's 176
Historical Society Museum 183
Hog Penny pub 177
Irish Linen Shop 176, 227–8
Little Theatre Cinema 184
Masterworks Foundation Gallery 115, 178
moongates 73, 172
National Gallery 113–4, 178, 185–6
nightlife 175, 177
Old Cellar 177
Old Cellar Lane 176–7
Par-la-Ville Park 143, 180
Pegasus 172
Perot's Post Office 181, 181
Phoenix drugstore 184
Pickled Onion restaurant 177
Post Office 186
Reid Street 183–4
Rosedon Hotel 172
Royal Bermuda Yacht Club 173
Sessions House 186, 187
shopping 171, 174, 175–6
sightseeing trips 174, 175
Spirit of Bermuda 116, 171, 180
Stockton House 173
The Spot 129
Trinity church 24
Victoria Park 185, 185–6
Visitors' Service Bureau 173
Walker Arcade 176
Washington Lane 176
Washington Mall 184
Waterfront 172
Waterloo House Hotel 172, 173
Windjammer Gallery 116, 176, 178
Windsor Place 184
Zurich Centre 172
Hamilton Harbour 135–7
Harbour Radio see Bermuda Harbour Radio
Harbour Road 203
Harrington Sound 217, 241–9
see also individual place names
Harriott, Henry 48–9
Harwood, Henry 64
Hayward, Martha 182
Hayward, William Brownell 18
Heydon, Sir John 50–51

Heyling, Margaret 50
Hildyard, Sir Reginald 21
historic houses
  Camden (Paget) 87, 143, *194*, 201–2
  Clermont 203
  Commissioner's House (Dockyard) 232
  Government House (Pembroke) *106*, *196*, 197
  Heydon Trust (Sandys) 51, 216, 225
  Palmetto House (Devonshire) 199, 216
  Springfield (Sandys) 88, 226
  Verdmont 87, 113, 158, *240*, 241–2
history 31–72
  America, relations with *56*, 57–62
  "overplus" scandal 47–8, 206, 215, 279
  Spanish hostilities 41, 43
  witch trials 51
  World War I 62, 64
  World War II 63, 64, 171
Holding, Carole 261
Homer, Winslow 115
  Bermuda Settlers 115
Horseshoe Bay 205
Horton, Randy 106
Hughes, The Rev. Lewis 16, 42–3, 44, 47, 48, 49
Hungry Bay 202

i

Indian John 217, 279
Ireland Island North *see* Dockyard
Ireland Island South 228–9
  Lagoon Park 229
  naval cemetery 229
  old convict cemetery 229
  Parson's Bay 229
Irving, Washington 39
  Three Kings of Bermuda 39

j

Jackson, Louise A. 156
"James, Edward" 113
Joell, Lillian 241
Joell, William 72
Jones, E. Michael 259
Jourdain, Silvester 34–5

k

Kendall, Captain 44
Kendall, Edwin 41
Kendall, Miles 48, 50, 69, 276
Khyber Pass 215

l

Lamb, Dennis *266*
Leather, Sir Edwin 91
Lefroy, Lady 113
  Fishes of Bermuda 34, *35*
Lightbourne, Kyle 106
Linberg, Jo Birdsey 116, 203
Lincoln, Abraham 59
Little, Douglas *234*
Little Sound 215
Lockwood, Bill 91
Long Bay Beach and Nature Reserve 227
Longbird Island 275
Louise, Princess 18, 62, 155
Lower Ferry 203

m

McCallan, E.A. 255
  Life on Old St David's 255
Maclarie, John 71
Madeiros, Jeremy 145
mail services 181–2, 186
Mangrove Bay *222*, 228
Mangrove Lake 248
Mansfield, Captain 44–5
May, Henry 32
media
  foreign newspapers 184
  Bermuda Harbour Radio 97, 101
  The Royal Gazette 105
Menuhin, Sir Yehudi 91, *92*
Middle Road 215
Middleton, John 51
money matters
  Bermuda Stock Exchange 189
  currency 21–2
  banking and finance houses 79, 188–9
  Hog Money 49, 184
  taxation 15, 24
  tobacco as currency 49
Moore, Richard 41, 42, 43
Moore, Tom 15, *248*, 256–7
Morgan's Point resort 223
motoring 21
  see also **vehicle rental**
  limitation on car ownership 21
  prewar ban on cars 21

Mowbray, Louis 144
Mowbray, Louis S. 145
Murphy, Dr Robert Cushman 145
museums and galleries
  Bermuda Maritime Museum (Dockyard) 99, 123, 223, 232, 234
  Bermuda National Trust Museum (St George's) *261*, 262
  Bermuda Natural History Museum (Flatts Village) 244–5
  Bermuda Underwater Exploration Institute (Hamilton) *180*
  Carter House Museum (St David's) *40*, 268
  City Hall (Hamilton) *91*, 113–4, 178, 185
  Colonial Gallery (Hamilton) 115
  Heritage Museum (St George's) 264
  Historical Society Museum (Hamilton) 184
  National Gallery (Hamilton) 113–4, 178, 185–6
  St George's Historical Society Museum (St George's) 265, 267
  Terrace Gallery (Dockyard) 115
  Treasury (Dockyard) 234
  Tucker House Museum (St George's) 88, 113, *257*
  Windjammer Gallery (Hamilton) 116, 176, 178
music and dance 118–9
  Gombey 78, *156*, 175

n

Napoleon 58
Natural Arches 248
nature reserves 241
  Castle Island 41, 43, *49*, 276, 277–8
  Edmund Gibbons (Devonshire) 199, 201
  Gilbert (Sandys) 226
  Gladys Morrell 228
  H.T. North 242
  Lagoon Park (Ireland Island South) 229
  Long Bay Beach and Nature Reserve 227
  Nonsuch Island 145, 277
  Paget Marsh 204
  Shelly Bay Park and Nature Reserve 217, 245
  Spittal Pond 32, 158, 242
  Springfield and the Gilbert Nature Reserve 216

Newport, Christopher 33
Nonsuch Island nature reserve
    145, 277
North, Nathaniel 125
North Shore Road 216, 246
Norwood, Richard 44, 47, 123–4,
    206, 215, 225

o–p

Outerbridge, Mary 108, 204
d'Oviedo, Gonzales Ferdinando 32
Paget 214
    Botanical Gardens 109, 143,
        201, *202*
    Camden 87, 143, *194*, 201–2
    Fourways Inn 131, 294
Paget Island 276
    Fort Cunningham 276
Paget Marsh nature reserve 204
Paine, Henry 33, 37
parks and gardens
    Barr's Bay Park (Hamilton) 173
    Botanical Gardens (Paget) 109,
        143, 201, *202*
    Palmetto Park (Devonshire) 216
    Palm Grove (Devonshire) *201*
    Par-la-Ville Park (Hamilton) 143,
        181
    Somers Garden (St George's)
        37, 264, *265*
    South Shore Beach Parklands
        215
    Spanish Point Park 197
    Victoria Park (Hamilton) *185*, 186
Patience 36, 37, 38, 259
Pembroke 171, 195–7
    Black Watch Pass 196
    Black Watch Well 196
    Government House *106*, *196*,
        197
    nightlife 195
    St Theresa's Cathedral 195–6
people 20, 22–3, 69, 77, 79, 158
    early settlers 17, 32–9
    slaves 23, 69–72, 229, 231,
        234
Perot, William B. 181
pirates and privateers 31, 41–2,
    44, 59, 69, 88, 123–5, 234
    see also **wrecking and salvaging**
plant life 17, 143, 157
    national flower 143
Pleissner, Ogden Minton
    St George's Bermuda 115
politics and government 20, 72,
    79–80, 179–80, 187
    membership of British
        Commonwealth 179

Progressive Labour Party 72,
    79–80
United Bermuda Party 72, 79–80
Pollard, William 46
Port's Island 278
Port Royal 42, 206
property 24
    restrictions on foreign ownership
        24
Prospect
    National Stadium 108
    Ruth Seaton James Theatre 91
public transportation
    buses 186

r

Railway Trail 206, 213–7, 223,
    228, 249
Rainey, Joseph 257
Raleigh, Sir Walter 31
Ramirez, Diego 31–2, 141–2
Restaurants 293–95
Rich, Robert 46
Richards, Sir Edward 72
Richardson, Brian *134*, 135
Robert E. Lee 61
Robinson, Robert 52
Rolfe, John 36
Royal Naval Dockyard *see*
    Dockyard

s

St David's 35, 64, 69, 255, 266,
    267, 268
    Bermuda airport 267
    Carter House Museum *40*,
        267–8
    Dennis's Hideaway 129, 266,
        268
    St David's lighthouse 268, *269*
St George's 41, 59, 87–8, 97–8,
    216, 255, 256–67
    Bermuda National Trust Museum
        261, 262
    Bridge House 88, 256–7
    Deliverance replica *36*, 259
    ducking stool 258
    Featherbed Alley 256, *261*
    Gwynn House 265
    Heritage Museum 263–4
    King's Square 258
    Masonic Hall 88, 264
    Old Maid's Lane 256
    Old Rectory *45*, 267
    One Gun Alley 256
    Ordnance Island 36, 259, *275*,
        279

Penno Wharf 78
post office 58, 263
Printery 265
Rosecote 116
St George's Historical Society
    Museum 267
St Peter's church 41, *47*, 49,
    52, 262–3
Shinbone Alley 256
Sir George Somers statue *32*,
    116
Somers Garden 37, 264, *265*
State House 49, 88, 263, *264*
Tom Moore bust 257
Town Hall *255*, 259
Tucker House Museum 88, 113,
    257
Unfinished Church 58, *262*,
    263
Visitors' Service Bureau 259
White Horse Tavern *260*, 261
sailing 97–101
    magnetic variations 101
Sandys, Sir Edwyn 47
Sandys 88, 224–6
    Bat 'n' Ball Lane 226
    Gilbert Nature Reserve 226
    Heydon chapel 225
    Heydon Trust 51, 216, 225
    Kingdom Hall 226
    St James' church *225*, 226
    Scaur Hill Fort 216, *224*
    Somerset Cricket Club 226
    Somerset Road 225
    Springfield 88, 226
    Visitors' Service Bureau 226
Saunders, Nicky 108
Scott, Herbert 246
Scott, Madeline 246
Sea Venture 33–4, *37*, 92, 230, 259
Shakespeare, William 15, 33, 92
    The Tempest 15, 33, 92
Sharples, Sir Richard 23, 197
Shelly Bay Park and Nature
    Reserve 217, 246
ship-building industry 50, *51*, 52
shipping 135–7
shipwrecks 16
shopping 22
sightseeing trips 174, 277
Sin Island 277
Smith, Hubert *118*, 119
Smith, The Hon. Jennifer M. 72
Smith's Island 39, 41, 275–6
Somers, Sir George 33–8, 50,
    264–5
Somers, Matthew 39
Somers Island Company 47, 48,
    51–2, 123

Somerset Village 216, 224, 227
  Railway Trail 228
  Woody's restaurant 129
Somerset Bridge 215, *216*, 224
Southampton 204
  Waterlot Inn 131
Southampton Princess Hotel 23–4
South Shore 204–6
South Shore Beach Parklands 215
"Southside" development 267
Spanish Point 31, 197, 216
  Spanish Point Park 197
Spanish Rock 32, 158, 243
Spittal Pond nature reserve 32,
  158, 242
sport and activities 105–9
  bowling 109
  cricket 105–6
  cycling 109
  diving and snorkelling 16, 206
  fishing 107
  golf 107, 206, 215, 248
  hiking and walking 21
  hockey 109
  National Stadium (Prospect) 108
  pot-holing 247
  rugby 109
  running and athletics 108–9
  sailing 97–101, 106
  soccer 106
  softball 109
  squash 109
  swimming 109
  tennis 107–8, 196, 203–4
  watersports 107
**Springfield and the Gilbert Nature
  Reserve** 216, 226
Strachey, William 33, 142
Strachey's Watch 35
Sugarloaf Hill 217
Swainson, Gina 177
Swan, Sir John 72, 80, 179

t

Tatum, Skipper 137
telephones 22, 186
Tew, Thomas 125

"three kings" 39, 41, 260
Timlin's Narrows 223
Tobacco Bay 57
tourism 18–19, 62, 77–80, 105,
  155
  eco-tourism 227
tourist information 174
  Visitors' Service Bureau
    (Hamilton) 174
  Visitors' Service Bureau (St
    George's) 259
  Visitors' Service Bureau (Sandys)
    226
treasure 16, 123–5
Treasurer 41–2, 125
Trimmingham, John 50
Trollope, Anthony 18
Trott, Chesley 116
Trott's Pond 248
Trunk Island 279
Tucker, Daniel 45–8, 50. 142–3,
  206, 215, 248, 279
Tucker, Sir Henry 72
Tucker, Nea 256–7
Tucker, Teddy 50, *123*, 234
Tucker, Mrs Terry 50, 257, 275
  Islands 275
Tucker's Island 206
Tucker's Town 248
Tudor Hill 223–4
Tumbridge, M.J. 109
Turtle Island 244
Twain, Mark *18*, 62, 155, 183

u–v

US military bases (former) 64,
  206, 223, 267
vehicle rentals 21, 249
Verdmont 87, 113, 158, *240*,
  241–2

w

Walker, Norman 60
Walsingham 143
Walsingham Bay 248
  Tom Moore's Tavern 131, 248

Warwick Long Bay 205
Warwick Parish 214
  Warwick Lanes 109
Washington, George *57*
Waters, Edward 36–7, 39
  see also **"three kings"**
water supply 22
Waterville 87, 203
Watford Bridge 228
Watford Island 228
Watlington, The Hon. Hereward 114
West End 223–34
  see also individual place names
West Whale Bay 206
  Whale Bay Battery 206
White's Island 278
wildlife 141–5
  amphibians 16, 144
  bird life 15, 144–5
  cahow 15, 17, 31–2, 41, 42,
    141, 142, 144–5
  rats 17, 41–2, 45, 125, 141,
    142, 216–7
  skink 15–16, 34, 141, 143
  wild hogs 16, 34–5, 37, 41, 141
Wilkinson, Henry C. 142
Wingate, Dr David 144–5
Wingood, Allan "Smokey" 230
Wood, Ensign 48
Wood, Lieutenant 276
Wood, Roger 50
Woodhouse, Henry 50
working in Bermuda 24
wrecking and salvaging 124, 234
Wyeth, Andrew 115
  The Bermudian 68, 115

z

Zuill, William 248, 257
  Bermuda Journey 257, 260
  Tom Moore's Bermuda Poems
    248

A
B
C
D
E
F
G
H
J
a
b
c
d
f
g
h
i
j
k
l

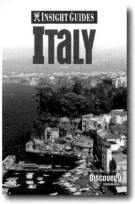

INSIGHT GUIDES
The classic series that puts you in the picture

✶ INSIGHT GUIDES
www.insightguides.com

Alaska
Amazon Wildlife
American Southwest
Amsterdam
Athens
Argentina
Arizona & the
   Grand Canyon
Asia's Best Hotels
   & Resorts
Asia, East
Asia, Southeast
Australia
Australia & New Zealand's
   Best Hotels & Resorts
Austria
Bahamas
Bali
Baltic States
Bangkok
Barbados
Barcelona
Beijing
Belgium
Belize
Berlin
Bermuda
Boston
Brazil
Bruges, Ghent, Antwerp
Brussels
Budapest
Buenos Aires
Bulgaria
Burgundy
Burma (Myanmar)
Cairo
California
California, Southern
Canada
Cape Town
Caribbean
Caribbean Cruises
Channel Islands
Chicago
Chile
China
China, Southern
Colorado
Continental Europe
Corsica
Costa Rica
Crete
Croatia
Cuba
Cyprus
Czech & Slovak
   Republics
Delhi, Agra & Jaipur

Denmark
Dominican Republic
   & Haiti
Dublin
East African Wildlife
Ecuador
Edinburgh
Egypt
England
Finland
Florence
Florida
France
France, Southwest
French Riviera
Gambia & Senegal
Germany
Glasgow
Gran Canaria
Great Britain
Great Gardens of
   Britain & Ireland
Great Railway Journeys
   of Europe
Great River Cruises
   of Europe
Greece
Greek Islands
Guatemala, Belize
   & Yucatán
Hawaii
Holland
Hong Kong
Hungary
Iceland
India
India, South
Indian Wildlife
Indonesia
Ireland
Israel
Istanbul
Italy
Italy, Northern
Italy, Southern
Jamaica
Japan
Jerusalem
Jordan
Kenya
Korea

Kuala Lumpur
Laos & Cambodia
Las Vegas
Lisbon
London
Los Angeles
Madeira
Madrid
Malaysia
Mallorca & Ibiza
Malta
Marine Life in the
   South China Sea
Mauritius, Réunion
   & Seychelles
Mediterranean Cruises
Melbourne
Mexico
Mexico City
Miami
Montreal
Morocco
Moscow
Munich
Namibia
Nepal
Netherlands
New England
New Mexico
New Orleans
New South Wales
New York City
New York State
New Zealand
Nile
Normandy
North American &
   Alaskan Cruises
Norway
Oman & the UAE
Orlando
Oxford
Pacific Northwest
Pakistan
Paris
Perth & Surroundings
Peru
Philadelphia
Philippines
Poland
Portugal

Prague
Provence
Puerto Rico
Queensland & The
   Great Barrier Reef
Rajasthan
Rio de Janeiro
Rockies, The
Romania
Rome
Russia
St Petersburg
San Francisco
Sardinia
Scandinavia
Scotland
Seattle
Shanghai
Sicily
Singapore
South Africa
South America
Spain
Spain, Northern
Spain, Southern
Sri Lanka
Sweden
Switzerland
Sydney
Syria & Lebanon
Taipei
Taiwan
Tanzania & Zanzibar
Tasmania
Tenerife
Texas
Thailand
Thailand's Beaches
   & Islands
Tokyo
Toronto
Trinidad & Tobago
Tunisia
Turkey
Turkish Coast
Tuscany
US National Parks West
USA On The Road
USA New South
Utah
Vancouver
Venezuela
Venice
Vienna
Vietnam
Wales
Washington D.C.
The Western
   United States

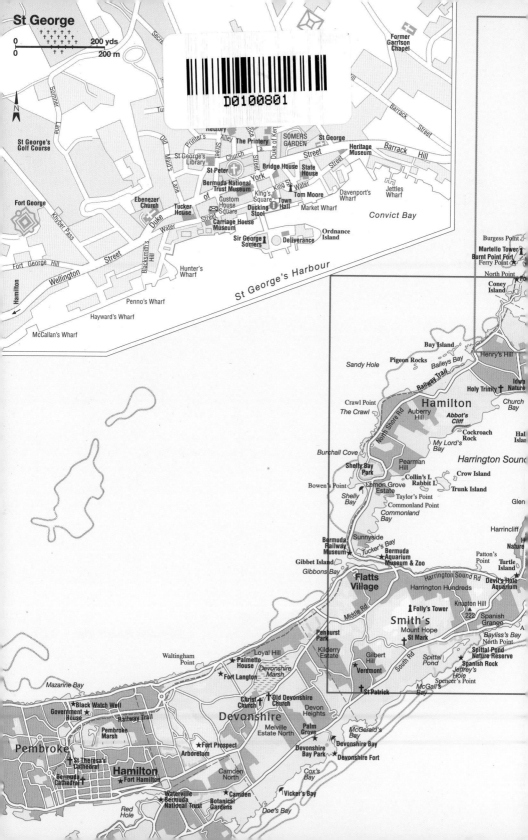

St George

| 0 | | | | 200 yds |
| 0 | | | | 200 m |

N

St George's Golf Course

Fort George

Sonnet Lane

Old Maid's Lane

Tulo

Secret

Printer's Alley
Rectory

The Printery
St George's Library

St Peter
Bridge House

Church La.

York Street

Duke of Kent

SOMERS GARDEN

St George Street

Heritage Museum

Barrack Hill

Barrack Street

Former Garrison Chapel

Ebenezer Church

Bermuda National Trust Museum

Tucker House

Custom House Square

Carriage House Museum

Sir George Somers

State House

King's Square

Town Hall

Water Street

Tom Moore

Ducking Stool

Deliverance

Davenport's Wharf

Market Wharf

Jettles Wharf

Convict Bay

Ordnance Island

Khyber Pass

Fort George Hill

Blacksmith's Hill

Duke of Water Street

Hamilton

Wellington Street

Hunter's Wharf

Penno's Wharf

Hayward's Wharf

McCallan's Wharf

St George's Harbour

Burgess Point

Martello Tower
Burnt Point Fort
Ferry Point

North Point

Coney Island

Bay Island

Sandy Hole

Pigeon Rocks

Bailey's Bay

Henry's Hill

Railway Trail

Idwa Nature

Holy Trinity

Crawl Point
The Crawl

Hamilton

Auberry Hill

Abbot's Cliff

Church Bay

Burchall Cove

My Lord's Bay

Cockroach Rock

Hal Islar

Harrington Sound

Shelly Bay Park

Bowen's Point

Pearman Hill

Collin's I.
Rabbit I.

Crow Island

Lemon Grove Estate

Trunk Island

Shelly Bay

Taylor's Point

Commonland Point

Commonland Bay

Glen

Bermuda Railway Museum

Sunnyside

Gibbet Island

Gibbons Bay

Tucker's Bay

Bermuda Aquarium Museum & Zoo

Harrinclliff

Nature

Patton's Point

Turtle Island

Flatts Village

Harrington Sound Rd

Harrington Hundreds

Devil's Hole Aquarium

Folly's Tower

Knapton Hill

222

Spanish Grange

A

Middle Rd

Smith's

Mount Hope
St Mark

Bayliss's Bay
North Point

Waltingham Point

Loyal Hill

Palmetto House

Devonshire Marsh

Fort Langton

Penhurst Park

Kilderry Estate

Gilbert Hill

Verdmont

South Rd

Spittal Pond

Spittal Pond Nature Reserve

Spanish Rock

Jeffrey's Hole
Spencer's Point

Mazarine Bay

Black Watch Well

Government House

Railway Trail

Pembroke Marsh

Christ Church

Old Devonshire Church

Devon Heights

Devonshire

Melville Estate North

Palm Grove

St Patrick

McGall's Bay

McGerald's Bay

Devonshire Bay

Pembroke

St Theresa's Cathedral

Bermuda Cathedral

Hamilton

Fort Hamilton

Fort Prospect

Arboretum

Fort Prospect

Camden North

Waterville
Bermuda National Trust

Camden

Botanical Gardens

Vicker's Bay

Doe's Bay

Cox's Bay

Devonshire Bay Park

Devonshire Fort

Red Hole